The Ego Made Manifest

The Ego Made Manifest

*Max Stirner, Egoism,
and the Modern Manifesto*

Wayne Bradshaw

BLOOMSBURY ACADEMIC
NEW YORK • LONDON • OXFORD • NEW DELHI • SYDNEY

BLOOMSBURY ACADEMIC
Bloomsbury Publishing Inc, 1385 Broadway, New York, NY 10018, USA
Bloomsbury Publishing Plc, 50 Bedford Square, London, WC1B 3DP, UK
Bloomsbury Publishing Ireland, 29 Earlsfort Terrace, Dublin 2, D02 AY28, Ireland

BLOOMSBURY, BLOOMSBURY ACADEMIC and the Diana logo
are trademarks of Bloomsbury Publishing Plc

First published in the United States of America 2023
Paperback edition published in 2025

Copyright © Wayne Bradshaw, 2023

Cover design: Eleanor Rose
Cover image: William Roberts' *The Vorticists at the Restaurant de la Tour Eiffel: Spring, 1915* © Mishcon de Reya / Tate Collections

All rights reserved. No part of this publication may be: i) reproduced or transmitted in any form, electronic or mechanical, including photocopying, recording or by means of any information storage or retrieval system without prior permission in writing from the publishers; or ii) used or reproduced in any way for the training, development or operation of artificial intelligence (AI) technologies, including generative AI technologies. The rights holders expressly reserve this publication from the text and data mining exception as per Article 4(3) of the Digital Single Market Directive (EU) 2019/790.

Bloomsbury Publishing Inc does not have any control over, or responsibility for, any third-party websites referred to or in this book. All internet addresses given in this book were correct at the time of going to press. The author and publisher regret any inconvenience caused if addresses have changed or sites have ceased to exist, but can accept no responsibility for any such changes.

Library of Congress Cataloging-in-Publication Data
Names: Bradshaw, Wayne (Literature scholar), author.
Title: The ego made manifest : Max Stirner, egoism, and the modern manifesto / Wayne Bradshaw.
Description: New York : Bloomsbury Academic, 2023. | Includes bibliographical references and index. |
Summary: "From Karl Marx to Wyndham Lewis, this book examines Max Stirner's influence on the modern manifesto"– Provided by publisher.
Identifiers: LCCN 2023007414 (print) | LCCN 2023007415 (ebook) | ISBN 9798765102565 (hardback) | ISBN 9798765102572 (paperback) | ISBN 9798765102589 (ebook) | ISBN 9798765102596 (pdf) | ISBN 9798765102602 (ebook other)
Subjects: LCSH: Egoism in literature. | Literary manifestos–Europe–History. | Political manifestos–Europe–History. | Stirner, Max, 1806–1856–Influence. | European literature–19th century–History and criticism. | European literature–20th century–History and criticism.
Classification: LCC PN56.E34 E34 2023 (print) | LCC PN56.E34 (ebook) | DDC 809.93352–dc23/eng/20230406
LC record available at https://lccn.loc.gov/2023007414
LC ebook record available at https://lccn.loc.gov/2023007415

ISBN: HB: 979-8-7651-0256-5
PB: 979-8-7651-0257-2
ePDF: 979-8-7651-0259-6
eBook: 979-8-7651-0258-9

Typeset by Integra Software Services Pvt. Ltd.

For product safety related questions contact productsafety@bloomsbury.com.

To find out more about our authors and books visit www.bloomsbury.com
and sign up for our newsletters.

Contents

Preface — vi
Acknowledgments — viii

Introduction: Manifestations of the Ego — 1

1. Germany: Stirner's Conquest of the Self — 15
2. France: The Rise of Literary Egoism — 53
3. Italy: The Ascent of the Poet Tyrant — 85
4. The Transatlantic Shift: Beyond Anarchism and Nationalism — 121
5. England: From Imagism to Vorticism — 153

Conclusion: A History of Possession — 179

Works Cited — 193
Index — 205

Preface

There is a prevailing tendency to depict Max Stirner as a forgotten figure from the fringes of nineteenth-century German idealism. From this perspective, he was the father of the philosophical dead end that was egoistic anarchism: a withered branch of a historically ineffectual movement, remembered largely because of its suggestion that criminal activity was a form of revolutionary action. Egoists subscribed to extreme forms of anarchism, such as the illegalism of the Bonnot gang, and defended theft, assault, and even murder. When Stirner's ideas found a wider audience, it was only briefly. His book, *Der Einzige und sein Eigentum* (The Ego and Its Own), was published in 1844 and—after being summarily dismissed by his contemporaries in the German intelligentsia—was almost immediately forgotten. Critics and historians acknowledged that it experienced a vogue at the end of the nineteenth century but suggested that interest in the book was once again brief. In any case, Stirner's egoism only held lasting appeal to rebels, nihilists, cranks, and criminals. All the better, then, that his ideas seem destined to be consigned to the dustbin of history. So went the established wisdom about Max Stirner.

It needs pointing out that many of these still widely accepted truisms about Stirner and his reception are false. Only recently has scholarship begun to recognize the geographical and temporal breadth of Stirner's readership, as well as his historical importance. With each year and each new book addressing Stirner's legacy the suggestion that he was merely an intellectual fad entertained at the turn of the twentieth century has become increasingly untenable. The persistent depiction of Stirner as an anarchist is anachronistic, and accusations that he was a nihilist ignore his troubled attempts to provide subjective foundations for love and creativity. In a variety of disciplines—chiefly philosophy, art history, and literary criticism—Stirner's influence on avant-garde and modernist conceptions of individuality is being recognized as of increasing importance. If the current trend continues, it is only a matter of time until he is acknowledged as a figure whose significance to the modernist project is comparable to the likes of Henri Bergson and William James.

In the pages that follow I have endeavored to demonstrate Stirner's important contribution, not only to the development of broadly modernist literary trends, but, more specifically, to the early development of the avant-garde literary manifesto between 1880 and 1914. Stirner provided an egoistic justification for individuals to write manifestos that not only rebelled against tradition, but took ownership of history, culture, and the movements they proselytized for. From *The Communist Manifesto*, published just four years after Stirner's magnum opus, through to English Vorticism's satirical approach to revolt, Stirner was never far from view, and his ideas proved popular with a diverse range of polemicists from a wide array of artistic and political movements. The trajectory of Stirner's reception placed him at the center of many developments in manifesto writing in the late-nineteenth and early-twentieth centuries, and while much remains to be written about Stirner's reception it is abundantly clear—as you will soon see—that his ideas were as crucial to the shape and tone of the modern manifesto as any of those put forward by Marx and Engels. Far from being a forgotten thinker from the dying days of German idealism, Stirner was a pervasive influence on the radical individualism that energized many literary responses to the modern condition, not least the manifesto.

Acknowledgments

The research that underpins this book was conducted with financial support from the Australian Government and James Cook University. My profound appreciation goes to Professor Richard Lansdown for his guidance and supervision from this project's inception. I thank Dr. Eduardo de la Fuente for his supervision during the first year of my PhD candidature and I am deeply indebted to Professor Michael Ackland for lending his intellectual and editorial support precisely when it was needed most. More than anything else, I am grateful for the limitless patience and never-ending editorial advice of my partner, Tenille McDermott, without whom I am convinced this book would never have seen its way to publication.

Introduction: Manifestations of the Ego

The relative silence on the subject of Max Stirner in literary discussion at times suggests a degree of censorship—or at least unwarranted neglect. Despite the fact that his only book, *Der Einzige und sein Eigentum* (1844),[1] "went through forty-nine printings from 1900 to 1929, and its ideas united an array of modernists" (Birmingham 79), Stirner remains in Lawrence Stepelevich's view "something more than a philosophical fad," but "much less than a major figure" (324). The fact that his ideas about individualistic rebellion variously informed a list of writers and artists that includes Stéphane Mallarmé, Maurice Barrès, Gustave Kahn, Gabriele D'Annunzio, Filippo Tommaso Marinetti, Dora Marsden, Rebecca West, Ezra Pound, James Joyce, Wyndham Lewis, Herbert Read, Tristan Tzara, Marcel Duchamp, and Francis Picabia has done little to shift the prevailing view that Stirner was not broadly read outside the fringes of anarchist theory. It remains true, for example, that no fewer than thirty references to Stirner continue to be excised from most English editions of Camus's *L'Homme révolté* (The Rebel, 1951), and that three hundred pages entirely devoted to Stirner are still regularly cut—albeit with acknowledgment—from standard editions and translations of Marx's *Die deutsche Ideologie* (1846). Similarly, the fact that perhaps the most well-known magazine in the history of English literary modernism, *The Egoist* (1914–19), drew its name from Stirner's thought has done little to secure his place in the modernist project. In short, his egoistic critique of values has frequently been downplayed, obliterated, or denigratingly associated with such intellectually aberrant groups as anarchists, fascists, and conspiracy theorists.

---

[1] Max Stirner was the pseudonym used by a German thinker named Johann Kaspar Schmidt. In 1907, Steven Byington very loosely translated the title of Stirner's book as *The Ego and His Own* and in 1995 David Leopold rendered it as *The Ego and Its Own*. In reality, the title is much closer to "the unique individual and its property," a title which captures the central premise of personal sovereignty that underpins Stirner's egoism. The book is radical in that it defines property in not only material but also conceptual terms.

Recently, greater justice has begun to be done to Stirner's intellectual contribution to the arts, and a reclamation project seems underway. Among others, Allan Antliff, Theresa Papanikolas, and David Ashford have all contributed to a reappraisal of Stirner's place in the history of art and literature. A picture of the extent to which his ideas found purchase in Paris Dadaism is beginning to emerge in *Anarchy and Art* (2007) and *Anarchism and the Advent of Paris Dada* (2010), by Antliff and Papanikolas, respectively. In *Autarchies* (2017), Ashford has further pursued these connections, as well as Stirner's influence on Marsden, Lewis, and Ayn Rand. What remains to be seen is Stirner's particular philosophical, historical, and literary role in the development of the modernist manifesto. The relationship between Stirnerian egoism, the European avant-garde, and British modernism is certainly worthy of such an investigation. Coincidence does not explain how Stirner's ideas became popular with so many of the individuals responsible for popularizing the manifesto in Germany, France, Italy, and Britain, at the same time that they were making their most important contributions to the manifesto-writing tradition.

Stirner's importance to literary movements in France, Italy, and the trans-Atlantic sphere was at its height in the years preceding the First World War, while by 1920 his readership extended as far as Japan and Australia. In the Russia of the Tsars and the Soviets alike, Stirner's importance was also felt: John Carroll has observed similarities between Stirner and Dostoevsky, and the Ego-Futurism of Igor Severyanin clearly owed a debt to Stirner's example. The perception that Stirner was a proponent of anarchism, nihilism, and terrorism has obscured the full extent of his influence in many cases. The latter suggestion that his thought helped lay the foundations for fascism and Nazism poisoned his reputation.[2] Overzealous efforts to safeguard the intellectual originality of Marx and Nietzsche have also contributed to an unwillingness to preserve and comprehend Stirner's intellectual legacy. In reality, Stirner's thought was crucial to the development of the avant-garde literary manifesto. His arguments for individual ownership of idealized concepts can be plotted directly onto the manifesto writer's relationship to the manifesto. His ideas help to explain not only the rhetorical style of some of the most famous manifestos of the twentieth century but also the intellectual and artistic positions they espoused.

---

[2] There is, perhaps, no better example of the tendency to read Stirner as a theorist of the far right than the edited translation of *Der Einzige und sein Eigentum* that was published by Jonathan Cape as part of its "Roots of the Right" series in 1971.

There is a long tradition of editing Stirner out of works important to the history of modern literature that the case of *L'Homme révolté* illustrates. A conceptual sibling of *Le Mythe de Sisyphe* (1942), *L'Homme révolté* was a sustained critique of philosophical justifications for rebellion. In it, Camus attempted to "face the reality of the present, which is logical crime, and to examine meticulously the arguments by which it is justified" (3).[3] Camus reconceived rebellion and revolution as crime justified by logic, and *L'Homme révolté* not only explored the history of political revolt, but also related currents of intellectual and philosophical rebellion, whether against God, society, or the human existentialist predicament. In the words of Herbert Read's foreword to the English translation, Camus "reviews the history of this metaphysical revolt, beginning with the absolute negation of Sade, glancing at Baudelaire and the 'dandies,' passing on to Stirner, Nietzsche, Lautréamont, and the surrealists" (viii). For both Read and Camus, it seems, Stirner's importance to the tradition of metaphysical revolt was self-evident, and in Camus's text Stirner is described as the predecessor to Nietzsche's metaphysical insurrection.

Stirner's place in that tradition was, in effect, negated by the publishers of the first English translation, Hamish Hamilton, in 1953. Beneath Read's commentary, the anonymous editor noted that "in the interests of economy certain pages relating to some of these figures have been deleted" (Camus, 1973, 8). Thus, Lautréamont disappeared from the narrative, and Stirner was reduced to three brief references instead of the four-page section and six additional passages devoted to him in the original. One instance was particularly telling. Camus's observation that "Il ne s'agit plus pour le révolté de se déifier lui-même comme Stirner ou de se sauver seul par l'attitude" (517)[4] was rendered in the abridged translation as: "It no longer suffices for the rebel to declare himself God or to look to his own salvation by adopting a certain attitude of mind" (78). By these means Stirner was written out of Camus's intellectual history, and his name omitted from one of Camus's most important works. Nevertheless, a remaining reference hinted at the extent of his influence by suggesting that "[e]verything has taken place as though the descendants of Stirner and of Nechayev were making use of the descendants of Kaliayev and Proudhon. The nihilists today are seated on thrones" (Camus, 1973, 213). Today there is nothing in the Penguin

---

[3] Unless otherwise stated, quotes from *The Rebel* are taken from the revised and complete translation currently published by Vintage.
[4] "It no longer suffices for the rebel to deify himself like Stirner or to look to his own salvation by adopting a certain attitude of mind" (107).

edition of *The Rebel* to indicate that Camus ever wrote at length about Stirner, as the section devoted to him—along with Read's foreword—remains absent.[5] No acknowledgment is made of the abridgment.

Camus's was by no means an unbiased account of Stirner, but *L'Homme révolté* is instructive in both its emphases and omissions. In the pages omitted from the Penguin, Camus suggested that Stirner had taken metaphysical revolt to its conclusion, and that it was only from this point that Nietzsche began his own search for meaning. Camus argued that "[e]ven before Nietzsche, Stirner wanted to eradicate the very idea of God from man's mind, after he had destroyed God himself" (62). Stirner rebelled against God, ideology, belief, and even against philosophy. Nothing was sacred to him, and "[e]ven revolution, revolution in particular, is repugnant to this rebel" (63). Stirner's egoism amounted to "a negation of everything that denies the individual and the glorification of everything that exalts and ministers to the individual" (64). For Camus, this logic represented the bitterest nihilism:

> And so, among the ruins of the world, the desolate laughter of the individual-king illustrates the last victory of the spirit of rebellion. But at this extremity nothing else is possible but death or resurrection. Stirner, and with him all the nihilist rebels, rush to the utmost limits, drunk with destruction.
>
> (65)

Such charges of extreme nihilism ignored Stirner's troubled efforts to provide an egoistic foundation for love, generosity, and artistic creation. Camus's accusations did, however, capture the prevailing perception that Stirner was an early proponent of anarchist terrorism: a perception that does not sit well with the fact that *Der Einzige und sein Eigentum* was more likely to be found in the libraries of poets and novelists than nihilistic revolutionaries. The book was indeed popular with rebels, but rebels in artistic spheres such as Mallarmé, Marinetti, Lewis, and Duchamp. Its warmest reception was among the propagandists and polemicists of the avant-garde, and its influence evident in the egoistic ideas espoused by many of the greatest manifesto writers of literature before the First World War.

---

[5] At the time of writing the unabridged Vintage edition is out of print in the United Kingdom and Australia. It is still available in the United States.

An Egoistic Tradition

Although his work was largely forgotten in his own lifetime, interest in Stirner experienced a rebirth in Europe and America in the 1880s and reached its height in the decade preceding the First World War. This renaissance brought his ideas into the orbit of the generation of writers who contributed to the development of recognizably modernist trends in English and European literature. Forty years before *L'Homme révolté*, the American critic James Huneker collected several of his own essays concerning "those modern poets, philosophers and prose masters whose writings embody the individualistic idea" (373) in a book he titled *Egoists: A Book of Supermen* (1909). Huneker suggested the existence of a tradition of authorship that stretched from Blake to Huysmans and included several authors crucial to the development of the concept of modernism, including Baudelaire, Flaubert, and Ibsen. In 1909, the young T. S. Eliot reviewed *Egoists* for the *Harvard Advocate*, where he suggested that the title of the book was "vague and unsatisfactory," but that "the Egoists are all men—French and German—of highly individual, some of perverse and lunary, genius" (16). Huneker's vague title was in fact a clear reference to the work of Stirner, whose ideas were discussed in the book's final chapter.[6] In *Der Einzige und sein Eigentum*, Stirner had implored his readers to "seek for *yourselves*, become egoists [*Egoisten*], become each of you an almighty ego" (149). Since its initial publication in 1844, Stirner's injunction had not been ignored, and some of his most influential readers—including Karl Marx, early in the piece—responded to this challenge in a range of countervailing and sympathetic manifestos with both political and artistic aspirations, themselves intermingled commonly enough.

Larger ideological conflicts between communism and fascism have blunted our perceptions of Stirner's importance to modernism and the avant-garde, and scholars have only recently begun to reappraise the historical reception of his ideas. His thought was certainly crucial to the development of individualistic tendencies within anarchism, provided a new conceptual foundation for libertarianism, informed elements of French nationalism and Italian fascism, and provided an important justification for manifesto writing in the radical wings of artistic modernism. The manifestos of the early twentieth century have often

---

[6] The subtitle of Huneker's book, *A Book of Supermen*, is an obvious reference to Nietzsche, and Huneker was only one in a long line of authors to suggest that Stirner had influenced his ideas, or to boost Stirner's status by hitching his wagon to the later philosopher's star.

been viewed as part of a collectivist tradition beginning with Marx's *Communist Manifesto*, but they can also be understood as part of a very different—perhaps antithetical—egoistic tradition of the kind identified by Huneker. With a few notable exceptions, literary and political manifesto writers of the early twentieth century tended to espouse and embody the qualities of elitism, individualism, and revolt that were central to Stirnerian egoism, as opposed to a Marxist perspective. Indeed, several openly acknowledged their affinities with Stirner's thought. Still, the propagandists of modernism and the avant-garde have only rarely been considered in terms of their shared interest in Stirner.

Although Stirner's ideas are regularly depicted as occupying the fringes of mainstream philosophy, Huneker was not the only critic to have recognized their importance in changing modernist conceptions of the individual's role in society. At various times in the nineteenth century, Stirner's thought secured the attention of a wide array of intellectuals, including Feuerbach, Marx, Eduard von Hartmann, John Henry Mackay, and Benjamin Tucker. In the twentieth century, this list grew exponentially. Camus, as we have seen, indicated Stirner's importance in *L'Homme révolté*, and Herbert Read also wrote at length about his ideas. More recently, David McLellan addressed the influence of Stirner on Marx's thought in *The Young Hegelians and Karl Marx* (1969). There he suggested that it is "likely that Marx's constant attacks on anything that appeared to be based on 'morality' or 'love' in true socialism was due to Stirner's ruthless criticism of all such notions" (132). Gareth Stedman Jones takes up the same argument in his biography, *Karl Marx: Greatness and Illusion* (2016), suggesting that Marx tacitly accepted Stirner's criticism of "the moralistic, normative and still quasi-religious character of socialist rhetoric" (190). More ambitiously, John Carroll has attempted to establish a philosophical tradition that brings together the writing of Stirner, Dostoevsky, and Nietzsche in *Break-Out from the Crystal Palace* (1974), calling it the "anarcho-psychological tradition" (1). Carroll describes a defiant moral philosophy that offers a "critique of ideology," a "critique of knowledge," and a "critique of *homo economicus*" (3). At the very least, Stirner's place in the history of individual revolt was comparable to other iconoclasts such as Bakunin, Nietzsche, and Dostoyevsky.

At the heart of Stirner's thought was a radical reconceptualization of the conventional meaning of egoism (*Egoismus*) as part of a wider assault on the foundations of Hegelian philosophy. Kant provided the standard philosophical interpretation of egoism in *Anthropologie in pragmatischer Hinsicht*

(Anthropology from a Pragmatic Point of View, 1798). There, he described egoism as a fundamental misunderstanding about the place of the individual in society, which resulted in a failure to recognize truth, beauty, or moral duty. Kant suggested that "Egoism may be thought of as containing three presumptions: that of reason, that of taste, and that of practical interest, that is, it may be logical, aesthetic, or practical" (11). Depicting egoism as a closed-off sense of self, Kant proposed that the "logical egoist considers it unnecessary to test his judgment by the reason of others," while the "aesthetic egoist is satisfied with his own taste, even though others may dislike, criticize, or even ridicule his verse, his painting, or his music" (11–12). By comparison, "the moral egoist limits all purposes to himself; as a eudaemonist, he concentrates the highest motives of his will merely on profit and his own happiness, but not on the concept of duty" (12). Kant concluded that "[e]goism can only be contrasted with pluralism, which is a frame of mind in which the self, instead of being enwrapped in itself as if it were the whole world, understands and behaves itself as a mere citizen of the world" (12). Feuerbach drew upon Kant's interpretation of egoism in *Das Wesen des Christentums* (The Essence of Christianity, 1841), and for both men the term described a devotion to the self which, when absolute, blinded the individual to the duties, values, ideals, and essences shared by society.[7]

In a direct repudiation of Feuerbach, Stirner proposed a radically different interpretation of egoism.[8] He rejected the idea that the egoist was somehow closed off from the world, and instead described egoism in terms of expansive self-ownership. From this perspective, the egoist was not blind to morality and beauty, but the sole creator and owner of values and ideals. Stirner effectively demolished the concept of essences which had come to dominate German philosophy and proposed that the subjective experience of the unique individual

---

[7] Feuerbach suggested that when "man places himself only on the practical stand-point and looks at the world from thence, making the practical stand-point the theoretical one also, he is in disunion with nature; he makes Nature the abject vassal of his selfish interest, of his practical egoism" (112).
[8] While it will be seen that Johann Gottlieb Fichte expressed ideas somewhat similar to those of Stirner, he did not place the same importance on the concept of egoism. In *Grundlage des Naturrechts nach Principien der Wissenschaftslehre* (Foundations of Natural Right, According to the Principles of the Wissenschaftslehre, 1796-7), Fichte used the word *Egoismus* only once: "*The security of the rights of all* is willed only through the harmonious will of all, through the concurrence of their wills. *It is only in this regard that all agree*; for in all other matters their will is particular and directed to their individual ends. In accordance with our assumption of universal egoism (which the law of coercion presupposes), no individual, no single part of the commonwealth, makes this an end for himself; rather, only *all* of them, taken as a whole do" (134). The word *Egoismus* does not appear at all in his *Grundlage der gesamten Wissenschaftslehre* (Foundations of the Science of Knowledge, 1794-5) or *Die Bestimmung des Menschen* (The Vocation of Man, 1799).

was the ineluctable basis for all abstractions. He concluded that everything that we might call religion, morality, ethics, ideology, good, evil—even the concept of humanity itself—was a product of the individual mind. There was no objective notion of good, but only the unique individual's abstract notion of good. If an abstract idea governed the behavior of an individual, it was only because that individual had surrendered ownership of that particular idea. By nature, egoism stood in direct opposition to every ideological position: as Stirner concluded, "humanity is nothing else than my humanity, my human existence, and everything that I do is human precisely because *I* do it, not because it corresponds to the concept of humanity" (*The Ego and Its Own* 159). Such audacity—or foolhardiness, perhaps—incensed the German intelligentsia but, despite a flurry of indignant responses, few could fault the logic which Stirner had used to dismantle the temple of idealism.

Stirner's insurrectionary ideas have been variously described as hedonistic, anarchic, dialectical, nihilistic, existentialist, and solipsistic, but none of these terms adequately characterize his thought. Egoism only resembles hedonism, for example, if the unique individual decides to embark on hedonistic pursuits— and why should he or she necessarily do that? While many strains of anarchism certainly contain elements of egoism, Stirner explicitly described the ideal of freedom as an abstraction that haunts the mind. Egoism does not allow for the existence of anything that does not originate in the self, so it is impossible to conceive of it as dialectical. It is not nihilistic either, because with his concept of the unique individual Stirner attempted to provide a solid foundation for love and creativity, rather than annihilate them. As in the case of anarchism, Stirner may have contributed to some aspects of existentialist thought through his influence on Camus and Martin Buber, but he allowed no room for existentialist notions of becoming. As the source of all meaning, there was nothing that the unique individual could become that would not involve self-abnegation. Egoism is undeniably solipsistic, but it is unusual insofar as it endeavors to use solipsism not as a means of narcissistic escape, but as a foundation for engagement with a world of the self's own creation.

Over time, the most effective response to Stirner's critique would prove to be silence and neglect. Marx was among the few to recognize the genuine threat posed by Stirner's egoism, but his 300-page review—characterized as it was by willful misreading, *ad hominem* attack, and vulgar insult—faced repeated rejections from publishers. Nevertheless, Stirner prompted Marx to break with the ideas of Feuerbach and redefine the meaning of communism along lines that later became known as historical materialism. Even years after *Der Einzige und sein Eigentum* had slipped from public memory, the father of modern communism rarely missed an opportunity to disparage "Sankt Max," or brand anarchist opponents as having lifted their ideas from the work of Stirner. In *The Tenth Muse* (1941) Herbert Read observed that "Marx triumphed over Stirner as he triumphed over Feuerbach and Bakunin: he had the last word and it is still echoing in the political events of the present day" (75). Through a remarkable chain of events Stirner's thought had survived in the most unexpected places, however, and Read went on to acknowledge that "the giants whom Marx thought he had slain show signs of coming to life again" (75). Stirner's book found generations of interested readers in the circles of avant-garde and modernist literature. While his name remains somewhat obscure, his ideas about the uniqueness of individual experience and the contingent nature of ideals are crucial to understanding the workings of the modern manifesto—for reasons I shall now explain.

The Egoistic Manifesto

The relatively consistent use of the term *manifesto* by avant-garde movements in the interwar period, as well as *The Communist Manifesto*'s ongoing status as the measure by which all manifestos are apparently to be judged, stands in sharp contrast to the diverse ways the word has been used throughout its history. Janet Lyon observes that "in seventeenth-century Italy 'manifesto' could refer to a document that publicized military intent or sovereign will, whereas a century earlier in that country 'manifesto' named a document refuting anonymous character assaults in academic communities" (13). The word has been used in a religious sense to describe manifestations of the divine; it has also been applied to political texts quite similar to the conventional use of manifesto today. Disparate individuals and groups have called all kinds of statements *manifests* and *manifestos*, but just as *The Communist Manifesto* helped to create a new interpretation of communism, its title produced a new kind of manifesto. Martin Puchner suggests that from 1848, "[g]enerically, the manifesto, at this juncture, can be seen as credo plus history" (21). According to Puchner, this noticeably modern iteration of the manifesto is "neither a declaration of self-evident principles nor an apocalyptic revelation but an instrument that gathers previous revolutionary events and channels them toward the immediate future, the immanent revolution" (21). It was this sense of the word that underpinned the first wave of literary programs produced by Symbolists, Futurists, Vorticists, and other avant-garde movements from the 1880s to around 1914. Nevertheless, when Jean Moréas's "*Le Symbolisme*" appeared under the heading "*Un manifeste littéraire*" in 1886, Anatole France could still mock the decision to call a literary treatise a manifesto. It was only then emerging as a recognizable trend in literary polemic.

Beginning with *The Communist Manifesto* it is easy to observe a superficial connection between the development of the avant-garde literary manifesto and the reception of Stirnerian egoism. In the years that preceded the writing of his manifesto Marx was obsessed with repudiating Stirner's ideas. *The Theses on Feuerbach* (1845)—a work that helped to provide a foundation for the *Manifesto*—owed a great deal to Stirner's criticism of Feuerbach. While Marx devoted significant energy to opposing the spread of egoism, it will be seen that the *Manifesto* relied on a Stirnerian critique "of Man in general [...] who exists only in the misty realm of philosophical fantasy" (Marx, *The Communist Manifesto* 103). After years of obscurity Stirner's work experienced resurgent interest in the mid-1880s, just as the first examples of self-described literary manifestos were beginning to appear. In fact, the primary vehicles for Stirner's reception in France were the Symbolist journals where pioneering developments in the literary manifesto were taking place. In the first decade of the twentieth century, *Der Einzige und sein Eigentum* was translated into Italian and soon after Italian Futurists led by Marinetti—a man who was among those familiar with Stirner's thought—produced a veritable flood of modern manifesto writing. In England, Stirner's book was published in 1907 and 1912 and was received most warmly by the circle that formed around *The New Freewoman*, a modernist-cum-feminist publication edited by Dora Marsden. Under the self-evident influence of Stirner's thought, *The New Freewoman* became *The Egoist* in 1914, and in the same year, Wyndham Lewis published the first volume of *Blast*, a journal brimming with the multifarious manifestos of his Vorticist movement.

Deeper connections between the development of the modern literary manifesto and the revival of Stirner's egoism hinge on the ways in which his notion of insurrection differs from other kinds of revolutionary thought. Stirner's use of *Empörung* is particularly important to understanding the manifesto as a form of egoistic rebellion. This term works against the efforts of a translator. As part of a tradition going back to Hamann and Hegel, wordplay was a fundamental element of Stirner's writing. In common usage, *Empörung* means something akin to indignation. Nevertheless, in the context of Stirner's writing the word is used in an archaic fashion to mean "insurrection" or "revolt." He avoids the more conventional German word for insurrection, *Aufstand*, for a variety of reasons. *Empörung* suggests the importance of indignation to Stirner's conception of rebellion against what appear to be society's morals and values. *Empörung* also recalls the word *empor*, meaning "up" or "upwards," to suggest an individual rising above the ideals that have hitherto governed him. By contrast, *Aufstand* implies a kind of collective—and therefore inherently political—action which is anathema to egoism's notion of individual revolt. Stirner suggests that "[r]evolution and insurrection [*Empörung*] must not be looked upon as synonymous," because while "revolution aimed at new *arrangements*; insurrection leads us no longer to *let* ourselves be arranged, but to arrange ourselves, and sets no glittering hopes on 'institutions'" (280). Insurrection involves taking personal ownership of value systems so that they can no longer govern individual behavior. All morals, values, and ideals are inevitably subject to the will of the unique individual and it is up to the individual—and nothing and nobody else—to assert ownership of them.

Stirnerian revolt can then be understood as the process by which the unique individual takes ownership of all abstract values, not as ends in themselves, but as property to be disposed of at will. Rules may be imposed on society, provided the individual possesses the might to do so, but society is also an ideal created in the mind of the individual. From the perspective of such egoism other people are not, at least in any meaningful sense, unique individuals. Stirner is broadly indifferent to the question of whether other unique individuals exist because the nature of reality confines him to the world he himself, alone, has created. Otherness is an abstraction that belongs to the realm of speculation. The only justifications for behavior are instinct, desire, and requisite might. Restrictions that lie outside the control of the individual—or, more accurately, desires that remain unattainable due to the limits of individual might—are deprived of their moral justification and obeyed out of mere self-interest. The law of gravity and the policeman's truncheon are both examples of an individual's limits rather than proof of external authority in either nature or the state. The fundamental principle of egoism is that all abstract notions have their ultimate origin in what Stirner calls the "creative nothing" (*schöpferisches Nichts*) of the unique individual (*The Ego and Its Own* 7).

Many of the manifestos of Symbolism, Futurism, and Vorticism—along with several important Dadaist manifestos—adapt Stirner's concept of egoistic insurrection to effect artistic revolts against tradition. Conscious of Stirner's work, a generation of avant-garde authors used the manifesto as a way of seizing control of abstract ideals, both as a way of liberating their own art and taking ownership of the work of others. When placed within the context of Stirner's thought, manifestos represent a self-appointed leader's effort to take ownership and control of a movement's values and ideals. In the case of literary manifestos, egoism underpins an effort to create new forms of artistic convention that remain within the manifesto writer's power. Many of Marinetti's manifestos, for example, purport to be written on behalf of the Futurist movement but in fact represent Marinetti's personal values at the time of writing. Such manifestos codify the values of a movement's founder and self-appointed leader and apply them to people who wish to be members of the group. Meanwhile, the manifesto writer remains free to produce a stream of manifestos that either reconfigure the existing movement or found a new movement according to individual whims. Egoism requires the seizing of personal control over abstractions and the manifesto, by its nature, transforms abstract ideals into personal property. In *The Communist Manifesto*—as Stirner would read the situation—the collective notion of communism became Marx's personal vision of communism. The manifesto turns the abstract into the personal, and serves the practical, political ends of the individual. By producing new programs, the manifesto writer repeatedly renews personal ownership and control of the movement's values. By this process, the values of the most recent manifesto remain the property of its creator.

As part of a document that converts abstract ideals into personal property, the collective "we" of the avant-garde manifesto is—at least from the perspective of its writer—less a statement of sub-Marxist revolutionary solidarity than an expression of expansive ownership. Nevertheless, from the perspective of the group at large the manifesto may appear to embody an egalitarian approach to artistic innovation. The manifesto may at the same time be revolutionary in the Marxist sense and insurrectionary in the Stirnerian sense, depending on whether it is viewed from the perspective of the group who subscribes to the manifesto or the individual writer who produces it. These contrasting attitudes coexist in the manifesto as a tension between the collective "we" the manifesto invokes, and the singular author who uses "we" as a rhetorical tool. On the one hand, the collective identity that the manifesto claims to speak for is revolutionary in character, symbolically creating a movement, declaring that movement's existence and calling for action. On the other hand, the singular author symbolically creates a fiefdom governed by the rules of the manifesto, rules determined by the leader rather than the collective. Even in cases like *The Communist Manifesto*, where there are ostensibly multiple authors, this collective enterprise is often something of an illusion—as Engels himself pointed out in later prefaces to the work. Ultimately, it is Marx's voice that reverberates through the text. The manifestos of Futurism and Vorticism were similarly strident examples of a manifesto writer's desire—Marinetti's, Lewis's desire—to take personal control of a given ideological and aesthetic program. The modern manifesto's style may originate in the writing of Marx, but its conceptual foundations are found in the work of Stirner. The egoistic desire to take personal control of abstract ideals underpinned manifestos produced by communists, fascists, and avant-gardists alike, and the reception of Stirner's ideas among these diverse groups helps explain why writers returned to this style of polemic again and again.

As a result of Stirner's influence, Symbolist, Futurist, and Vorticist manifestos were conscious attempts by individual writers to take ownership and control of the aesthetic ideals of the groups they were members of. Although it is undeniable that the influence of *The Communist Manifesto* helped to shape the literary manifestos written in this period, Stirnerian egoism also made a vital contribution to the style, tone, and content of these works. Indeed, Stirner's influence on Marx sheds further light on some of the driving forces behind the production of one of the most important examples of modern manifesto writing. The fact that many of these manifesto writers rejected communism brought them even closer to the egoism of Stirner. Egoism's popularity with important polemicists such as Barrès, D'Annunzio, Marinetti, and Lewis led to the production of a series of manifestos that decried tradition, convention, and morality, and which championed egoistic qualities of elitism, individualism, and revolt. Stirner's radical reconceptualization of individual experience retains the capacity to shock and disturb, and he provides a crucial way of understanding ideology as a manifestation of individual will.

1

Germany: Stirner's Conquest of the Self

A discussion of Stirner's life and the influence of his work on avant-garde manifesto writing necessarily begins in 1887, some thirty years after his death. It was in the summer of that year that the German poet and anarchist, John Henry Mackay,[1] began his efforts to rescue Stirner's legacy from obscurity.[2] Mackay's work on Stirner was an important factor in the revival of his thought in the early twentieth century, and by extension in the popularity of egoism with dissidents, writers, and artists in that period. In his biography, *Max Stirner: Sein Leben und sein Werk* (1897), Mackay recalled that it was while "buried in my study of the social movement of our century in the British Museum in London […] that I read the name Stirner and the title of his work for the first time" (5). He had discovered a reference to Stirner in the second volume of Friedrich Albert Lange's *Geschichte des Materialismus und Kritik seiner Bedeutung in der Gegenwart* (The History of Materialism and Criticism of Its Present Importance, 1866), one of a few works to consider Stirner since his death in 1856. In it, Lange devoted a mere three paragraphs to Stirner, but noted that "[e]verything that in any way, whether it be external force, belief, or mere idea, places itself above the individual and his caprice, Stirner rejects as a hateful limitation of himself. What a pity that to this book—the extremest that we know anywhere—a second positive part was not added" (256). It took Mackay a further year to acquire his own copy of *Der Einzige und sein Eigentum*, but on reading it he was galvanized,

---

[1] Born in Scotland but raised in Germany from the age of two, Mackay was a writer of nonfiction, poetry, and novels. Under the pseudonym *Sagitta* he wrote a series of works in defense of pederasty titled *Die Bücher der namenlosen Liebe* (The Books of Nameless Love, 1906–26). Today he is perhaps best known as the lyricist of one of Richard Strauss's *Four Last Songs*. Peter Morgan observes that "Mackay advocated a particular set of views about homosexuality that rendered him an outsider even among the small cohort of public advocates of 'the love that bears no name.' For Mackay, 'nameless love' (*namenlose Liebe*) referred to the pederastic relations of younger and older males rather than to homosexuality *per se*" (119). For this reason, Mackay was personally invested in a philosophy that rejected traditional moral impositions on the will as ghosts haunting the mind.

[2] Another proponent of Stirnerian egoism, James L. Walker, was similarly responsible for introducing the English-speaking world to *Der Einzige und sein Eigentum*. His role in popularizing Stirner in America and England is considered in the chapter titled "The Transatlantic Shift."

and recalled "the tremendous, incomparable impression that the work made on me then, as well as since on every new approach to it" (*Max Stirner* 5). He devoted most of the following thirty years to excavating the intellectual life of the theorist of insurrectionary egoism.

In 1892, Mackay's obsession saw him return to Berlin after a long absence, where he continued his research, installed a plaque at Stirner's former residence, and had a headstone placed at his grave. While engaged in these reclamation efforts, he was surprised to discover that "[i]n the meantime Stirner experienced a kind of rebirth" (*Max Stirner* 10), and wrote:

> These public events, which often brought his name into the press, the dedication of my poems *Sturm*, and the reference to him in the introduction of *Die Anarchisten*—above all the great influence that Friedrich Nietzsche more and more exercised every day, especially on the young generation—drew attention to his book, which was again much read, often mentioned, and now has been made available to the widest circles through an inexpensive edition in the Reclam Universal-Bibliothek.
>
> (10)[3]

Recognition of Stirner's contribution to anarchist thought had indeed received a significant boost from the perception that he had been a direct influence on Nietzsche—whose own oeuvre was growing in popularity day by day in the *fin de siècle*. The increasing public interest in *Der Einzige und sein Eigentum* spurred on Mackay's efforts to uncover the events of Stirner's life and restore his place in the history of German thought. The timing was fortuitous, and although Mackay lamented that Stirner "has gone and has left nothing behind except his immortal work" (16), Stirner had not yet slipped from living memory.

A Philosophical Apprenticeship

Besides a few scattered publications, references, and *Der Einzige und sein Eigentum*, almost all the knowledge that remains about Stirner the man comes from Mackay's interactions with those who knew Stirner in life, including the remaining members of his intellectual circle, *Die Freien* (the free ones); the

---

[3] *Die Anarchisten* was also the work of Mackay and was published in both English and German in 1891. The semi-autobiographical novel about its protagonist's conversion to individualist anarchism was widely read and well received. It was one of several key texts responsible for promoting Stirner's ideas in France, Britain, and America.

composer Hans von Bülow; and Stirner's second wife, Marie Dähnhardt. The only reliable images of Stirner that remain are two sketches by Frederick Engels that he drew from memory in 1892, fifty years after his time with *Die Freien*.[4] One depicts Stirner's face in profile; his eyes hidden behind spectacles, his head tilted back, and his lips parted. The impression is one of cold detachment. The other drawing depicts *Die Freien* collectively, and Stirner occupies a position in the middle distance, assuming an aristocratic pose and smoking a cigar while others engage in fierce argument and gesticulate wildly. Both sketches caricature an immense sloping forehead—the German for forehead, *Stirn*, being the origin of his pseudonym—along with a certain aloofness of character. Mackay imagines that "[b]ehind the glasses his clear, blue eyes looked at people and things calmly and gently, neither dreamily nor staring," while on his "fine, small-lipped mouth" there "often played a friendly smile, which with the years sharpened and which betrayed an inner irony, just as many noticed in Stirner a 'quiet inclination to ridicule'" (86). The portrait of Stirner that emerges from Mackay's biography is one of a difficult and anti-social man, whose bombastic prose stood in marked contrast to his personal reticence.

Der Einzige und sein Eigentum was the culmination of Stirner's life and career. The book was the definitive work of insurrectionary egoism, and its indignant critique of liberal values provided a theoretical justification for generations of rebels against moral, intellectual, philosophical, and artistic authority. Stirner did not develop his theories over the course of a single book, however, and his earlier works foreshadowed the fully realized egoism of his only major publication. Beleaguered by years of personal hardship and intellectual isolation by his contemporaries, Stirner's failed attempt to establish an academic career for himself helped to cement his reputation as a philosophical outsider and a rebel to be championed by anarchist and artist alike.

Although Stirner attended the same institutions and moved in the same circles as his contemporaries Feuerbach and Marx, his life was dominated by personal rather than political circumstances. On October 25, 1806, Johann Caspar Schmidt—the later Stirner—was born in the town of Wagner's birth, Bayreuth,

---

[4] A third drawing of Stirner exists, though it comes from a less reliable source. Carroll notes that Rolf Engert, in conducting his own research into the life of Stirner for *Das Bildnis Max Stirners* (The Portrait of Max Stirner, 1921), "received a pencil drawing of 'Joh. Kasp. Schmidt' from a Berlin worker who had claimed that his grandfather had known Stirner" (*The Ego and His Own* 20). Unlike Engels' sketches, this "is a romantic sketch of a signally handsome young man, in the style of Byron: large intense eyes, long fluted nose, pursed sensual lips [...] square-set jaw and the long hair casually brushed back from a high, aristocratic brow" (20).

"where his family had lived for several generations, in a house located in the center of town" (Shone 207). He was the first and only child of Albert Christian Heinrich Schmidt, a maker of flutes, and Sophia Eleonora, the daughter of a postman. His father died six months after he was born, and two years later, in 1809, his mother married the manager of the court apothecary, Heinrich Friedrich Ludwig Ballerstedt. The family soon moved to "Kulm on the Weichsel River in West Prussia" (Mackay, *Max Stirner* 30),[5] but in 1818, the young Johann was sent back to Bayreuth to live with his godparents and attend the gymnasium there. He performed admirably in school, and Mackay notes that "[i]n his leaving certificate of 8 September 1826 he was given the mark I and the grade 'very worthy'" (31). These few facts—along with considerable conjecture—represent the full extent of Mackay's discoveries about the boy who would become Max Stirner. Nothing else remains in the published record.

Stirner's character and the influences on his thought become clearer once he encountered the intellectual world of nineteenth-century Berlin and the radical politics of the *Junghegelianer* (Young Hegelians). Mackay links the crucial phase of Stirner's intellectual development to his arrival "in Berlin for the Michaelmas term of 1826 fresh from Bayreuth as a young student of twenty" (*Max Stirner* 37). It was here, during his second semester at the University of Berlin, that Schmidt had the opportunity to study directly under the titan of German idealism, Georg Wilhelm Friedrich Hegel.[6] Ronald Paterson notes that Schmidt attended lectures by "[August] Neander [...] on ecclesiastical history and Christian antiquity, and [Philip] Marheineke [...] on dogmatics, Church symbolism, and recent philosophical theology; he heard [Friedrich] Schleiermacher lecture on ethics; and he listened to the great Hegel himself, as the oracle pronounced on the history of philosophy, philosophy of religion, and the philosophy of spirit" (37).

---

[5] Now the town of Chełmno in northern Poland, it is located near the banks of what is now the Vistula. During the Second World War, the invading German forces once again imposed the name Kulm on the town, and in 1941 it became the site of the first of Hitler's extermination camps, *Vernichtungslager Kulmhof*.

[6] Hegel's contributions to the dialectical method dominated the German intellectual landscape in the nineteenth century, influencing an entire generation of thinkers ranging from Kierkegaard to Marx. It was the most influential concept that Stirner would have learned from him. Hegel uses the word dialectic to describe "the process by which one proposition (the 'thesis') fights with another (the 'antithesis') and both are finally overcome by a third ('the synthesis')" (Kenny 113). Like many of his contemporaries, Stirner reacted against the theological aspects of Hegel's dialectic, but his opposition went further still. He attempted to use the dialectical method to prove that the dialectical method itself was incorrect, and that all contradictory propositions were preceded by the unique individual.

These lectures presumably provided the young Schmidt with a foundation in dialectical idealism, and almost certainly its rhetorical language. He would adapt both to the cause of undermining the foundations of idealism less than twenty years later in his magnum opus. He also appears to have embraced the name Max Stirner while studying at the University of Berlin.

The progress of Stirner's studies shared several similarities with those of Ludwig Feuerbach, a man who would go on to become the target of Stirner's most savage attacks in *Der Einzige und sein Eigentum*. Both men were students at the University of Berlin in the 1820s, and both attended Hegel's lectures while there. They also "attended the University of Erlangen at the same time, in the fall of 1828" (Shone 208), although there is no suggestion that the two were acquainted with each other at this stage. The first signs of mutual recognition—and conflict—would not occur for more than a decade, when Stirner joined *Die Freien* at Hippel's local *Weinstube* (wine-bar) in the early 1840s. At this earlier point in his career, Stirner had left Berlin to study at two other universities "in accordance with custom," and he attended lectures on "divinity, logic and metaphysics" at Erlangen before leaving for the University of Königsberg in 1829 (Paterson 5). Mackay suggests that even at Erlangen, Stirner's studies began to falter, and that he "heard only two series of lectures in the winter semester: one with the well-known theologian Georg Benedikt Wiener on the Letters to the Corinthians, the other with Christian Kapp, the philosopher, on Logic and Metaphysics" (38), before undertaking a three-month-long tour of Germany. The appeal of academia seemed to dissipate, and at Königsberg Stirner was entirely absent from lectures.

Stirner's interrupted studies at the University of Königsberg constitute one of many unresolved mysteries about the writer of *Der Einzige und sein Eigentum*. It is generally believed that his mother's deteriorating mental condition forced Stirner to abandon his studies for a time in order to care for her. Paterson suggests that "in 1831, although still nominally a student of Königsberg, he was compelled to devote another year to 'family affairs,' the nature of which must be conjectural, but which may have arisen from his mother's increasing mental instability" (5). Admitted to Berlin's *Charité* hospital in 1835, Frau Ballerstedt was released "with indefinite leave as uncured" in 1836 and, it seems, spent the rest of her life in care (Mackay, *Max Stirner* 49). Family demands and personal illness plagued the second half of Stirner's university education, and surely contributed to the collapse of his fledgling academic career. Having returned to the University of Berlin in 1832, Stirner would not take his oral exam for another three years, and even then, would only be "granted the qualified *facultas docendi*" (Mackay, *Max Stirner* 46), preventing him from teaching in the upper forms of the gymnasium. While his markers appear to have recognized talent in the now 28-year-old Stirner, they certainly perceived serious gaps in his knowledge, the inevitable result of his intermittent studies.

After leaving the University of Berlin for the last time, Stirner largely disappears from the historical record for a period. Mackay notes that his marriage in 1873 to Agnes Clara Kunigunde Burtz at St Marien's Lutheran church in Berlin ended a year later in childbirth when "[t]he skill of those attending her was unable to save her or the child" (Mackay, *Max Stirner* 50). While *Max Stirner: Sein Leben und sein Werk* freely speculates about the time devoted to private study in order to account for gaps left in its subject's education, Mackay suggests only one other confirmed development relevant to Stirner's intellectual life. Between 1839 and 1844—a period that includes the writing of *Der Einzige und sein Eigentum*—Stirner was in the regular employ of "Madame Gropius's 'Institute for the Instruction and Cultivation of Superior Girls'" (Paterson 6), a private school where he taught history and literature. The certainty of a modest but regular income seems to have provided Stirner with a degree of freedom, and it was during this time that he began to appear in the intellectual circle of *Die Freien*.

This rowdy group of intellectuals, malcontents, and radicals represented the heart of Berlin's *Junghegelianer*.[7] They frequented several of Berlin's beer houses, including *Zum Kronprinzen* and Walburg's, as well as Hippel's famous establishment. Mackay described them as a group of "very disparate individuals, who had only one thing in common: they were more or less dissatisfied with the political and social conditions of the time and were fighting against them more or less fiercely in public" (*Max Stirner* 57). Steve Shone adds that "*Die Freien* was an assemblage known for its partying prowess as well as for its continuation of intellectual position-taking" (208). Before leaving for Cologne in 1841, "Karl Marx attended its discussions while he was completing his studies; and Engels, during his year of military service in Berlin [1841], frequently took an enthusiastic part in its proceedings" (Paterson 8). The fact that Stirner never met Marx—who had left to write for the *Rheinische Zeitung* in the early months of 1841—but did meet

---

[7] The entire section of Mackay's biography titled "'The Free' at Hippel's in the Fifth Decade of the Century" remains the most comprehensive source of information on the Berlin faction of the Young Hegelian movement. Mackay provides a detailed account of *Die Freien*'s membership and of the personalities who spent their evenings arguing and proselytizing at Hippel's.

Engels in that or the following year suggests that he joined the ranks of *Die Freien* in the second half of 1841. The 35-year-old Stirner quickly became part of the inner circle of this crowd of "mostly young journalists, teachers, officers, university students and lecturers in their twenties and thirties" (Paterson 8). The theologian Bruno Bauer informally led its inner circle, which included his brothers Edgar and Egbert; the writer Ludwig Buhl; the gymnasium teacher Carl Friedrich Köppen; the publicist Eduard Meyen; the journalists Friedrich Sass, Hermann Maron, Adolf Rutenberg, and Arthur Müller; the translator Ludwig Eichler; a philologist by the name of Lehmann; and the jurist and politician Gustav Lipke. Mackay notes another visitor of *Die Freien*, Lieutenant Saint-Paul, who was "[s]ent as a censor to Cologne to observe the *Rheinische Zeitung*," but who "much preferred cozy evenings with its editors" in Berlin (*Max Stirner* 65).

It was while immersed in this climate of boisterous debate and revolutionary speculation that Stirner wrote his contributions to the field of egoism. He began with two short essays published in the *Rheinische Zeitung* in 1842.[8] The first, appearing in April, was a critique of contemporary trends in schooling titled "Das unwahre Prinzip unserer Erziehung" (The False Principle of Our Education).[9] In it, Stirner characterized the nineteenth-century German education system as consisting of two philosophical camps engaged in a "struggle for victory," where the humanist and the realist "each wants to recommend his principle of education as the best and truest for our needs" ("The False Principle of Our Education" 12). Stirner borrowed the terms "humanism" and "realism" from *Konkordat zwischen Schule und Leben, oder Vermittlung des Humanismus und Realismus, aus nationalem Standpunkte betrachtet* (Concordat Between School and Life, or Mediation of Humanism and Realism, viewed from a national Standpoint, 1842), by Professor Theodor Heinsius, and suggested that "[f]or the contradictions of the opposing enemy camps, Heinsius chose the names humanism and realism, and, inaccurate as they are, we will retain them as the most commonly used" (13). He described humanist teaching as that which relies on reading the classics while realist pedagogy places everything in the context of practical life, and attacked "the empty elegance of the humanist, of the dandy," and the realist for producing "people of principles who act and think

---

[8] The *Rheinische Zeitung* was still under the editorial leadership of Moses Hess when Stirner submitted his two essays for consideration, so it remains a matter of speculation whether Marx—who was appointed to the editorial board in October—read them while working for the paper.
[9] Literally "The *Untruthful* Principle of Our Education." Stirner depicts contemporary teaching methods as founded on false ideals, while the only true foundation for education is self-knowledge.

according to maxims [...] legal minds, not free ones" (24). Anticipating his later preoccupation with the need to be conscious of one's own egoism, Stirner suggested that "[i]f a child does not learn self-awareness, then he plainly does not learn that which is most important" (24). All knowledge, Stirner seemed to imply, was predicated on knowing one's self.

Stirner suggested that neither tradition nor normative values should underpin the education system, but rather the pursuit of self-awareness. He proposed that "to grasp the past as humanism teaches and to seize the present, which is the aim of realism, leads both only to power over the transitory," whereas "the spirit which understands itself is eternal" (15). The essay is without doubt the product of a troubled relationship with the German education system, but Stirner was already approaching some of the concepts that would be fully realized in *Der Einzige und sein Eigentum*. His persistent concern with the importance of self-awareness to the development of young minds hints at the increasing importance he placed on the individual as a foundation for understanding human experience. Self-knowledge provided the only way of adjudicating between abstractions like humanism and realism. The notion that all knowledge was contingent on individual experience would become a linchpin for Stirner's later justification of philosophical egoism.

Stirner's second published essay, "Kunst und Religion" (Art and Religion), appeared in the *Rheinische Zeitung* in June, and more directly foreshadowed the philosophy of egoism that he developed two years later in *Der Einzige und sein Eigentum*. In this second essay, Stirner addressed "the very Hegelian subject of the relation between art and religion" (McLellan 118). He proposed that art both creates and destroys religion, first by providing its archetypes and then by providing new archetypes which challenge the established ones in turn. He depicted a fluid process through which:

> Not only have the poets Homer and Hesiod "made the gods of the Greeks," but others, as artists, have established religions, although one hesitates to apply the superficial name "Artist" to them. Art is the beginning, the Alpha of religion, but it is also its end, its Omega. Even more—it is its companion. Without art and the idealistically creative artist religion would not exist, but when the artist takes back his art unto himself, so religion vanishes.
>
> (Stirner, "Art and Religion" 331)

Artists are the founders of religions; clergy are merely those who uphold the ideals produced by inspired artists. Stirner proposed that "[o]nly the founder of a religion is inspired, but he is also the creator of Ideals, through whose creation any further genius will be impossible" (329). The masses take up the values created by the artist and exhaust them through use and familiarity. At this point the artist resumes possession of the ideal and subjects it to comedic use. Stirner suggested that "[c]omedy, in openly displaying the emptiness, or better, the deflation of the Object, frees men from the old belief, and so their dependency upon this exhausted being" (333). "Kunst und Religion" is both an early attempt by Stirner to work through the ideas he later elaborated on in *Der Einzige und sein Eigentum* and a prescient description of the insurrectionary forces that dominated the manifesto writing culture of the avant-garde.

In the years between joining *Die Freien* in 1841 and the publication of *Der Einzige und sein Eigentum* in 1844 Stirner also published a number of smaller essays and reviews. Some were influential, and David McLellan notes that he "published two articles a little later in the *Berliner Monatsschrift*, a review edited by one of the *Freien*, the first rejecting any ideas of the state, while in the second [...] Stirner elevates the self at the expense of any fixed moral norms" (118). Stirner also found time to marry Marie Dähnhardt in 1843, in an eccentric ceremony culminating in the exchange of brass rings obtained at the last minute. Mackay described Dähnhardt as "a slim, lovely blonde of short, full figure with noticeably rich ornaments in her hair" (*Max Stirner* 118). Dähnhardt was a confirmed radical who "was seen with a long pipe in the rooms of the students, played billiards—and in fact excellently—and drank the Munich beer [...] out of the same large mugs as the men" (Mackay, *Max Stirner* 118).[10] The marriage of two such pronounced iconoclasts was perhaps bound to be problematic; however, Stirner still contrived to devote his productive energies to writing. For the rest of 1843 and the first four months of 1844, work on what would become *Der Einzige und sein Eigentum* consumed Stirner's free time and efforts.

Composition of the book began in 1843, and although the first edition listed the year of publication as 1845, Otto Wigand in Leipzig had published it by the end of 1844. Mackay proposed that among "the circle of 'The Free' a rumor had spread in the course of time that Max Stirner was working on an extensive work," although he "betrayed the 'secret of his life' only to the extent that he occasionally used to point to his desk where his 'I' lay hidden"

---

[10] The unconventional marriage does not seem to have been a happy one, and although Stirner dedicated his book to Marie, she rebuffed Mackay's early efforts to interview her, before informing him that Stirner had been "very sly" and "too selfish to have true friends" (12).

(*Max Stirner* 125).[11] McLellan suggests that "Stirner spent most of 1843 writing *Der Einzige und sein Eigentum*," and that "[i]t was finished by April 1844 and published in November of that year" (118). At its core, the book was a response to Feuerbach's *Das Wesen des Christentums* (The Essence of Christianity, 1841) that "turned Feuerbach's argument against itself, adding humanists to the religious domain" (Shone 214).[12] The implications of this line of argument, however, were more far-reaching than merely polemical, and sent a set of short-lived but intense shockwaves through the ranks of the German intelligentsia.

Der Einzige und sein Eigentum

Der Einzige und sein Eigentum was divisive at the time of its publication, and it has remained so ever since. Stirner's central proposition was that Feuerbach had failed—despite his best efforts—to escape theological concerns and had simply substituted an abstract conception of "Man" for the previously ubiquitous abstract conception of "God." He also claimed that it was with "the strength of *despair* Feuerbach clutches at the total substance of Christianity, not to throw it away, no, to drag it to himself, to draw it, the long-yearned-for, ever-distant, out of its heaven with a last effort, and keep it by him forever" (Stirner, *The Ego and Its Own* 34). Like Feuerbach, Stirner proposed that theology had governed German thought up until Hegel, but Stirner suggested that the post-Hegelian attempt to throw off the shackles of faith had only served to institute a new god, "Man," who proved to be no less tyrannical than the Christian one.[13] McLellan proposes that Stirner can "be seen as the last of the Hegelians, last perhaps because he was the most logical, not attempting to replace Hegel's 'concrete universal' by any 'humanity' or 'classless' society since he had no universal, only the individual, all-powerful ego" (119). Stirner's critique was controversial among his peers, not only because of its strident atheism, but also because it proposed itself to be a final inversion of Hegel's dialectical method that rendered all further philosophical inquiry irrelevant.

[11] Allegedly, Stirner had originally intended to call his book "*Ich*," but later moved this title "to appear over the second principal section of the work" (Mackay 125).
[12] Like many members of the *Junghegelianer*, Feuerbach desired to free the dialectical method from its theological basis. Where Hegel suggested that God was creator of man, Feuerbach proposed that man was the creator of an abstract conception of God. If the idea of God was a human creation, then abstract qualities associated with God—such as love, justice, and mercy—were human qualities. Becoming more Godly then, Feuerbach speculated, was a case of becoming more human.
[13] This is the sense in which Stirner used the term "humanist" to condemn Feuerbach's thought. He was referring to a moral philosophy that depended on the idea of a transcendental conception of the human essence.

Stirner's book was the full realization of insurrectionary egoism, insofar as it subordinated all ideals to the will of the individual—the very point that would make it attractive to manifesto writers. It set out to overturn the entire basis of German idealism by demonstrating that its values had no foundation beyond individual experience. In place of abstract ideas of humanity, love, nationality, and a good cause, Stirner founded his thought on self-will and self-satisfaction. The egoist as envisaged by him was the antithesis of all liberal ideals (in particular those that, in effect, were only substitutes for religion), and a model for political and artistic rebellion. His criticism of the religious foundations of secular ethics proved to be a highly influential line of argument for both artistic and political firebrands. Marx, for instance, went on to incorporate elements of Stirner's critique of Feuerbach by replacing the ego with a socio-economic foundation for philosophy, and Engels proposed that "Proudhon's harmless, purely etymological anarchy [...] would never have resulted in the present anarchist doctrines had not Bakunin laced it with a good measure of Stirnerian 'rebellion'" ("Engels to Max Hildebrand" 394). When Mackay published *Max Stirner: Sein Leben und sein Werk* in 1897, he introduced Stirner's work to a new generation of political and artistic dissidents. Because he argued only for conscious ownership of personal causes at the expense of all other notions of duty, writers and insurgents could easily adapt Stirner's egoism to insurrectionary causes as diverse as fascism and Dada.

The extent to which Stirner achieved his own desired ends inevitably fell somewhere between Mackay's glowing praise and the derisive response of his opponents. *Der Einzige und sein Eigentum* is an uneven work that does not progress logically through its arguments and engages in poorly conceived and sustained forays into dialectical rhetoric. However, its central proposition—that all abstractions are the creations and properties of the individual—so entirely assaulted the basis of post-Hegelian thought that it could "at once quicken the anxiety, inflame the indignation, and for a time monopolize the thunderbolts of such reigning giants as Marx, Engels, Feuerbach and Hess" (Paterson 7). David Leopold suggests that this was an intended effect, and that "almost every feature of [Stirner's] writing seems calculated to unnerve" (xiii). His "use of aphorism and metaphor, the neologisms, the mixture of self-consciously obscure terminology with colloquial language, the excessive italicization and hyperbole, all confound the received framework in which philosophical argument is conducted" (Leopold xiii). *Der Einzige und sein Eigentum* was not only an assault on the principles of German idealism; it was an assault on its style. Indeed, the similarities between Stirner's frequently outrageous style and some literary manifestos produced in the early twentieth century may provide another reason for his particular popularity with writers and artists of Futurism, Vorticism, and Dada.

It is unusual, then, that a book so incendiary begins with one of the most conventional of all Hegelian devices, a dialectical triad that describes the history of society as analogous with the personal development of a child into youth and maturity. In fact, the entire structure of *Der Einzige und sein Eigentum* borders on parody of Feuerbach's most famous work. McLellan explains that "[t]he layout of the book is clearly modelled on Feuerbach's *Das Wesen des Christentums*, being divided into two parts entitled 'man' and 'myself,' which correspond to the two parts of Feuerbach's work that dealt respectively with God and man" (120). Similarly, Stirner used a dialectical triad to mock Feuerbach's early suggestion in his book that "Religion is the childlike condition of humanity; but the child sees his nature—man—out of himself; in childhood a man is an object to himself, under the form of another man" (*The Essence of Christianity* 14). Stirner responded:

> The child was realistic, taken up with the things of this world, until little by little he succeeded in getting at what was behind these very things; the youth was idealistic, inspired by thoughts, until he worked his way up to where he became the man, the egoistic man, who deals with things and thoughts according to his heart's pleasure, and sets his personal interest above everything.
>
> (*The Ego and Its Own* 18)

Civilization—and Feuerbach—had not yet managed to develop from youth into adulthood and remained transfixed by the world of abstract ideas. McLellan describes the use of Hegel's dialectical rhetoric as "only an outer shell, for Stirner was very weak on history as he had no room to allow for a historical development whether of the world spirit, self-consciousness or the class struggle" (119). The way Stirner adopted the structure of *Das Wesen des Christentums* instead provided him with an opportunity to take ownership of Feuerbach's ideas and to mock them at length.

The early sections of *Der Einzige und sein Eigentum* describe three stages of a human life, and the remainder of the first half of the book sets out to compare these stages to the ancients (*Die Alten*), the moderns (*Die Neuen*),[14] and the free

---

[14] Stirner opened his discussion of *Die Neuen* by quoting 2 Corinthians 5:17, that "If any man be in Christ, he is a *new creature*; the old is passed away, behold, all is become *new*" (27). The tone is ironic, and the implication is that "[t]o pure warm-heartedness or pure theory men exist only to be criticized, scoffed at, and thoroughly despised; to it no less than to the fanatical cleric, they are only filth and other such fine things" (28). According to him, even the so-called atheist philosophers were arrogant zealots whose praise of an abstract humanity matched their contempt for actual human beings. To be *modern* for Stirner meant to be religious.

(*Die Freien*).¹⁵ Stirner suggested that one "feels with particular vividness what changes have taken place in himself when he has before his eyes the unrolling of another's life," so proposed to "look into the activities our forefathers busied themselves with" (*The Ego and Its Own* 19). What follows is a hasty account of pre-Christian Europe that begins with the observation that "we will not throw it up against them that, in comparison with us experienced people, they ought properly to be called children" (19).¹⁶ He unconvincingly proposed that the entire thrust of ancient history from Pericles to Cicero was founded on "the feeling that the world and mundane relations (such as the natural ties of blood) were the truth before which the powerless 'I' must bow" (20). Then, having barely begun a historical discussion of the moderns, he dismissed the topic with the suggestion that "[i]f the ancients have nothing to show but wisdom of the world, the moderns never did nor do make their way further than to theology," while "even the newest revolts against God are nothing but the extremist efforts of 'theology,' that is, theological insurrections" (30). With this indictment, Stirner abandoned his task of establishing a dialectical triad in favor of an extended diversion into identifying and condemning the "fixed ideas" of the moderns. McLellan calls this a "sort of demonology of the spirits to which humanity has been successively enslaved" (121); again, the apparent intent was a polemical one to confound and unnerve.

The account in *Der Einzige und sein Eigentum* of the spooks, spirits, fixed ideas, and wheels in the head that possess the modern mind is the most powerful element of Stirner's critique.¹⁷ It has provoked the ire of his opponents, exhilarated his supporters, informed an entire stream of anarchist thought, and left a lasting impression on the nature of the modern manifesto. Stirner insisted that "not only is the God of religion a projection of man's alienated self, but so is

---

¹⁵ An explicit reference to *Die Freien*, whom he proceeded to castigate for their failure to escape the theological thinking of the moderns.

¹⁶ Stirner also briefly outlined a second dialectical framework here, this time structured around race. In reality, it was a blatant attempt to insult his opponents using racial slurs. Stirner proposed that "[t]he history of the world, whose shaping properly belongs altogether to the Caucasian race, seems till now to have run through two Caucasian ages, in the first of which we had to work out and work off our innate *Negroidity*; this was followed in the second by *Mongoloidity* (Chineseness), which must likewise be terribly made an end of" (*The Ego and Its Own* 62). From this point he suggested that materialists belong to the "Negroid age," while idealists belong to the "Mongoloid age" (63). Though only a few pages long, this crass interlude continues to prove repellent, though not for the reasons Stirner intended.

¹⁷ While Byington's translations of *Spuk*, *Geist*, and *fixe Idee* are conventional, "wheels in the head" requires some explanation. The German idiom used by Stirner is "Du hast einen Sparren zu viel!" (You have a rafter too many!) but Leopold recommends an "alternative, if equally unliteral, translation" of "you have a screw loose!" as perhaps better capturing Stirner's meaning for a contemporary reader (*The Ego and Its Own* 333).

every ideal, every cause, every 'fixed idea,' for they all entice men into following a *spook* which is neither of their creation nor within their power" (Carroll, *Breakout from the Crystal Palace* 21). He proposed that the foremost of these was what Feuerbach identified as "the essence of man" (Feuerbach, *The Essence of Christianity* 8), a cornerstone of humanism, liberalism, and socialism. Stirner proposed that "*Man* reaches beyond every individual man, and yet—though he be 'his essence'—is not in fact *his* essence (which rather would be as single as he the individual himself) but a general and 'higher,' yes, for atheists 'the highest essence'" (Stirner, *The Ego and Its Own* 39).[18] From the fixed idea of humanity emerged an entire pantheon of modern gods including "right, law, a good cause, majesty, marriage, the common good, order, the fatherland, and so on," with all being examples of "[a]n idea that has subjected the man to itself" (43). He derided Christians, humanists, liberals, and socialists alike for their fixation on phantom ideals that had no relevance outside the realm of pure thought and labeled appeals to such ideals the delusions of fanatics.

It is only after having likened modern society to a lunatic asylum that Stirner saw fit to return to his triad of the ancient, the modern, and the free. He warned not to "think I am jesting or speaking figuratively when I regard those persons who cling to the higher, and [...] almost the whole world of men, as veritable fools, fools in a madhouse" (Stirner, *The Ego and Its Own* 43). Having dismissed the ancients as mere children at the whim of the elements and the moderns as lunatics possessed by spirits, convention suggests that Stirner had arrived at the point of Hegelian synthesis, where "the free" come to liberate themselves from both their physical and spiritual shackles. However, this was not the case, and Stirner again played on expectations by observing that "it may seem as if the free were here to be described in a third division as independent and distinct," but "are only the more modern and most modern among the 'moderns'" (89). His ruse of a dialectical triad had provided him with the very opportunity to seize upon the Hegelian fixed ideas that monopolized the thought of his liberal compatriots. He began the process of exorcising *Die Freien* with an account of the demons that possessed their champions.

Stirner identified three strains of liberalism in *Der Einzige und sein Eigentum*, political, social, and humane, and ascribed to each the respective fixed (abstract)

---

[18] Stirner's choice of words to denote "the highest essence" are "das höchste Wesen" which Leopold observes can also connote "the Supreme Being" (*The Ego and Its Own* 333). The implication is, of course, that some transcendental fantasy of a collective and superlative notion of man has essentially become the god of the modern atheist.

ideas of state, society, and humanity. What Stirner called the political, social, and humane iterations of liberalism, Mackay identified by the end of the century as the philosophies of the "liberals, socialists and ethicists" (*Max Stirner* 138). Stirner had managed to single out for derision the founding principles of three of the most important philosophical movements in the history of Western thought: liberalism, socialism, and humanism. If *Der Einzige und sein Eigentum* exasperated conservative audiences with its mockery of the Christian faith, its discussion of "the free" ensured that progressive thinkers joined the ranks of the incensed.

Stirner first turned his attack to the foundations of classical liberalism. Far from defending the rights of the individual as they claimed to, Stirner asserted that political liberals had imposed a tyranny of the state. He proposed that the political liberal's "commonalty is nothing else than the thought that the state is all in all, the true man, and that the individual's human value consists in being a citizen of the state" (Stirner, *The Ego and Its Own* 90). The liberal citizen may be "filthy rich or as poor as a church mouse—the state of the commonalty leaves that to your choice; but only have a 'good disposition,'" lest the state have cause for your censorship or arrest (95). He argued that liberals had surrendered any aspirations of political self-will to the mechanisms of the state in return for having limited property rights conferred upon them. Through the provision of property rights, the state—a spirit—had become "proprietor and master" over the people whom it purported to represent, for the individual "who must have something 'granted' to him cannot be regarded as absolute" (91). Having claimed that the liberal ideal of "a community of those who know their human dignity and hold together as 'human beings'" was a sham (90), Stirner turned his attention to his most revolutionary foes: the socialists.

Where the liberal had only surrendered power to the idea of the state, Stirner proposed that the socialist had also surrendered *ownership* to the idea of society.[19] He suggested that "social liberalism concludes, *no one must have*, as according to political liberalism *no one was to give orders*; as in that case the *state* alone obtained the command, so now *society* alone obtains the possessions" (Stirner, *The Ego and Its Own* 105). The socialist had recognized the "fundamental contradiction" in liberalism's "theoretical equality of men as

---

[19] Stirner's discussion of socialism and communism never mentions Marx, and he does not seem acquainted with his work at this stage. This is unsurprising, given that in 1844 Marx was still developing his own theories of communism. The only thinker singled out for direct criticism in this section of *Der Einzige und sein Eigentum* is Proudhon, whose collectivist anarchism seemed to Stirner tantamount to communism. In later parts of the book, Stirner also identified Wilhelm Weitling and Moses Hess with socialism.

'persons' simultaneously with their actual inequality in respect of property" and sought to resolve it by "placing all property in the impersonal and impartial hands of Society" (Paterson 75). In reply to the socialist declaration that, in surrendering property to society "all may have," Stirner asked "Who is this person that you call 'all'?" (Stirner, *The Ego and Its Own* 105). He rejected the collective identity of society because while "the united society may indeed have bodies at its service," it has "no one body of its own" (105). The socialists had not even considered the possibility that "society is no ego at all, which could give, bestow, or grant, but an instrument or means, from which we may derive benefit; that we have no social duties, but solely interests for the pursuance of which society must serve us" (111). Bluntly, he suggested that under communism "we are all ragamuffins [*Lumpen*] together, and as the aggregate of communistic society we might call ourselves a 'ragamuffin crew'" (106). He proposed that the socialists had placed the idea of society above its constituent individuals and by doing so reduced people to mere units of labor possessed by an idea.

In his critique of humane liberalism, Stirner upbraided his friend, Bruno Bauer, for his appeals to a human essence. He proposed that the "self-criticising, 'critical' liberalism" of Bauer had brought to a conclusion the liberal project of doing away with self-will (Stirner, *The Ego and Its Own* 111). The goal of what Stirner branded humane liberalism was "to strip away every peculiar characteristic limited to a particular group, thereby liberating our essential and universal humanity" (Paterson 76). For Stirner, ideology founded on universal humanity was an even greater threat to the unique individual than earlier forms of liberalism. He suggested that both political and social liberalism at least provided room for a degree of individuality, but that humanistic liberalism sought to extinguish the differences that allowed for a sense of unique selfhood. Political liberals "thinking to abolish *personal will*, self-will or arbitrariness, did not observe that through *property* [*Eigentum*] our *self-will* [*Eigenwille*] gained a secure place of refuge" (Stirner, *The Ego and Its Own* 115). Socialists then attempted to extinguish self-will by "taking away property too," but "do not notice that this secures itself a continued existence in *self-ownership* [*Eigenheit*]" (115).[20] Humanism was both the beginning and end of efforts to overcome the individual ego because "in the 'human society' which the humane liberal promises, nothing

---

[20] Stirner's use of *Eigenheit* represents another challenge for translators. A better alternative is perhaps a notion of "owness." The implication is that individuals' peculiarities defy efforts to reduce people to examples of a wider class. Stirner claimed that humanism was an assault on owness because it sought to create a universal class that ignored the properties which made the individual unique—and inherently unequal.

'special' which one or another has is to find recognition, nothing which bears the character of 'private' is to have value" (115). In humanism Stirner perceived a desire to render everyone equal by assigning all individual value to the universal characteristic of being human. If the political liberal had branded the egoist a criminal and the social liberal had branded the egoist a thief, only the humanist had the gall to brand the individual inhuman (*unmenschlich*) for claiming to be more important than society. Stirner responded that "[l]iberalism as a whole has a deadly enemy, an invincible opposite, as God has the devil: by the side of man stands always the un-man, the individual, the egoist" (125). To be an egoist then was to be the nemesis of every liberal ideal.

Stirner's criticism of the religiosity of liberal values readily translated to the realm of art. He had already suggested in "Kunst und Religion" that the inspired artist effectively founds a faith by creating an essence for others to aspire to, but his critique of such essences in *Der Einzige und sein Eigentum* implied a deeper connection between art, morality, and politics. Stirner proposed that while the "discoverer of a great truth doubtless knows that it can be useful to the rest of men," he produces his book, painting, or symphony "for his own sake and for the satisfaction of *his* want" (Stirner, *The Ego and Its Own* 119). Artists had created great works out of an egoistic desire "to offer *oneself* to the world in a work, to work out and shape *oneself*" (119). As in politics so in art essences such as beauty and truth—as well as whole systems of values such as the Enlightenment and Romanticism—had guided the hands of the individuals possessed by them. Artistic innovation had been the product of individual artists rising above these essences to produce works that met a desire for self-realization. These works had provided the models for the revolutions—artistic, moral, and political—that followed. Great artists were crucial figures, able to bring about widespread social change if—and only if—they could rise above the fixed ideas established by their forebears and become founders of new traditions.[21]

The second half of *Der Einzige und sein Eigentum* is concerned with uncovering the means by which an individual may overcome the fixed ideas that govern people's thoughts and actions. While Stirner had convincingly argued that the world of ideas was the product of a religious mindset, he struggled with the matter of what to do about it. He concluded that it was not sufficient

---

[21] It has already been noted that Stirner singled out Homer and Hesiod as having created new gods for the Greeks, and he also observed that "Raphael's portrayal of Christ casts him in such a light that he could be the basis of a new religion—a religion of the biblical Christ set apart from all human affairs" (Stirner, "Art and Religion" 332).

to be liberated from ideals, because "the craving for freedom as for something absolute, worthy of every praise, deprived us of ownness" and "created self-denial" (Stirner, *The Ego and Its Own* 142). Freedom was itself an ideal, and simply another spirit that haunted the mind. Once stripped of its theological associations with being "delivered from the 'bonds of this earth-life!'" the goal of "[b]eing free from anything—means only being clear or rid" of it (142). Freedom from a thing necessarily meant relinquishing control over it. Stirner argued that "the completest self-denial is nothing but freedom—freedom namely from self-determination, from one's own self" (142). Instead of total freedom then, he proposed the goal of total ownership. He observed that "I am free from what I am *rid* of, owner of what I have in my *power* or what I *control*" (143). The goal of the egoist was not to become free from moral constraint, but to become the sole arbiter of moral values. Nevertheless, it was one thing to aspire to total dominion, another thing to obtain it.

The first difficulty Stirner faced with granting total ownership to the unique individual was determining what individuality amounted to once separated from all external values. On this topic, he turned to the work of Johann Gottlieb Fichte. In *Wissenschaftslehre* (Science of Knowledge, 1794), Fichte had already proposed that reality was the product of the self-positing ego. Fichte argued that in order to "arrive at a self-justifying basis for our claims to knowledge" philosophy needed to "find something that is posited in the act of thinking itself" (Scruton 157). The only thing that he could conceive of that met this requirement was the self, "for when the self is the object of thought, that which is 'posited' is identical with that which 'posits'" (157). Nevertheless, Fichte's concept of the ego was too abstract for Stirner and threatened to be yet another abstract idea. Stirner rejected Fichte's contention that "the ego is all," and proposed instead that "it is not that the ego *is* all, but the ego *destroys* all, and only the self-dissolving ego, the never-being ego, the—*finite* ego is really I" (Stirner, *The Ego and Its Own* 163). In contrast to Fichte's position that the "self-positing of the self is the true ground of the law of identity, and hence of logic itself" (Scruton 157), Stirner described a "transitory ego" that existed only insofar as it was able to destroy everything outside of itself (Stirner, *The Ego and Its Own* 163). In order to avoid the inevitable criticism that his conception of the self was nothing more than yet another ideal to aspire to, Stirner founded it on the act of insurrection (*Empörung*).[22] This rhetorical flourish had liberated the unique individual from

---

[22] The concept of *Empörung* and how it differs from the idea of revolution is discussed further in the introduction of this book.

the realm of ideals, but this freedom had come at the cost of confining the egoist to the role of consuming or destroying every idea ever created.

The second problem with proposing a limitless and all-powerful ego was that there were obvious material limits to the unique individual's power. If egoism was to overturn the realism of the ancients as well as the idealism of the moderns, it seemed to demand total ownership not only of the spiritual world of thoughts, but also of the corporeal world of things as well. At the very least, Stirner needed to accommodate the physical limitations placed upon individuals by the brute force of others. Acknowledging the limits of individual power, Stirner conceded that "[h]e who has might has—right; if you have not the former, neither have you the latter" (Stirner, *The Ego and His Own* 172). He maintained, however, that even the most powerful opponent "who would break your will has to do with you, and is your *enemy*," while "even if as a power you overawe your opponent, still you are not on that account a hallowed authority to him, unless he be a simpleton" (176). Material constraints only limited the extent to which individuals could realize their egoistic desires. Faced with the overwhelming physical power at the disposal of the state, Stirner proposed that "[t]he state's behaviour is violence, and it calls its violence law," (176).[23] It was "only by crime [*Verbrechen*]," he continued, that the egoist could "overcome [*bricht*] the state's violence when he thinks that the state is not above him, but he is above the state" (176). While no individual could claim total control of the physical world, Stirner suggested that every individual was capable of challenging authority through willfully criminal acts. Logic had once again forced Stirner into an apparently nihilistic position in which the only way an individual could demonstrate self-ownership was by rejecting notions of authority.

The fact that Stirner's own logic forced him to found egoism on insurrection and crime has led some critics to suggest that his was a fundamentally nihilistic philosophy. For example, Paterson proposes that "[r]esting as it does on an ontology of negation, in which vacuity, purposelessness, and disintegration are the constitutive concepts, [Stirner's] total egoism is essentially grounded in a world-view which is starkly nihilistic" (ix). Still, Carroll suggests that

---

[23] Nevertheless, a logical inconsistency appears to arise at this juncture of Stirner's thought. He had already acknowledged "the fixed idea of the State itself" (Stirner, *The Ego and Its Own* 44), so it is peculiar that the state is considered as an external force to be struggled against. The state, like all abstractions, is surely a creation of the unique individual. One way to make sense of this apparent inconsistency is to interpret crime as a rejection of authority on an intellectual level and, as a result, a denial of the state's existence. From this standpoint the individual follows—or breaks—rules out of self-interest rather than out of a perceived duty to the idea of the state.

"Stirner is not the prophet of callous isolation in spite of his caustic words; his intention is to put that focus of much of human hope and philosophy—love—on an honest, concrete footing" (*Break-Out from the Crystal Palace* 29). Stirner did not set out to abolish inter-personal relationships but reinterpret them as the joyful outpourings of the unique individual. He conceived of love as "not a commandment, but, like each of my feelings, *my property*" (*The Ego and Its Own* 259). When an individual genuinely cared for another person, it was not because of a shared duty to a human essence or Christian ideal, but because of the self-satisfaction that such feelings produced. Love was not an obligation but an act of will. For Stirner, individual experience was the only solid foundation in what would otherwise be a nihilistic universe.

Because he argued it was the source of all meaning, Stirner could only describe the self as that which remained after he excluded everything that it had created. When he proposed that "[i]n the *unique one* [*Einzigen*] the owner [*Eigner*] himself returns into his creative nothing, of which he is born" (*The Ego and Its Own* 324), he did not suggest a nihilistic conception of the self, but one that precluded language, thought, and meaning. Stirner both begins and ends *Der Einzige und sein Eigentum* with the opening line of Goethe's poem "Vanitas! Vanitatum vanitas!": "Ich hab' mein' Sach' auf Nichts gestellt [I have set my affair on nothing]" (326). Stirner, however, saw no contradiction between setting his affairs on nothing and setting his affairs on himself. Once he had excluded all meaning, only his self-will remained. The ego was "nothing" because it created everything, and Stirner proposed that "no concept expresses me, nothing that is designated as my essence exhausts me; they are only names" (324). For him, the repossession or rejection of all alienated abstractions, and the continual creation and destruction of personal ideals within the control of their owner—effectively the founding of a contingent, personal manifesto—was the ultimate expression of creative self-will.

The Immediate Reception

The response of the German intellectual community to the assaults of *Der Einzige und sein Eigentum* was swift and intense. Engels was among the first to read Stirner's book, and he wrote to Marx about it within days of its publication. He described Stirner as "the most talented, independent and hard-working of the 'Free'" ("Engels to Marx" 13), but labeled his egoism "the essence of present society and present man brought to consciousness, the ultimate that can be said against us by present society, the culmination of all the theory intrinsic to the prevailing stupidity" (11). Nevertheless, he conceded that it was "certainly true that we must first make a cause our own, egoistic cause, before we can do anything to further it—and hence that in this sense, irrespective of any material relations, we are communists out of egoism also" (12). Engels further suggested to Marx that Stirner was "right in rejecting Feuerbach's 'man,' or at least the 'man' of *Das Wessen des Christentums*," because "it is from God that he arrives at 'man,' and hence 'man' is crowned with a theological halo of abstraction" (12). The egoism that Engels saw as an inevitable component of communism demanded that communists "must not simply cast [*Der Einzige und sein Eigentum*] aside, but rather use it as the perfect expression of present-day folly and, *while inverting it*, continue to build on it" (11). In order to combat the egoism of Stirner, Engels considered it necessary both to break with Feuerbach's idea of a human essence and to account for the role of the ego within a broader theory of communism.

Marx's initial impression of Stirner's book—in his response to Engels' 1844 letter—has not survived, but circumstantial evidence suggests he was unmoved. Paterson speculates that "Engels' modified rapture must have been chilled by Marx's reply, for in his next letter we find him dismissing *Der Einzige*" in contrite terms (103). Engels admitted to Marx that "[w]hen I wrote to you, I was still too much under the immediate impression made upon me by the book," and that having "laid it aside and had time to think it over, I feel the same as you" ("Engels to Marx" 16). He added that Moses Hess too had, "after several changes of mind, come to the same conclusion as yourself" (16). It seems that Marx decreed there was to be no room for egoism in his conception of communism. In fact, he had already set out to respond to Stirner in a review for the upcoming *Vorwärts! Pariser Deutsche Monatsschrift* (Forward! Parisian German Monthly), a journal edited by Heinrich Börnstein and due for publication on January 16, 1845.

The review did not go as planned. Marx wrote to Börnstein in early January, informing him that it was "impossible for me to let you have the review of Stirner before next week," and instructing him to "deliver the specimen copy without my contribution; [Heinrich] Bürgers will let you have an article in its stead" ("Marx to Heinrich Börnstein" 14). Whereas Engels' comments suggest that Marx regarded *Der Einzige und sein Eigentum* as of little consequence, Marx's own response seems to have demanded considerable time and effort. The fact that he had not completed his review in a timely manner, however, proved irrelevant. The French government's decision to expel many of the journal's contributors—including Marx—torpedoed the first issue of *Vorwärts! Pariser Deutsche Monatsschrift* entirely. Nevertheless, Marx continued work on his review of Stirner's book, and he soon enlisted the assistance of Engels. The pair eventually spent over a year working on a reply to *Der Einzige und sein Eigentum*, and by the time it was complete, it had become an unpublishable tirade of epic proportions. The difficulty of refuting Stirner's arguments seems to have proved taxing beyond Marx's early expectations. By the time that he and Engels moved to publish the manuscript of *Sankt Max*, Stirner's book had already begun to fade from public attention, and other offended parties had long since printed their own responses to the book.

By the end of 1845 Feuerbach, Hess, and a disciple of Bruno Bauer writing under the pseudonym of Szeliga had all published replies to *Der Einzige und sein Eigentum*.[24] The first to come forward was Szeliga, publishing his response in the March 1845 edition of the *Norddeutsche Blätter für Kritik, Literatur, und Unterhaltung* (North-German Pages for Criticism, Literature, and Entertainment). In his review, Szeliga dismissed Stirner's egoist as itself an abstraction, and suggested that "[m]easured by his own principle, to see ghosts everywhere in the ideal, the Unique Individual [...] becomes the ghost of all ghosts" (my trans.; 18).[25] Although Szeliga noted Stirner's failure to recognize the difficulty of meaningfully cordoning off his egoist from his social and historical context, he ignored the extent to which Stirner had already anticipated—and countered—any suggestion that the individual was itself an ideal.

Feuerbach was the next to respond, in the form of an anonymous review for the July number of *Wigands Vierteljahrsschrift* (Wigand's Quarterly) titled "*Über das Wesen des Christentums in Beziehung auf den Einzigen und sein Eigentum*" (On *The Essence of Christianity* in Relation to *The Ego and Its Own*). Like Szeliga, Feuerbach argued that "the 'Egoist' has still, despite everything, also based his affairs on God" and, for this reason, belonged to the same category of "pious atheists" as the political liberal ("On *The Essence of Christianity* in Relation to *The Ego and Its Own*" 81). Feuerbach decried "the absolute idealism of 'Egoism'" and called Stirner's claim to have based his affairs on nothing "an expression of religion" founded on the principle that "God is nothing" (81). He reduced *Der*

---

[24] Szeliga was a pseudonym for Franz Zychlinski, a follower of Bauer's school of criticism. Bauer himself remained Stirner's firm friend, and "was the only one, apart from Buhl, to attend Stirner's funeral and pay him this last mark of respect" (McLellan 125).
[25] "Mit seinem eigenen Principe gemessen, dem Princip überall Gespenster zu sehn, wird der Einzige, wie wir gesehn haben, zum Gespenst aller Gespenster" (Szeliga 18).

Einzige und sein Eigentum to an idealization of selfishness and nothingness, and completely ignored Stirner's argument that only the individual ego provided a concrete foundation for ideals. Hess also joined the fray in July, releasing "a pamphlet entitled *Die letzten Philosophen* (The Recent Philosophers), in which he held Stirner's "Union of Egoists" to be nothing new, since "[o]ur whole history up to now has been nothing but the history of egoistical unions, whose fruits are known to all of us—ancient slavery, Roman bondage, and our modern principled and universal serfdom" (373-4). Conspicuously, all three reviewers avoided Stirner's criticism of the moral foundations of post-Hegelian philosophy, and instead chose to write at length on Stirner's efforts to establish a dialectical triad using a simplistic rendering of ancient and modern history. As David Ashford suggests, "[n]one of Stirner's contemporaries seem to have understood (or—been prepared to accept) the extent to which this egoism marked a break with essentialist thought" (15). Only Marx and Engels seriously attempted to refute Stirner's indictment of socialism's religiosity.

Marx and Engels finished work on their response to Stirner in 1846 and moved to publish it—along with criticism of Feuerbach and Bruno Bauer—as a book that would later be given the title of *Die deutsche Ideologie*. Despite the "urgings of Jenny [Marx], of Engels and of [Georg Gottlob] Jung and other friends [...] to get on with his *Critique of Politics and of Political Economy*" (Stedman Jones 190), Stirner's book seems to have become an ongoing obsession for Marx, and over the course of two years, he wrote more than 300 pages on the subject. In short, Marx devoted almost as much time—and paper—to criticizing Stirner as Stirner had devoted to writing *Der Einzige und sein Eigentum* in the first place. The resulting manuscript essentially "comprises a criticism of Feuerbach which borrows elements from Stirner and a criticism of Stirner which tacitly admits the validity of his attack on Feuerbach but maintains that it no longer applies" (McLellan 129). However, the invective that Marx directed against Stirner was so bellicose as to render the manuscript virtually unpublishable. Despite the diligent efforts of Marx and Engels to find a printer for the book, by December 1847 Marx accepted that his "German manuscripts are not being published as a whole," and even the parts that could be printed had to be supplied "gratis, simply in order to launch them on the world" ("Marx to Engels" 150). As *Die deutsche Ideologie*, an abridged version of the book was first printed in 1932, and most editors continue to excise the lengthy and tedious chapter on Stirner that represents two-thirds of the original work.

In *Die deutsche Ideologie*, Marx took an unconventional approach to combatting Stirner's ideas. Rather than challenge his assaults on the foundations of socialism, he tacitly accepted Stirner's critique of Feuerbach, claimed it as his own, and provided a line-by-line re-reading of *Der Einzige und sein Eigentum*, portraying the book as the very embodiment of religious idealism.[26] Marx laid claim to Stirner's most powerful insight—the religious foundations of liberalism, humanism, and "true" socialism—and used it to establish a new ideological program of his own design. He declared that "[t]he entire body of German philosophical criticism from Strauss to Stirner is confined to criticism of religious conceptions," whereby "[t]he world was sanctified to an ever-increasing extent till at last the venerable Saint Max was able to canonise it *en bloc* and thus dispose of it once for all" (Marx, *The German Ideology* 29).[27] Marx conceded that "[t]he first premise of all human history is, of course, the existence of living human individuals," but added that "what individuals are depends on the material conditions of their production" (32). Like Stirner, Marx proposed that German philosophers had never succeeded in escaping theological concerns, but rather than finding firm ground in the uniqueness of the individual, "for Marx the basis to which philosophy had to be reduced was socio-economic" (McLellan 122). Marx and Stirner had come to diametrically opposed conclusions about the future of philosophy. In *Der Einzige und sein Eigentum*, Stirner had ignored society's role in shaping the individual ego, while in his response, Marx had ignored the role of individual self-will in social relations in order to propose a socio-economic foundation for philosophy.

Despite being a work of "monomaniac prolixity" (Paterson 107), *Die deutsche Ideologie* is important to understanding the history of the modern manifesto because it documents the effect of *Der Einzige und sein Eigentum* on Marx in the

---

[26] In *Specters of Marx* (1993), Jacques Derrida described Marx's misapprehension of Stirner's thought as the result of his own eagerness to banish the supernatural: "After having determined the spirit to be something other than (the) self ('*Der Geist ist etwas Andres als Ich*'), a definition, we dare say, not lacking in insight, Stirner poses yet another excellent question ('But this other, what is it? [*Dieses Andre aber, was ist's?*]'), a big question which Marx, it seems, is too quick to scoff at and too eager to do whatever necessary to exorcise in his turn" (151). Stirner's answer to this second question was, of course, "I take the world as what it is to me, as *mine*, as my property [*Eigentum*]; I refer all to myself" (Stirner, *The Ego and Its Own* 17).

[27] The derisive nickname "Saint Max" is directed at Stirner's supposed desire to sanctify everything in order to exorcise the world of all spirits. It is yet another example of Marx's willful mischaracterization of Stirner's arguments.

years immediately preceding the writing of *The Communist Manifesto*. In turn, *The Communist Manifesto* is so important to understanding later political and artistic manifestos that Martin Puchner has proposed that "[t]he predominance of the [*Communist*] *Manifesto* over the subsequent history of the genre means that a history of the manifesto must also entail a history of socialism" (2). *Der Einzige und sein Eigentum* forced Marx to abandon "the moralistic, normative and still quasi-religious character of socialist rhetoric" (Stedman Jones 190) and redescribe communism as "the *real* movement which abolishes the present state of things" (Marx, *The German Ideology* 49). Marx's response to Stirner was to fall back from an ideological position in favor of a practical one, and Stirner could have certainly answered that Marx nevertheless demanded the willful actions of individuals to abolish present socio-economic conditions. Just as Engels had proposed in 1844, Marx needed to account for the role of individual will in communism, and he did so in the *Theses on Feuerbach*.

Marx wrote the *Theses on Feuerbach* in the spring of 1845, within months of reading *Der Einzige und sein Eigentum* and at the height of his preoccupation with Stirner. In no small way, they represented an effort to redefine communism in order to account for Stirner's criticisms. In order to counter Stirner's attack on the mysticism inherent in Feuerbach's essence of man, for example, Marx argued that "the essence of man is no abstraction inherent in each single individual," but instead "the ensemble of the social relations" (*Theses on Feuerbach* 7). Nevertheless, in his efforts to break away from Feuerbach's materialism—a position he saw as demolished by Stirner's assault—Marx repeatedly co-opted many of Stirner's ideas without any kind of attribution. Marx argued that "[t]he chief defect of all previous materialism" is that it has not conceived of reality "as *human sensuous activity, practice*," and "not *subjectively*" (6; emphasis added). Like Stirner, he asserted the need to "prove the truth" with practical displays of "reality and power" (6). He even rejected the "materialist doctrine that men are the products of circumstances and upbringing" and instead proposed that "it is men who change circumstances and the educator must himself be educated" (7). The eleventh thesis in particular—a statement that Puchner suggests *The Communist Manifesto* was "forged in accordance with" (1)—ultimately advocated a willful display of individual might. In it, Marx proposed that "[t]he philosophers have only *interpreted* the world in various ways; the point, however, is to *change* it" (*Theses on Feuerbach* 8). With a singular statement, Marx allowed for the possibility that superior individual minds—such as his own—could exert their will on the course of history.[28] Egoism entered communism just as Engels had suggested it must, and *The Communist Manifesto* became a powerful demonstration of the potentially transformative role of individuals on existing socio-economic conditions.

The opportunity to write what would become *The Communist Manifesto* fell into Marx's lap in 1847. Leaving the exiled Marx behind in Brussels, Engels had returned to Paris to "at once set up a propaganda community" ("Engels to Marx" 138), and he soon secured a position in the Paris District Committee of the Communist League. He wrote to Marx on October 26, updating him on recent developments. Before Marx's expulsion from Paris, the London Central Authority of the Communist League had distributed Engels' attempt at a "Communist Confession of Faith" to the various international branches. In Engel's absence, Hess had responded by proposing his own version of a "Communist Catechism" to the Paris District Committee. Upon his return, Engels subjected this catechism to a savage and systematic assault. He explained to Marx that "Mosi" had "put through a delightfully amended confession of faith. Last Friday at the district I dealt with this, point by point, and was not yet half way through when the lads declared themselves *satisfaits*" (Engels 138). He succeeded in having what had been a majority decision in favor of Hess's catechism overturned. Engels informed Marx that "*Completely unopposed*, I got them to entrust me with the task of drafting a new one which will be discussed next Friday by the district and will be sent to London *behind the backs of the communities*" (138–39). In November he wrote to Marx on the subject again, asking him to "[g]ive a little thought to the Confession of Faith. I think we would do best to abandon the catechetical form and call the thing Communist *Manifesto*" ("Engels to Marx" 149). Marx, working largely alone, completed *The Communist Manifesto* by January 1848, and the Workers' Educational Association in London published it in German a month later.

From the standpoint of Marx's theory, the writing of a manifesto seems to be an unwarranted endeavor. This is because his interpretation of communism considered revolution to be the inevitable outcome of changing socio-economic conditions rather than the product of propaganda. Even *The Communist Manifesto* itself proposed that the fall of the bourgeoisie "and the victory of the

---

[28] Mikhail Bakunin certainly framed Marx's motives in egoistic terms, suggesting that "there is no intrigue so sordid that he would hesitate to engage in it if in his opinion (which is for the most part mistaken) it might serve to strengthen his position and his influence or extend his power" (*Statism and Anarchy* 141).

proletariat are equally inevitable" (*The Communist Manifesto* 79). Marx wrote that "not only has the bourgeoisie forged the weapons that bring death to itself; it has also called into existence the men who are to wield those weapons—the modern working class—the proletarians" (68). It was not the propagandizing of individuals, but "with the development of industry" that "the proletariat not only increases in number; it becomes concentrated in greater masses, its strength grows, and it feels its strength more" (72). Indeed, even the role set out for the communist party in *The Communist Manifesto* was quite nebulous, and Marx proposed that "[t]hey merely express, in general terms, actual relations springing from an existing class struggle, from an historical movement going on under our very eyes" (81). The closest he came to justifying the need for a manifesto was his suggestion that there was a need to confront "the *spectre of communism* with a manifesto of the party itself" (55). On this point, Stedman Jones proposes that *The Communist Manifesto* was "not designed for posterity or even the wider world," but instead "for the members of the League alone, and its aim was to bind the various branches—particularly those in Paris—to a single agreed programme" (221). Nevertheless, Marx did provide a theoretical justification for *The Communist Manifesto*, but not in the manifesto itself.

While *The Communist Manifesto* promoted Marx's materialist conception of history, it was not beholden to it for justification. Instead, its existence relied as Puchner suggests on the eleventh of the *Theses on Feuerbach*, and its notion that the duty of the philosopher was to change history rather than understand it. The idea that the will of an individual could break the shackles of moral training was, however, the closest that Marx ever came to agreeing with Stirner's intellectual position. At the very least, it was an idea that first emerged in his application of Stirner's critique to Feuerbach's humanism. In order to advocate any kind of willful action, *The Communist Manifesto* needed to provide some space for the operation of individual will. Like Stirner, Marx found a place for the ego in its capacity to destroy, and proposed that "Communists everywhere support every revolutionary movement against the existing social and political order of things" (*The Communist Manifesto* 116). Revolutionary will was the path to socio-economic improvement, and the "theory of the Communists may be summed up in the single phrase: Abolition of private property" (82). Stirner's greatest impact on *The Communist Manifesto* was not a contribution to communist ideology, but that he provided a theoretical justification for the actual writing of a manifesto.

There are, of course, other interesting similarities to Stirner's ideas in *The Communist Manifesto*. For example, the *Manifesto* described the proletarian in almost the same terms that Stirner had previously used to describe the individual beleaguered by liberalism. It asserted that "[t]he proletarian is without property; his relation to his wife and children has no longer anything in common with the bourgeois family relations" and he has been stripped "of every trace of national character" (Marx, *The Communist Manifesto* 76). Under such conditions, "[l]aw, morality, religion, are to him so many bourgeois prejudices, behind which lurk in ambush just as many bourgeois interests" (76). Whereas Stirner had argued that law, morality, and religion were the tools with which the idea of the state overcame the will of the individual, Marx insisted that they were the tools the bourgeoisie used to deny the destiny of the proletariat. Social forces had brought history to this point, but with the *Manifesto* Marx could change the course of history. Marx was but one of many authors to co-opt aspects of Stirner's thought, and his case was typical of the way Stirner's presence has been subsequently understated.

While Marx's engagement with Stirner was characterized by intense antagonism and hostility, anarchism has had a more conflicted relationship with the founder of insurrectionary egoism. Marx and Engels were perhaps the first to propose a link between Stirner and the anarchist movement. Engels recalled in 1889 that "Stirner enjoyed a revival thanks to Bakunin," and that "[a]s a result the anarchists have themselves become nothing but a collection of '*Unique Ones*,' so much so that no two of them can abide one another's company" ("Engels to Max Hildebrand" 394). Marx even proposed that the conclusion made by Pierre-Joseph Proudhon—one of the fathers of organized anarchism—that "[r]eligion, the State, etc., having become impossible, only 'individuals' remain," was "a discovery he has lifted from Stirner" ("Marx to Engels" 135). Similarly, he labeled Karl Heinzen's "aristocrat of the intellect" a "ludicrous second-hand rehash of Feuerbach-Stirner" ("Marx to Engels" 161). Marx and Engels sweepingly branded anarchist theorists as substandard egoists who had stolen insights from the pages of *Der Einzige und sein Eigentum*. Stirner's influence on early continental anarchists such as Proudhon, Heinzen, and Bakunin was, however, more complex than Marx credited and—as in the case of Stirner's influence on Marx himself—is primarily apparent in the unattributed reproduction of his ideas.

When anarchists were compelled to agree with Stirner's conclusions they did so only grudgingly and they rarely conceded any kind of credit. Bakunin, for instance, described a philosophy that frequently attempted to resolve Marx's materialism with Stirner's egoism, but made no mention of Stirner in the process.[29] In 1871, he proposed that "[o]ne can distinguish the main elements in the attainment of freedom. The first is eminently social" and "is the fullest development of all the faculties and powers of every human being, by education, by scientific training, and by material prosperity" (*Bakunin on Anarchy* 238). In contrast, "[t]he second element of freedom is negative. It is the revolt of the individual against all divine, collective, and individual authority" (238). According to Bakunin, revolution demanded both the destructive efforts of the individual and the productive efforts of the community, and "revolt against the society in which he was born is indispensable for the humanization of the individual" (238). Despite drawing upon Stirner's conception of individual revolt, Bakunin made no mention of Stirner's contribution to this second, "negative," conception of freedom. Nevertheless, E. H. Carr proposed in his biography of Bakunin that "where he moved beyond Hegel, [Bakunin] was influenced less by the Young Hegelians than by the extreme idealist and individualist, Max Stirner" (451). The reluctance to concede the weight of Stirner's influence on his thought was yet another example of the disregard that contributed to Stirner's disappearance from revolutionary thought following his death in 1856.

Like Bakunin, Proudhon frequently alluded to Stirner's ideas without direct attribution. There are more than twenty instances of the word *égoïsme* in *Système des contradictions économiques ou Philosophie de la misère* (The System of Economical Contradictions: or, The Philosophy of Misery, 1846). While conventionally rendered as "selfishness," Benjamin Tucker instead chose to translate the word to "egoism" in his 1888 English translation of the work.[30] The context does provide some justification for this choice. Proudhon invited comparison to Stirner's critique of humanism when he suggested that "with the cessation of the worship and mystification of humanity by itself, the theological problem is for ever put aside. [...] The gods have gone: there is nothing left

---

[29] Bakunin was familiar with Stirner and suggested in *Statism and Anarchy* (1873) that Marx was "the soul and center of the notable circle of progressive Hegelians" that "also included the brothers Bruno and Edgar Bauer, Max Stirner, and later, in Berlin, the first circle of German nihilists" (142).

[30] Tucker was justified in using the word egoism here, but it needs to be acknowledged that he played an important role in the popularization of Stirner's thought in the United States and England. Tucker was introduced to Stirner's ideas by James L. Walker in 1887. Nevertheless, Tucker was known foremost for his many translations of Proudhon, and as a founding figure in a movement called philosophical anarchism.

for man but to grow weary and die in his egoism" (*System of Economical Contradictions: or, The Philosophy of Misery* 12). He conceded a point made by Stirner when he accepted that selfishness provided a foundation for philanthropy. Proudhon admitted that "[t]he sympathy which we feel for the proletaire is like that with which animals inspire us; delicacy of organs, dread of misery, pride in separating ourselves from all suffering—it is these shifts of egoism that prompt our charity" (412). Most importantly, Proudhon reiterated Stirner's conclusion that "Humanity is a spectre to God, just as God is a spectre to humanity" (466). Despite these apparent allusions to his ideas, Proudhon did not once mention Stirner or *Der Einzige und sein Eigentum* in his book. Still, there is clear evidence that Marx was correct when he suggested that Proudhon had lifted a number of his later ideas from Stirner's thought.

Regardless of the immediate impact Stirner made on prominent socialists and anarchists, any direct influence that he had once possessed had already dissipated by the time Marx and Engels conspired to expel the anarchist contingent from the First International at The Hague Congress in 1872. Interest in egoism that remained now came indirectly, through the shadows of egoism left in works of Marx, Bakunin, and Proudhon, rather than through *Der Einzige und sein Eigentum* itself. Outside of a few scholarly works—such as those by Friedrich-Albert Lange and Eduard von Hartmann—Stirner's ideas persisted largely as an individualistic tendency within the broader field of anarchist theory. This was, however, an attenuated version of egoism, adapted to the promotion of socialist and egalitarian values that Stirner would surely have decried as hauntings of the mind. It would not be until Nietzsche emerged as a proponent of egoism in the 1880s that readers would again confront such a radical critique of morality and affirmation of self-will. It was Nietzsche's rise to fame that set the stage for renewed interest in Stirner, and by 1920, scholars, dissidents, and poets from France to the United States, and as far afield as Japan, had become acquainted with the insurrectionary appeal of *Der Einzige und sein Eigentum*.

Nietzsche and the Path to Rediscovery

In 1872—the same year that Marx engineered the expulsion of Bakunin and the other anarchists from the First International—Friedrich Nietzsche published his first book, *Die Geburt der Tragödie aus dem Geiste der Musik* (The Birth of Tragedy from the Spirit of Music). While Marx had been working to stamp out what he saw as the remaining traces of egoism in revolutionary politics, another German proponent of self-will was gathering his thoughts at the University of Basel. Marx succumbed to pleurisy in 1883, however, and did not live to witness the effect that the increasing popularity of Nietzsche's philosophy would have on resurrecting interest in Stirner's thought. In the interim, Nietzsche himself had to learn to embrace a philosophy founded on self-will. Unlike Stirner, Nietzsche's conversion to egoism was a gradual process that took place over the course of a decade. While he began as an elitist, critical of the threat egoism posed to true culture, by 1882 Nietzsche was one of the few thinkers whose opposition to conventional moral norms could rival that of Stirner.

Although the *Übermensch* was the culmination of Nietzsche's own approach to morality, he did not begin his intellectual development as a proponent of egoism in the same way as Stirner. In fact, Nietzsche actively disparaged egoism in his early writings. Like Stirner, one of Nietzsche's first works was a critique of the German education system that anticipated some of his later preoccupations. Where Stirner's *"Das unwahre Prinzip unserer Erziehung"* foreshadowed the development of his philosophical egoism, the series of lectures that Nietzsche delivered between January and March in 1872—published under the title *Über die Zukunft unserer Bildungsanstalten* (On the Future of Our Educational Institutions)—instead demonstrated the extent of the 27-year-old professor's elitism. He perceived egoism to be anathema to high culture and, in the fourth of his lectures, suggested that "true culture would scorn to contaminate itself with the needy and covetous individual; it well knows how to give the slip to the man who would fain employ it as a means of attaining to egoistic ends" (94). Nevertheless, there was an insurrectionary element to Nietzsche's elitism, as he demonstrated when he suggested that:

> the aristocratic nature of true culture is feared, because the people endeavour in this way to drive single great individuals into self-exile [...] in order that the many may in this way endeavour to escape the rigid and strict discipline of the few great leaders, so that the masses may be persuaded that they can easily find the path for themselves—following the guiding star of the State!
>
> (89)

Nietzsche expressed his contempt for both the masses and the state for their opposition to the will of the superior individual. Despite his criticism of the needy and covetous intentions of egoism, Nietzsche's early portrayal of the aristocrat driven out of society by the state bears a marked resemblance to Stirner's egoist, a figure equally beleaguered by Christians, liberals, and communists for a desire to assert ownership over society and its values.

Nietzsche reversed his opinion of egoism over the course of his intellectual development, and with the publication of Die fröhliche Wissenschaft (The Gay Science, 1882), he arrived at a position comparable to that of Stirner. In book three of this work, Nietzsche pursued a critique of the religious foundations of secular values that led him to many of the same conclusions that Stirner reached in part one of Der Einzige und sein Eigentum. First, Nietzsche proclaimed that "God is dead; but given the way people are, there may still for millennia be caves in which they show his shadow. [...] we must still defeat his shadow as well" (109). He argued that "[u]nder the rule of religious ideas, one has got used to the idea of 'another world (behind, below, above)' and feels an unpleasant emptiness and deprivation at the annihilation of religious delusions—and from this feeling grows now 'another world,' but this time only a metaphysical and not a religious one" (131). From this point, Nietzsche completely overturned his opinion of egoism and wedded it to his pre-existing advocacy of elitism.

In his next book, Also sprach Zarathustra (Thus Spoke Zarathustra, 1883–85), Nietzsche drew conclusions that inspired generations of critics to compare his thought to Stirner's egoism. Zarathustra repeats and expands upon several ideas that are close to those Stirner developed in the second half of Der Einzige und sein Eigentum. Like Stirner, Zarathustra is preoccupied with the creative power of crime, and proclaims, "Behold the good and the just! Whom do they hate most? Him who smashes their tables of values, the breaker [Brecher], the law-breaker [Verbrecher]—but he is the creator" (Nietzsche, Thus Spoke Zarathustra 51).[31] Just as Stirner had, Zarathustra observes the falsehood inherent in the state's claim that "I, the state am the people," and he calls it "the coldest of all cold monsters" (75). He reiterates Stirner's argument that the ego alone is able to overcome secular mythology, and suggests that "My Ego taught me a new pride. [...] No longer to bury the head in the sand of heavenly things, but to carry it freely, an earthly head which creates meaning for the earth!" (60). Zarathustra also finds the most meaningful foundation for the self in its destructive capacity, describing a self that is "always listening and seeking: it compares, subdues, conquers, destroys. It rules and is also the Ego's ruler"

---

[31] Nietzsche chooses the word Verbrecher to describe the individual who overcomes secular morality. Normally translated as "criminal," Nietzsche's use of Verbrecher recalls Stirner's argument that the egoist achieved self-ownership through Verbrechen, or crime.

(62). Unlike Stirner, however, Zarathustra recognizes the dangers implicit in an insurrectionary approach to selfhood and observes that it "is not the danger for the noble man—that he may become a good man—but that he may become an impudent one, a derider, a destroyer" (71). Unlike Stirner, Nietzsche recognized the fine line between self-realization and total nihilism inherent in egoism's call for rebellion against moral values.

While many of Nietzsche's ideas are reminiscent of Stirner's, there are important points of difference between the egoist and the *Übermensch*. Zarathustra describes two potential fates for humanity: the *Übermensch* and the *Letzter Mensch* (last man). His apparent goal is to foretell the arrival of the *Übermensch*, a being who overcomes all human limitations and represents "the meaning of the earth" (Nietzsche, *Thus Spoke Zarathustra* 42). The *Letzter Mensch*, on the other hand, is the potential outcome of man's failure to bring about the arrival of the *Übermensch*. The world of the *Letzter Mensch* is described as "[n]o herdsman and one herd," in which "[e]veryone wants the same thing, everyone is the same: whoever thinks otherwise goes voluntarily into the madhouse" (46).[32] To avoid this potential fate, Zarathustra proposes that "[w]hat is great in man is that he is a bridge and not a goal; what can be loved in man is that he is a *going-across* and a *down-going*" (44). Nietzsche's vision of the *Übermensch* is entrenched in a notion of human transcendence which is totally at odds with Stirnerian egoism. Stirner broadly mocked the notion of transformation or becoming, and proposed that "[a] man is 'called' to nothing, and has no 'calling,' no 'destiny,' as little as a plant or a beast has a 'calling'" (288). For Stirner, Nietzsche's *Übermensch* would have seemed yet another alienated abstraction, requiring self-abnegation.

Nevertheless, the many similarities that did exist between the thought of Stirner and Nietzsche added a sense of timeliness to Stirner's rediscovery. In 1893 *Der Einzige und sein Eigentum* became more widely available than ever with its inclusion in the Reclam Universal Bibliothek. Stirner's denunciation of conventional morality invited comparison with Nietzsche's oeuvre. The introduction by Paul Lauterbach went so far as to address Nietzsche as Stirner's "great successor" (Paterson 146). Although a direct relationship between the two was not obvious, the fact that they shared a "radically new perspective on religion, on morals, on political and social life" (Carroll, *Break-Out from the*

---

[32] By comparison, Stirner suggested that the world was already such a madhouse, and he asked: "Is not all the stupid chatter of most of our newspapers the babble of fools who suffer from the fixed idea of morality, legality, Christianity, and so forth, and only seem to go about free because the madhouse in which they walk takes in so broad a space?" (Stirner, *The Ego and Its Own* 43).

Crystal Palace 39) implied a connection, or at least profound affinities between the two. The perception that Stirner influenced Nietzsche was encouraged by the proselytizing of devotees such as Mackay, who were more than willing to seize on any resemblances in order to popularize their hero.

Mackay was not alone in promoting the importance of *Der Einzige und sein Eigentum*, or in comparing it to the work of Nietzsche. In fact, he had the support of such luminaries as Hans von Bülow and Richard Strauss. Von Bülow claimed to have personally known Stirner and his "final performance with the Berlin Philharmonic [in April 1892] closed with a speech by the conductor exalting the ideas of Stirner" (Youmans 91). In the same year, "[t]wo drafts for a Don Juan opera [...] show Strauss immersed in Stirner, particularly the latter's explicitly antimetaphysical view of sexual love" (Youmans 91). Strauss had already read *Die Anarchisten*, and in April, he met with Mackay and heard von Bülow's speech. Two years later, he set two of Mackay's poems to music, "Morgen!" (Morning!) and "Heimliche Aufforderung" (Secret Call). The former went on to become one of his most recognizable works, incorporated in the *Four Last Songs*. In fact, in the 1890s interest in Stirner's book experienced a rebirth; James Huneker recalled visiting Bayreuth in 1896 and being "[a]ll fire and flame at that time for Nietzsche," when "a member of the Wagner Theatre" proposed that Stirner's "name will be green when Jean Paul and Richard Wagner are forgotten" (351). The encounter led the American to read *Der Einzige und sein Eigentum* for the first time and conclude that "Nietzsche [was] the poet of the doctrine," and "Stirner its prophet, or, if you will, its philosopher" (Huneker 352). Like many others, Huneker assumed some connection between the philosopher of egoism and the poet of the *Übermensch*.

Nevertheless, it proved difficult to substantiate a line of influence between the two. As Nietzsche never directly referred to Stirner in his own work, arguments about their putative relationship depended on a few pieces of tenuous circumstantial evidence. Nietzsche may have encountered Stirner in the same way as Mackay, "through the medium of Friedrich-Albert Lange's 1866 book" *Geschichte des Materialismus und Kritik seiner Bedeutung in der Gegenwart* (Shone 209). In the first edition that Nietzsche read, however, Lange only dedicated a single paragraph to Stirner. A more substantial point of contact was Eduard von Hartmann's discussion of Stirner's egoism in *Philosophie des Unbewussten* (Philosophy of the Unconscious, 1869) and *Phänomenologie des sittlichen Bewusstseins* (Phenomenology of Moral Consciousness, 1879). Thomas Brobjer confirms that "Nietzsche read Hartmann carefully, and with the exception of Schopenhauer and Lange, Hartmann is likely to have been the philosopher who taught Nietzsche most about philosophy" (111). For his part, von Hartmann certainly "thought it was possible that Nietzsche might have been stimulated to read *Der Einzige* as a result of his own discussion of Stirner" (Paterson 149).[33] In *Stirner et Nietzsche* (1904), Albert Lévy noted that "Nietzsche's favorite student," the "son of Mme Baumgartner-Kochlin, who translated the *Untimely Meditations* into French," had borrowed *Der Einzige und sein Eigentum* from the library at Basel in 1874 (10). Baumgartner claimed that "it was on Nietzsche's advice that he read Stirner" (10). Franz Overbeck insinuated a connection when he cryptically proposed that Nietzsche was "'economical' with his knowledge of Stirner" (Löwith 187), while his wife Ida directly alleged that Nietzsche was aware of the similarity of Stirner's ideas to his own work. She recalled him telling her in the early 1880s that he felt an affinity with Stirner and stating that "[t]hey will be talking about plagiarism" (Löwith 114). The evidence suggests that Nietzsche had acquired—at the very least—a second-hand familiarity with *Der Einzige und sein Eigentum* no later than 1869.

Critics have variously responded to these details, ranging from accusations of plagiarism through to denials that Nietzsche ever read *Der Einzige und sein Eigentum*. Lévy concluded that Stirner "perhaps contributed to keeping Nietzsche for a time within the realm of Schopenhauer's metaphysics," but "was doubtless little by little forgotten afterwards" (my trans.; 19).[34] Huneker waded into the debate in *Egoists*, when he cited the work of Lévy and proposed that "Nietzsche had used Stirner as a springboard, as a point of departure, and that the Individual had vastly different meanings to those diverse temperaments" (352). In 1911 Paul Carus alleged that Nietzsche had effectively plagiarized Stirner, but that "the common rules of literary ethics cannot apply to individualists who deny all and any moral authority" (396). Mackay suggested in the 1914 edition of *Max Stirner: Sein Leben und sein Werk* "that Nietzsche knew *Der Einzige* and shyly buried in himself the overwhelming force of its influence, until he was able to free himself of it in his own creating" (19).

---

[33] Hartmann addressed Stirner in the third volume of *Philosophie des Unbewussten*, in a chapter that Nietzsche subsequently criticized at length in "Vom Nutzen und Nachteil der Historie für das Leben" (On the Use and Disadvantage of History for Life), the second essay of *Unzeitgemässe Betrachtungen* (Untimely Meditations, 1873–6).

[34] "Bref, il ne semble pas que Stirner ait eu sur Nietzsche une influence décisive; il a peut-être contribué à retenir quelque temps Nietzsche dans le domaine de la métaphysique de Schopenhauer; il a été sans doute peu à peu oublié dans la suite" (19).

Scholarship continues to remain divided on the question of Stirner's impact on Nietzsche, and positions vary from Saul Newman's declaration that Nietzsche "was clearly influenced" by Stirner (56), to Brobjer's conclusion that it is "highly unlikely that Nietzsche in any sense was profoundly influenced by Stirner" (112). John Glassford suggests there is perhaps "no other example of two philosophers whose works bear such a strong similarity, but where no debt of acknowledgement took place" (78). Still, the debates of the 1890s and 1900s about Stirner's effect on Nietzsche's thought demonstrate the extent of a perceived kinship between the ideas of these two philosophers at a time when they were both widely known and read.

Regardless of whether they were the product of plagiarism, influence, or coincidence, there were significant similarities between Stirner and Nietzsche in terms of biography, rhetorical style, and the content of their works. Paterson suggests that there were "many striking resemblances between the two thinkers," with each having been "a great solitary, who utterly rejected the existing culture and who sought to present, in his own person, a living alternative to the philistinism by which he was surrounded" (146). Each of them "relinquished a teaching career in order to devote himself […] to the definition and contemplation of his philosophy" (Paterson 146). Each had a short but intense period of philosophical output that "ended early and abruptly" and each "spent his last years in a kind of twilight" before dying "at a comparatively young age" (Paterson 146). Glassford proposes that "[s]tylistically speaking, Stirner uses hyperbole and metaphor in much the same way as Nietzsche, although most would agree that Nietzsche's technique is the more successful" (74). It is in terms of abrasive, controversial content, however, that the most remarkable similarities emerge. Glassford goes on to observe that "Nietzsche, like Stirner, denies God, he rejects the traditional boundaries available to moral agents, he undercuts the more plausible conceptions of truth, and he glorifies the use of power to settle disputes between competing interests" (74). Both men made "a persistent call to authenticity, whatever the costs" and both noted the "potentially tyrannising effects" of language (Glassford 74). Most importantly, "they have in common a consciously epoch-making relationship towards Christianity, from which follows their idea of a 'surmounting of man'" (Löwith 187). Stirner's egoist and Nietzsche's *Übermensch* are distinct from each other but they share the common aim of overcoming the Christian foundations of secular morality in order to impose a value system founded on individual self-will.

While it is tempting to regard the insurrectionary egoism of Stirner and Nietzsche as a revolutionary new phase in European philosophy, their ideas are better understood as nineteenth-century developments in a much older tradition. Elements of their assaults on conventional morality were markedly similar to the ideas that Plato attributed to Callicles and Gorgias. Similarly, their approaches to power recalled the work of Machiavelli. John Carroll has suggested that "[k]ey passages in the work of both Stirner and Dostoevsky echo Christ's parables," and that "[s]trains of a sometimes similar type of psychological anarchism are to be found in the writing of Charles Fourier" (*Break-Out from the Crystal Palace* 15). Carroll also suggests that Blake's radical aphorisms from *The Marriage of Heaven and Hell* (1793) represented a "remarkable anticipation" of the "anarcho-psychology" of Stirner and Nietzsche (16). Even Bakunin preconceived the egoistic call to creative destruction in an essay written in 1842, in which he suggested that "the eternal spirit which destroys and annihilates [...] is the unfathomable and eternal source of all life. The passion for destruction is a creative passion too!" (*Bakunin on Anarchy* 57). Where Stirner and Nietzsche succeeded was in combining the moral cynicism of the sophists, the *Realpolitik* of Machiavelli, and the revolutionary reading of Christ common to Blake and Dostoevsky into a singular mode of self-awareness, expressed in terms that both drew upon and countered the work of their mentors. In Stirner, this philosophy produced a thoroughly Hegelian assault on idealism; in Nietzsche it resulted in a sustained attack on Wagner and Schopenhauer.

By the time of Nietzsche's death in 1900, readers across Europe were familiar with his major works, and as his readership grew so did a recognition of Stirner's importance. *Der Einzige und sein Eigentum* had already begun to attract the interest of translators, and by 1920, it was available in French, Danish, Spanish, Italian, Russian, English, Dutch, Swedish, and Japanese. Mackay noted that "the translations of Stirner into foreign languages announce, as incorruptible witnesses, how successfully he too has now finally started his path throughout the world" (*Max Stirner* 23). The translations of Stirner and Nietzsche accompanied the arrival of prolific Manifesto writers who established themselves as the egoists and *Übermenschen* of their respective movements.

By the end of the nineteenth century, themes were beginning to emerge that would characterize much of Stirner's reception in Europe, the United States, and England. Continually read outside of the context in which he was writing, his ideas became closely associated with—and attenuated by—elements of anarchist and Nietzschean philosophy. Increasingly, Stirner's critique of the tyrannizing power of abstract ideals was ignored in favor of reading him as a founding philosopher of elitism, terrorism, and extreme libertarianism. *Der Einzige und sein Eigentum* had been published as a direct assault on the idealism of Hegel and Feuerbach, but from 1887 it was primarily read in dialogue with Marx, Nietzsche, and Proudhon. Proudhon had been the only one of these men to have any real bearing on Stirner's ideas, and only to the extent that Stirner had dismissed him as a communist. By contrast, all three were familiar with Stirner's work, and had responded to him by tacitly accepting his critique of ideals without providing any form of acknowledgment. As a result, Stirner remained a largely ignored but unresolved stumbling block in the history of Marxist communism, Nietzschean philosophy, and anarchism alike. It was Stirner who had delivered the final blow to Hegelian idealism, but credit for the victory had been handed to Marx. Nevertheless, abstractions continued to haunt the modern mind, and Stirner's criticisms remained undigested. Communism, socialism, anarchism, and nationalism all depended on abstract notions of right and wrong, and all were prime targets for egoistic attack. The question was whether Stirner's insights could survive the process of transmission and translation in such leading centers of intellectual debate as Paris, Milan, and London.

2

France: The Rise of Literary Egoism

Pinning down Stirner's impact on the development of the literary manifesto in France is a task complicated by the fact that his ideas were available from a wide variety of sources. The translations of *Der Einzige und sein Eigentum* into French by Robert L. Reclaire in 1899 and Henri Lasvignes in 1900 contributed significantly to the spread of egoism in the Parisian literary scene, but there were also earlier, indirect sources where his ideas could be encountered. Word of Stirner's assault on German idealism had certainly reached France in the aftermath of his immediate reception, and Saint-René Taillandier warned French readers about the dangers of Stirner's thought in an essay for *Revue des deux mondes* titled "De la crise actuelle de la philosophie hégélienne: Les partis extrêmes en Allemagne" (Of the Current Crisis in Hegelian Philosophy: Extreme Parties in Germany, 1847).[1] John Henry Mackay and James L. Walker began popularizing Stirner's ideas in 1887 and a French translation of Mackay's *Die Anarchisten* in 1891 provided a more positive introduction to his work. Perhaps the greatest force in promoting egoism in France was an interest in tracing the origins of anarchist philosophy. Throughout the 1880s and 1890s, Paris remained in the grip of terrorist hysteria, and both supporters and opponents of anarchism attempted to explain the philosophical foundations of the movement. Some writers pursued the implicit connections leading from existing anarchist thought to Stirner and, like Mackay, encountered *Der Einzige und sein Eigentum*. Others, such as Maurice Barrès and Stéphane Mallarmé, merely perceived analogues between artistic and anarchist rebellion. If they were unaware of their

---

[1] In 1853, this essay was republished as "La demagogie et l'athéisme" (Demagoguery and Atheism) in the first volume of Taillandier's *Études sur la révolution en Allemagne* (Studies on the Revolution in Germany). He suggested that Stirner's egoism was the final, logical, and abhorrent conclusion of post-Hegelian atheism, and that the only remaining avenues were to "either return to universal belief; […] or if your insane dialectic binds you, follow your dark path to the end and proclaim with M. Stirner that the individual exists alone!" ("ou bien revenez à la croyance universelle; […] ou bien, si votre dialectique insensée vous enchaîne, suivez jusqu'au bout votre voie ténébreuse et proclamez avec M. Stirner que l'individu existe seul!"; my trans.; *La demagogie et l'athéisme* 378).

role in a tradition beginning with Stirner, their contemporaries were quick to enlighten them. Finally, Stirner's ideas began to resonate with the development of the still nascent literary manifesto and transform the genre into a vehicle for egoistic, insurrectionary revolt.

An interesting and indeed crucial development in Stirner's French reception was the way writers and radicals frequently adopted egoism before they had become conscious of his importance to it. A number of authors, of varying political allegiances, independently recognized the individualistic strains within anarchist thought and developed them to their logical "Stirnerian" conclusions. A few did eventually adopt Stirner's ideas consciously and openly—most notably the illegalist movement in the 1900s[2]—but in the 1890s insurrectionary writers were much more likely to have their previously unrecognized connections to Stirner pointed out to them by their contemporaries. Such was the case for important figures in the literary avant-garde, such as Mallarmé and Barrès, who provide crucial examples of the circuitous paths that led back to Stirner. Barrès, for instance, developed an explicitly egoistic program of individualism in the form of his *culte du moi*, but only recognized Stirner's importance retrospectively. Mallarmé's critics were responsible for connecting his ideas to anarchism and, more specifically, Stirner's egoism. Stirner's reception in France at the end of the nineteenth century was a multifaceted phenomenon that included the translation of *Der Einzige und sein Eigentum* into French, efforts to uncover the philosophical foundations of anarchism, and a long-existing preoccupation with elitist individualism among French decadents and Symbolists.

Translating Stirner

There is evidence that Stirner's influence on French literature and politics began not with Reclaire's complete translation in 1899, but more than a decade earlier. In the 1880s, radical individualism proved popular among French literary circles due to the influence of Baudelaire. He had already described

---

[2] David Ashford suggests the important role illegalism played in popularizing egoism when he suggests that "[e]goism returned to prominence in Western Europe [...] on the back of a criminal rampage" (18). The most notorious of the illegalists were the Bonnot Gang—a group of professional criminals led by the automotive mechanic Jules Bonnot. As Ashford notes, "the Bonnot Gang took their inspiration from Albert Libertad, the editor of the journal *l'anarchie*, the only anarchist paper in the Republic at that time which positively promoted crime as a form of political rebellion through a controversial 'illegalist' reading of Stirner" (19).

"the perfect dandy" who was confident in his "aristocratic superiority of mind" (Baudelaire, "The Painter of Modern Life" 27), and Symbolists could easily find similar vindications of the elite artist in the thought of Stirner and Nietzsche. Anarchist ideas also played an important part in laying political foundations for egoism, particularly those of Bakunin and Proudhon. By 1890 several French poets had arrived at conclusions similar to Stirner's about the role of the individual in society and the relationship between the ego and the world of abstract ideas. Peter Marshall suggests that "[w]ith the lifting of restrictions on political activity in France in 1881, anarchism became recognizable for the first time as an identifiable movement" (437). A stream of anarchist publications including *Le Révolté* (1879–85),[3] *Le Père Peinard* (1889–1902), and *Le Libertaire* (1895–1914) began to pour out of Paris in the 1880s and a canon of anarchist theorists began to take shape.

Chief among the recognized fathers of anarchism were Proudhon and Bakunin, two of the men Marx had singled out as having pilfered Stirner's ideas in their later writings. Their programs of rebellion against the state helped popularize the cause of radical individualism in the 1890s. Marshall notes that "[a]narchism at the turn of the century undoubtedly attracted many bohemian individualists, and for a while it became a broad cultural movement, giving expression to a wide range of social disenchantment and artistic rebellion" (440). Richard Parry confirms that interest in Stirner was "reawakened around the turn of the century due to a conjunction of two main factors: the current fad for all things German [...] and the keen interest in individualist philosophy among artists, intellectuals, and the well-read, urban middle classes in general" (8). Unlike prominent anarcho-communists such as Jean Grave and Pyotr Kropotkin, Symbolist poets were primed to take up the cause of philosophical egoism. Under the influence of Baudelaire, they had long considered the artist to be a "solitary, gifted with an active imagination, ceaselessly journeying across the great human desert" (Baudelaire, "The Painter of Modern Life" 12), fascinated with but superior to his contemporaries. From their perspective, Stirner's ideas were not so much revolutionary as yet another justification of current aesthetic approaches to individuality. It was these bourgeois artists and writers, drawn to anarchism mostly as a political expression of their own existing elitism, who proved the most influential proponents of Stirner's ideas.

---

[3] *Le Révolté* was renamed *La Révolte* in 1887 in a futile attempt to avoid responsibility for a fine the journal had incurred.

Ironically, French opponents of Stirnerian egoism played an important role in bringing attention to his thought. In 1853 Taillandier republished his essay condemning Stirner and thirty years later Théophile Funck-Brentano drew upon these criticisms in *Les sophistes allemands et les nihilistes russes* (The German Sophists and the Russian Nihilists, 1887). Quoting Taillandier's article, he once more portrayed egoism as a logical conclusion of post-Hegelian philosophy. Suggesting that Bakunin's support of anarchist violence had developed directly out of egoism, Funck-Brentano proposed that "Stirner's absolute self was to end with an apology for the Russian brigand and for political assassination; the two indeed represent the 'self' in its entire power and complete independence" (my trans.; 210).[4] As Marx had in Germany, these authors depicted Stirnerian egoism as an important precursor to nihilism and anarchist violence. Hostile interpretations of egoism by Taillandier and Funck-Brentano went on to inform Stirner's Italian translator, Ettore Zoccoli, in 1902, and in France they ensured that Stirner's name continued to be associated with anarchism and terrorism.

The first favorable point of contact with Stirner for many French readers was Louis de Hessem's 1892 translation of *Die Anarchisten*, the novel in which John Henry Mackay had first referred to Stirner. A review of the book—which was published as *Anarchistes: mœurs du jour*—in the August issue of *Entretiens* noted that Mackay "wanted to show—and it was easy enough for him—that anarchism is an established doctrine, having its theoreticians, poets, fighters and martyrs, too" (my trans.; Lazare 97).[5] In fact, *Die Anarchisten* was above all a panegyric on the virtues of egoism. In the introduction to the novel, Mackay suggested:

> The nineteenth century has given birth to the idea of Anarchy. In its fourth decade the boundary line between the old world of slavery and the new world of liberty was drawn. For it was in this decade that P. J. Proudhon began the titanic labor of his life with *Qu'est-ce que la propriété?* (1840), and that Max Stirner wrote his immortal work: *Der Einzige und sein Eigenthum* (1845).
>
> (Mackay, *The Anarchists* ix)

While Stirner's name does not appear again in the work, his ideas dominate the action of the novel. In his depiction of the various competing cliques within the anarchist movement, Mackay repeatedly pits egoistic ideas against socialist ones.

---

[4] "Le moi absolu de Stirner devait finir par l'apologie du brigand russe et par celle de l'assassinat politique; les deux représentent en effet le 'moi' dans son entière puissance et sa complète indépendance" (210).
[5] "Il a voulu montrer aussi, et cela lui a été facile, que l'anarchie est une doctrine établie, ayant ses théoriciens, ses poètes, ses combattants et ses martyrs aussi" (97).

The protagonist of *Die Anarchisten*, Carrard Auban, is a convert to egoism who takes issue with the dogmatic collectivism of his compatriots. Walking the streets of London with an old acquaintance at the beginning of the novel, Auban first raises his concerns about prevailing attitudes in anarchist circles. Whilst acknowledging that "[t]he future is Socialism," he condemns it as "[t]he suppression of the individual into ever-narrower limits. The total lack of independence. The large family. All children, children ... But this, too, must be passed through" (Mackay, *The Anarchists* 26). His friend Otto Trupp is a collectivist and counters by deriding individualism for "giving free rein to all the low passions of man, above all, egoism," and for producing the very misery that surrounds the two men. Auban retorts that "we are living under a Communism more complicated and brutal than ever before," where "the individual, from the cradle to the grave, is placed under contribution to the State" (29). For Auban—as for Mackay—egoism was not the cause of modern misery but the means of achieving the genuine liberty to which anarchism aspired. He sardonically quips: "these slowly ripening thoughts of egoism (I use this word deliberately)—they are in the same way dangerous to the present conditions as they will be dangerous to the conditions prevailing when we shall have entered the haven of the popular state that will make all things happy, the haven of condensed Communism" (29). Even Trupp's communism, Auban suggests, cannot withstand the will of the self-assured egoist. In the closing pages of the story, Auban is again wandering the streets of London, this time musing that "[s]oon he would have friends and comrades. Already an individualistic Anarchistic movement was noticeable among the Communists of Paris, championing private property" (282). Only a year after the first publication of *Die Anarchisten* in German and English, Mackay could count some of these French individualists among his growing readership.

The reception of *Anarchistes: mœurs du jour* and its promotion of Stirner's philosophy in Parisian literary circles was positive and immediate. In September 1892, *Entretiens* included a ten-page polemic by Théodore Randal dedicated to the revolutionary implications of *Der Einzige und sein Eigentum*. Titled "Le livre libérateur," the essay declared that "[i]t seems paradoxical to say so, but the truth is obvious: There was only one free man in our century of freedom. [...] His name was Max Stirner" (my trans.; Randal 117).[6] Even beyond the confines of the nineteenth century, Randal suggested that to Stirner, "Machiavelli alone can be

---

[6] "Il semble paradoxal de le dire, mais la vérité en crève les yeux: Il n'y a eu qu'un seul homme libre en notre siècle de liberté. [...] Il s'appelait Max Stirner" (117).

compared for cynical serenity and impassive daring" (my trans.; 117).[7] "Le livre libérateur" largely consisted of a summary of *Der Einzige und sein Eigentum*, but Randal approached this task as an advocate and devotee. He proclaimed "[i]t is enough to have read this book to feel at that moment purified of sin, protected from error and free from yoke, to be a free man at last, as Stirner was" (my trans.; 117–18).[8] Published alongside the work of Élie Reclus, Paul Adam, and Bernard Lazare, Randal's article was a sure sign that Stirner's ideas were taken seriously by the anarchist and literary circles of Paris even before the publication of *l'Unique et sa propriété*.

As in Germany, a particular aspect of Stirner's renewed importance was his apparent connection to Nietzsche. On March 16, 1893, the *Journal des débats politiques et littéraires* published an article connecting the thought of Stirner to Nietzsche, written by Jean Bourdeau, titled "Nouvelles modes en philosophie: Max Stirner et Frédéric Nietzsche." Bourdeau, a friend and correspondent of the radical philosopher George Sorel, had already translated works by Schopenhauer and Heine, and in the course of his essay contributed some of the earliest French translations from *Der Einzige und sein Eigentum*. Indeed, Bourdeau included two sizable passages from Stirner's book, addressing both his notion of the fixed idea and his critique of morality. Bourdeau also reproduced Stirner's inflammatory accusation that the modern man was a fool in a madhouse, and that "*Homme, tu as des revenants dans ta tête, tu as une fêlure dans le cerveau!*" (Bourdeau 1).[9] Furthermore, Bourdeau confirmed developing interest in Stirner's ideas both at home and abroad, suggesting that "[t]oday, it is two Germans, Max Stirner and Friedrich Nietzsche, who are, in Europe and America, in circles of the initiated that are still quite small, it is true, the craze and the vogue" (my trans.; 1).[10] He was right; by 1890 Stirner's ideas were indeed spreading in the United States, largely because of the work of James L. Walker and Benjamin Tucker. Like others before him, Bourdeau depicted Stirner as an important precursor of Nietzsche and proposed that "[t]o explain Nietzsche [...] we need Stirner" (my trans.; 1).[11]

---

[7] "Machiavel seul lui peut être comparé par la sérénité cynique, et par l'audace impassible" (117).
[8] "Il suffit d'avoir lu ce livre pour se sentir à l'instant même purifié de péché, garanti d'erreur et exempt de joug, pour être un homme libre enfin, comme Stirner le fut" (117–18).
[9] Bourdeau renders Stirner's idiomatic "Mensch, es spukt in Deinem Kopfe; Du hast einen Sparren zu viel!" as "Man, you have ghosts in your head, you have a crack in the brain!" (1).
[10] "Aujourd'hui, c'est à deux Allemands, Max Stirner et Frédéric Nietzsche, que vont, en Europe et en Amérique, dans de petits cercles d'initiés encore assez restreints, il est vrai, l'engouement et la vogue" (1).
[11] "Pour expliquer Nietzsche, dont nous parlerons dans un prochain feuilleton, nous avons besoin de Stirner" (1).

Over the course of two pages, Bourdeau attempted to summarize Stirner's thought, taking an approach that was characterized by its even-handedness.

In his assessment Bourdeau carefully avoided resorting to either the invective of Stirner's contemporaries or the proselytizing of his recent converts. Instead, his article addressed the ways in which Stirner's conception of the ego differed from Fichte's, his notion of an egoistic foundation for love, and the similarities between his ideas and those of Proudhon. The essay was far from a token gesture to a forgotten thinker, and Bourdeau proposed that "Stirner and Proudhon appear as harbingers of the storm; they announce the revolution" (my trans.; Bourdeau 2).[12] He even suggested that "the anarchist school, philosophical and militant, venerates Stirner as the father of its church, and strives to propagate his doctrine" (my trans.; 2).[13] In contrast to the unreserved rebukes of Marx and Feuerbach, Bourdeau's essay addressed both the strengths and weaknesses of Stirner's line of argument and—like Engels upon first reading *Der Einzige und sein Eigentum* in 1844—he stressed the need to reconcile individualism and collectivism. He proposed that "[t]o pretend to bring everything back to the self, like the egoists or to sacrifice the individual to the collective, like the socialists, are errors born from narrow minds, which only see one side of the question, while the two are inseparable" (my trans.; 2).[14] Ultimately, however, Bourdeau saw in anarchism an inevitable path to tyranny and the rise of "the great Egoist, the Dictator, the Caesar or Caesarion, who will tame all these rival egoisms, organize them, discipline them, lead them to loot, carnage and collapse" (my trans.; 2).[15] The article was a prescient warning of the outcomes that the spread of egoism would have in the following century, but it went unheeded.

As articles on Stirner proliferated, commentators began to explore the further connections between Stirner, Nietzsche, and the anarchist movement. Within a month of Bourdeau's essay, the April number of the *Revue bleue* opened with an article by the translator and playwright, Jean Thorel, titled "Les pères de l'anarchisme: Bakounine, Stirner, Nietzsche." Working backwards from Bakunin,

---

[12] "Stirner et Proudhon apparaissent comme des oiseaux avant-coureurs de la tempête; ils annoncent la révolution" (2).
[13] "[…] l'école anarchiste, philosophique et militante, vénère en Stirner le Père de son Eglise, et s'efforce de propager sa doctrine" (2).
[14] "Prétendre tout ramener au moi, comme les égotistes, ou sacrifier l'individu à la collectivité, comme les socialistes, ce sont des erreurs qui ne peuvent naître que dans des esprits étroits, qui s'appliquent à ne voir qu'un côté de la question, alors que les deux sont inséparables" (2).
[15] "le grand Égoïste, le Dictateur, le César ou le Césarion, qui va dompter tous ces égoïsmes rivaux, les organiser, les discipliner, les conduire au butin, au carnage et à la débâcle" (2).

Thorel set out to delineate the origins of anarchist philosophy, suggesting that "if one does not find in the militant anarchists powerful defenders of individualism, there exists, however, one in particular, whose work has been a constant point of support for the further development of the anarchist doctrine. It is the German, Max Stirner, I want to talk about" (my trans.; Thorel 451).[16] "It is impossible," Thorel proposed, "to read a single anarchist pamphlet, by any companion whatsoever, without finding the ideas of [*Der Einzige und sein Eigentum*], incomplete, disfigured, less clearly stated, but all, if not borrowed from this book, can at least be found there" (my trans.; 451).[17] Rather than regarding Stirner's thought as an important step in the development of Nietzsche's more fully realized ideas, Thorel suggested that "Stirner's work is the product of the intellect," whereas "that of Nietzsche is the outlet for a temperament that has found no other way to assert itself" (my trans.; 453). Where "Stirner had made the sovereign self the basis of his philosophy," Thorel argued that "Nietzsche seems rather to approach Schopenhauer; but instead of summarizing everything in the 'will to live' (*Wille zum Leben*), as he had done, modifies this fundamental formula, restricts it, I would say, relates everything to the 'will to power' (*Wille zur Macht*)" (my trans.; 453).[18] The contributions of Thorel, Bourdeau, and Randal demonstrate the way in which French intellectuals began to consider Stirner as a central figure in the development of anarchist philosophy in France. But he soon became associated with revolutionaries in the arts as well.

Gustave Lanson[19] was possibly the first to claim that there was a connection between Stirner's egoistic philosophy and Symbolist poetry. On July 15, 1893, his essay titled "La poésie contemporaine: M. Stéphane Mallarmé" was published in the *Revue universitaire*. In it, the eminent historian and literary critic proposed that it was "true to say that M. Mallarmé is a literary anarchist. Concepts, logic, sentences, words, all the forms, all the intellectual and verbal institutions that

---

[16] "si l'on ne trouve pas chez les anarchistes militants de puissants défenseurs de l'individualisme, il en existe cependant, un en particulier, dont l'œuvre a été un point d'appui constant pour le développement ultérieur de la doctrine anarchiste. C'est de l'Allemand Max Stirner que je veux parler" (451).

[17] "Il est impossible de lire une seule brochure anarchiste, de quelque compagnon que ce soit, sans y retrouver les idées de ce livre, incomplètes, défigurées, moins clairement dites, mais toutes, sinon empruntées à ce livre, pouvant du moins s'y retrouver" (451).

[18] "Stirner avait fait du moi souverain la base de sa philosophie; Nietzsche semble plutôt se rapprocher de Schopenhauer; mais au lieu de tout résumer dans le 'vouloir vivre' (*Wille zum Leben*), comme avait fait celui-ci, il modifie cette formule fondamentale, il la restreint, dirai-je, il rapporte tout au 'désir de pouvoir' (*Wille zur Macht*)" (453).

[19] A historian and literary critic who taught at the Sorbonne and the *École Normale Supérieure*, Lanson influenced the development of sociological and historical approaches to French literary criticism.

human society has created, he breaks them, he blows them up, the right of his individuality aspires to 'modulate itself' freely" (my trans.; Lanson 130).[20] Lanson did not merely associate Mallarmé with the established ideas of Proudhon or Bakunin; he explicitly likened his poetry to the newly rediscovered philosophy of Stirner. He argued that the "words of Max Stirner, which we have recently read in the *Revue bleue*, could serve as an epigraph for the work of M. Mallarmé. He wants to manifest his unspeakable self, which is not his thought, and must get rid of his thought for it to appear in its purity" (my trans.; 130).[21] Mallarmé's poetry was not anarchist in the sense that it advocated literal violence—or the political views of Proudhon, Bakunin or Kropotkin, come to that—but in the sense that it expressed a desire for the radical assertion of selfhood. Such a conception of anarchism as a philosophy founded on expressing an "unspeakable self" reflected Stirner's increasing influence on perceptions of anarchist theory in France in the 1890s. Furthermore, it marked out a line of influence between Stirner and arguably the most important contributor to Symbolism since Baudelaire.

The *Revue universitaire* published Lanson's article within days of the first anniversary of Ravachol's[22] execution on July 11, 1892, at a time when Paris remained preoccupied with the ongoing threat of anarchist violence. The continued concerns about terrorism were certainly justified. On December 9, 1893, Auguste Vaillant hurled a bomb from the public gallery of the *Chambre des députés* in a violent reprisal for Ravachol's execution. Two days later, the French government passed the first of the *lois scélérates* (villainous laws),[23] condemning the anarchist press. In the following April "came the anarchist bombing most pertinent to Mallarmé's personal and literary life: the attack on the restaurant Foyot, in which [Mallarmé's friend Laurent] Tailhade was gravely wounded and for which [the editor and critic Felix] Fénéon was arrested" (McGuiness 170). As Roberto Calasso points out, *Der Einzige und sein Eigentum* arrived in French "right in the most lively literary arena of those years, between symbolism and

---

[20] "Il est encore vrai de dire que M. Mallarmé est un anarchiste littéraire. Concepts, logique, phrases, mots, toutes les formes, toutes les institutions intellectuelles et verbales que l'humanité sociale s'est créés, il les brise, il les fait sauter, du droit de son individualité qui aspire à 'se moduler' librement" (130).
[21] "Ces paroles de Max Stirner, que l'on a pu lire récemment dans la *Revue Bleue*, pourraient servir d'épigraphe à l'œuvre de M. Mallarmé. Il veut manifester cet indicible moi, qui n'étant pas sa pensée, doit se défaire de sa pensée pour paraître en sa pureté" (130).
[22] François Claudius Koenigstein, better known as Ravachol, was an infamous anarchist bomber whose execution was used by supporters and opponents alike as a symbol of the anarchist struggle against the state.
[23] A pejorative name for a series of anti-terrorism laws which made it a crime to express public support for criminal acts.

anarchy" (*The Forty-Nine Steps* 168). Literary publications such as the *Mercure de France* and the *Revue blanche* became increasingly responsible for translations and discussions of Stirner's work. While "France was in many ways the cradle of the historic anarchist movement" (Marshall 431), the newly arrived immoralism of Stirner provided an alternative to the collectivism espoused by prominent anarchists such as Grave and Kropotkin. In particular, egoistic insurrection proved to be a far more palatable prescription for the bohemian tastes of an already individualist literary community.

Mallarmé as Literary Anarchist

After Stirner's ideas began to appear in the French press, Symbolists were quick to incorporate them into a long tradition of French elitism. When Lanson accused Mallarmé of being the literary equivalent of Stirner, what he actually identified was a marked similarity between the bohemian elitist tradition and Stirnerian egoism. It was potentially the first time Mallarmé himself had considered the similarity of his own ideas to those of the recently rediscovered Stirner. In fact, Stirner and Nietzsche proved popular in French literary circles partly because many Symbolists had already reached similar conclusions about the role of the superior individual within society. For example, ideas comparable to those of Stirner and Nietzsche had begun to appear in the work of Mallarmé more than a decade before the translation of *Der Einzige und sein Eigentum* into French. In "critical poems" such as "Un spectacle interrompu" (An Interrupted Performance, 1875), "Crise de vers" (Crisis in Verse, 1886), and "L'Action restreinte" (Restricted Action, 1886), Mallarmé questioned society's conception of the real and repeatedly returned to the idea that the poet was an intellectual aristocrat among the mundane masses. In 1885 Mallarmé suggested the unique importance of the poet in a letter to Maurice Barrès:[24]

> anyone who thinks he has understood [the symbol], must be that Magus called God, whose honor lies in not being himself but the very last one still to be reabsorbed into pure simplicity, in order to return to life: from which it follows that it's not even to the entire crowd of a whole day that one must deliver the

---

[24] Barrès would soon play a more direct role in the popularization of egoism in Paris by publishing a trilogy of novels titled *Le culte du moi* (1888–91). His importance to the spread of Stirner's ideas is discussed later in this chapter.

meaning of that abstruse letter [...] but to Humanity. All is vain save for this
ransoming through Art, and the artist remains a rogue.

("Maurice Barrès" 141)

Going further, Lanson contentiously suggested that Mallarmé wanted, like Stirner, to express his unspeakable self through his poetry. If Lanson was right, Mallarmé had adopted egoism primarily under the influence of Baudelaire, and without any knowledge of Stirner or Nietzsche. Nevertheless, Lanson's article strengthened the perceived connections between egoism and the avant-garde. The French Symbolist movement went on to introduce Filippo Tommaso Marinetti to Stirner, and Marinetti, in turn, imbued the still nascent literary manifesto with the spirit of egoistic rebellion. As the first Symbolist poet compared to Stirner, Mallarmé was, then, an important figure in the history of the egoistic avant-garde manifesto.

Lanson identified Mallarmé as a proponent of Stirnerian values, but Mallarmé also had a profound role in the development of the avant-garde literary manifesto. Guy Michaud suggested that "Mallarmé managed to remain an astonishing paradox in [the Symbolist] battle against literary conformism and bourgeois common sense," because although "[h]e always refused to enter the lists or to print a manifesto [...] he was in fact the involuntary promoter and undisputed victor in the battle" (Michaud 121). Mallarmé's penchant for precise language combined with semantic ambiguity contributed to his Delphic status in the Symbolist literary scene, and his works continue to thwart efforts at lucid interpretation. Mallarmé's cultural influence was pervasive, yet Michaud suggested that he "in no way claimed to teach a doctrine" (123).[25] "Crisis in Verse" and "Restricted Action" rank among the most important programs of the Symbolist movement, but are not polemics in any conventional sense. Mallarmé's writing does, however, continually struggle with the relationship between the individual and the ideal. Peers and critics alike branded him an anarchist even though his poetry eschewed political concerns, even by Symbolist standards. Despite all these paradoxes, Lanson proclaimed that "[t]here will be no efficacy,

---

[25] From the mid-1880s, Mallarmé's Tuesday-night salons—known as *Mardis*—became a polestar for the Parisian avant-garde and attracted some of the most important writers, painters, and thinkers of the period. Attendees included Whistler, Munch, Gauguin, Monet, Degas, Manet, Rodin, Jarry, Valery, de Gourmont, Tailhade, Quillard, Gide, Yeats, Wilde, and Arthur Symons. Michaud noted that "the small salon on the rue de Rome could scarcely contain the Tuesday night inundation" as *Mardistes* from across Paris and the world assumed "a contemplative silence" while "the 'master' improvised without a trace of pedantry" (121–2).

there will be no fertility in what is called Symbolism but on the condition of absolutely repudiating the essential dogma of M. Mallarmé" (my trans.; 132).[26] The dogma that Lanson referred to was "literary anarchism" and he equated it with the ideas of Stirner.

The foundation of Lanson's argument was that Mallarmé sought to realize an all-encompassing self in his poetry by stripping away the vestiges of his own will and intellect. He proposed that "M. Mallarme concludes—this is the bold originality of his effort—that we must do without ideas if we wish to enclose the whole self and all the infinite in the work of art" (my trans.; Lanson 128).[27] Lanson suggested that the ultimate aim for both Mallarmé and Stirner was the expression of an unspeakable and absolute self that encompassed all of creation, and Mallarmé:

> destroys or stops in him, will, consciousness, reflection, judgment, the whole machine to make ideas; he strips himself of all his personal reality, and when he is sure to have suspended all intellectual action, he listens to the words sung in him, in agreements that are often incoherent, unintelligible, but all the more expressive, it seems to him, the *ego* and the infinite.
>
> (my trans.; 128–9)[28]

The argument followed that Mallarmé's desire to express an unintelligible and infinite self was founded on the same logic as Stirner's claim that "*I* am the criterion of truth, but I am not an idea, but more than idea, that is, unutterable" (*The Ego and Its Own* 314). Reducing anarchism to egoism and Mallarmé's poetry to a kind of Quietism,[29] Lanson proposed that "[w]hat in theology is *Quietism* is called *anarchism* in sociology; basically, from one science to another, the two terms are equivalent; both mark the supreme exaltations of individuality, which is equal to the infinite" (my trans.; 130).[30] Mallarmé's dissolution of the

---

[26] "Il n'y aura d'efficacité, il n'y aura de fécondité dans ce qu'on appelle le symbolisme qu'à condition de répudier absolument le dogme essentiel de M. Mallarmé" (132).

[27] "M. Mallarmé en conclut—voilà l'originalitié hardie de son effort—qu'il faut se passer d'idées, si l'on veut enfermer tout le *moi* et tout l'infini dans l'œuvre d'art" (128).

[28] "M. Mallarmé en conclut—voilà l'originalité hardie de son effort—qu'il faut se passer d'idées, si l'on veut enfermer tout le moi et tout l'infini dans l'œuvre d'art. Soigneusement il détruit ou arrête en lui volonté, conscience, réflexion, jugement, toute la machine à fabriquer des idées; il se dépouille de toute sa réalité personnelle, et quand il est bien sûr d'avoir suspendu tout acte intellectuel, il écoute des mots chantés en lui, en accords souvent incohérents, inintelligibles, mais d'autant plus expressifs, lui semble-t-il, du moi et de l'infini" (128-9).

[29] A branch of seventeenth-century Christian mysticism most prominently associated with Miguel de Molinos and François Malaval. It is hard to see what the intellectual stillness of Quietism had in common with Stirner's advocacy of permanent revolt beyond a heretical approach to Catholic convention. There was, however, a similarity between the passivity of the Quietist mystic and that of the contemplative poet described by Mallarmé in works such as "Glory."

[30] "Ce qu'est en théologie le *quiétisme*, s'appelle en sociologie l'*anarchisme*; au fond, d'une science à l'autre, les deux termes s'équivalent; tous les deux marquent les exaltations suprêmes de l'individualité, qui s'égale à l'inifini" (130).

world of ideas into pure music and Stirner's insurrectionary revolt against ideas differed in their approaches, but both began with a fundamental belief that the innermost-self of the superior individual—Stirner's egoist or Mallarmé's poet—created meaning for the world.

There is evidence for reading Mallarmé's poetry as an attempt to express individuality by taking personal ownership of invented ideals. In his letter to Barrès, Mallarmé cited the importance of Wagner and described a desire to produce "at last, a fragment of the only drama I have to create, which is that of Man and Idea" ("Maurice Barrès" 142). In an earlier letter to the physician and poet, Henri Cazalis, Mallarmé suggested that human beings "are merely empty forms of matter, but we are indeed sublime in having invented God and our soul" ("Henri Cazalis" 60). Written in 1866, Mallarmé's sentiments were, like Stirner's, focused on the notion that the divine is a human creation with no foundation in material reality:

> I want to gaze upon matter, fully conscious that it exists, and yet launching itself madly into Dream, despite its knowledge that Dream has no existence, extolling the Soul and all the divine impressions of that kind which have collected within us from the beginning of time and proclaiming, in the face of the Void which is truth, these glorious lies!
>
> (60)

Unlike Stirner, however, Mallarmé was at times troubled by the falsity of ideals, and the poet's role in creating beautiful lies that mask the meaninglessness of reality. He observed that portraying this process is "the plan of my lyrical volume and that it might also be its title: *The Glory of the Lie* or *The Glorious Lie*. I shall sing it as one in despair!" (60). Mallarmé and Stirner were united by their recognition that ideals were inventions of the human mind, and by a shared understanding that the artist played a crucial role in their formation and propagation.

Lanson proposed that Mallarmé had set himself the impossible task of using poetry to express the infinite and unspeakable ego. Itself the product of intellectual action, poetry could only give the sensation of surmounting the realm of ideas, an illusory escape produced by the workings of the mind. Mallarmé gave "art the object of realizing the unreal, of expressing the inexpressible, of communicating the incommunicable" (my trans.; Lanson 131).[31] In doing so Mallarmé ignored the limitation that "[c]reation of the intelligence, like

---

[31] "Il donne à l'art pour objet de réaliser l'irréel, d'exprimer l'inexprimable, de communiquer l'incommunicable" (131).

science, cannot be otherwise than intellectual, and if sometimes it aspires to give the sensation, the communication of the unintelligible, it does it by means of signs and reports which express intelligibly the unintelligible character" (my trans.; 131).[32] A poetry that sought to give voice to the infinity of the ego faced the same impasse encountered by Stirner in *Der Einzige und sein Eigentum*: that once separated from all external values the ego could only be represented as the negation of meaning. For Lanson, Mallarmé's desire to uncouple poetry from intellectual action was the literary equivalent of an anarchist's bomb, signifying only the destruction of "all the intellectual and verbal institutions that social humanity has created" (my trans.; 130).[33] It was a colorful—if not entirely accurate—analogy.

There are a number of problems with Lanson's argument for a correlation between anarchism, the ideas of Stirner, the poetry of Mallarmé, and the Symbolist aesthetic in general. The allegation that Mallarmé was a literary anarchist relied, as Thierry Roger suggests:

> upon two implicit, indeed unthought, ideas: a certain idea of anarchism, equated here with the thought of Stirner, which is brandished as an interpretative grill in the very midst of the era of bombings; and a certain idea, frozen in 1893, of Mallarmé's work.
>
> (61)

Whereas Stirner had contributed to the individualist elements of anarchism through his influence on Bakunin and Proudhon, it was an overstatement to call Stirner's own philosophy anarchist. Furthermore, it is important to recognize that Mallarmé's positions—particularly regarding anarchism—were not always clear or consistent.[34] The Mallarmé that Lanson criticized was not, Roger suggests, "the author of the […] 'critical poems' in which he will, precisely, clarify his 'politics' so as, perhaps, to respond in part to this Lansonian attack" (61). More recently, Patrick McGuiness warns that "[t]he topic of Mallarmé's politics has made whole

---

[32] "Création de l'intelligence, comme la science, il ne peut pas être autrement qu'intellectuel, et si parfois il aspire à donner la sensation, la communication de l'inintelligible, il le fait au moyen de signes et de rapports qui en expriment intelligiblement l'inintelligible caractère" (131).
[33] "Concepts, logique, phrases, mots, toutes les forms, toutes les institutions intellectuelles et verbales que l'humanité sociale s'est créés, il les brise, il les fait sauter, du droit de son individualité qui aspire à 'se moduler' librement" (130).
[34] For instance, Mallarmé enigmatically suggested in "Accusation": "Devices whose explosion lights up the houses of Parliament with a summary glow, but pitifully disfigures the passers-by, I would be interested in this because of the light—without the brevity of its ability to teach, which permits the legislator to allege a definitive incomprehension; I refuse to stock up on bullets and nails" (*Divagations* 257).

books," and "[t]he danger [...] with cherry-picking statements and prising them out of their often extremely dense and interconnected passages is that we end up with a series of convenient soundbites, topped and tailed to their argument's occasion" (140). As Stirner was not an anarchist, connecting Mallarmé to Stirner did little to advance the argument that Mallarmé was a literary anarchist. Because Mallarmé was never clear about his political allegiances, it remains impossible to confirm his connection to anarchist politics.

Nevertheless, Mallarmé's pronouncements did at times indicate affinities with the ideas of Stirner and Nietzsche. Like the German philosophers of egoism, Mallarmé pondered the socially constructed foundations of reality. In "An Interrupted Performance" he went so far as to suggest that "*Reality* is just an artifice, good for anchoring the average intellect among the mirages of a fact; but it therefore rests on some universal agreement" (Mallarmé 23). Before Nietzsche had even begun work on *Also sprach Zarathustra*, Mallarmé had already proposed that only the poet could rise above the mundane ideals agreed upon by the masses. As Stirner had argued in "Kunst und Religion," Mallarmé suggested that the poet's role was to write new ideals into existence. To this end, he announced his desire "for my own sake, to write down the way this Anecdote struck my poetic eye, before the mass of reporters have chewed it over into the pabulum required to give everything its common character" ("An Interrupted Performance" 23). Nevertheless, where Stirner and Nietzsche demanded rebellion against old values, Mallarmé invited poets to find ever-new combinations of words to create ever-higher ideals.

Mallarmé's poetry also contained an individualism that correlated with Stirner's egoism. In "Hamlet" (1897) he proposed that "[t]he one available act, forever and alone, is to understand the relations, in the meantime, few or many: according to some interior state that one wishes to extend, in order to simplify the world" (188). As Stirner suggested in "Kunst und Religion," the material world is meaningless until the poet suggests the existence of transcendental ideals. The ego of the poet imposes relations on the material world in order to create meaning. Symbolism represented a collective effort to suggest universal ideals by superior individuals expressing their interior states in poetic language. This is similar to the kind of mysticism expressed in parts of Proudhon's later works, and is perhaps best summarized as an idealism that recognizes the ego as the origin of all ideals. Of course, the notion that all ideals originated in the ego was the fundamental conclusion of *Der Einzige und sein Eigentum*, and the element of Proudhon's thought that Marx attributed to Stirner.

Still, Mallarmé came to his conclusions about the creation of ideals and the role of the poet in that process without any direct knowledge of Stirner, or even Nietzsche. Christopher E. Forth points out that "Nietzsche remained unknown to most Parisians until Teodor de Wyzewa's 1891 article—in the midst of a structural shift of the French literary field away from decadence" (102). Whatever limited contact Mallarmé had with Stirnerian egoism could only have come through the philosophy of anarchists such as Bakunin and Proudhon. Even then, Baudelaire was a far greater influence on Mallarmé's thought than anarchism. As with the relationship between Stirner and Nietzsche, however, an important aspect of the similarity between Mallarmé and Stirner was that it was publicly recognized and brought to the attention of both Mallarmé and his contemporaries. Once Lanson suggested that Mallarmé was the literary equivalent of Stirner, and once Mallarmé responded (however obscurely, and in however otiose a fashion), the connection between Symbolism and egoism became a matter of public record within the literary circles of Paris.

Importantly, Mallarmé's pronouncements also indicated important differences from Stirnerian egoism. Mallarmé's conception of the ego was always dreamlike and suggestive. When the ego extended itself into the world of ideas, it did so through the mystical act of writing. In "Restricted Action," for example, Mallarmé described writing as a "fold of dark lace, which holds the infinite, woven by thousands, each according to his own thread or extension, not knowing the secret, [that] assembles distant spacings in which riches yet to be inventoried sleep: vampire, knot, foliage; and our job is to present them" (216). The infinite realm of ideas only became meaningful when the writer connected words to one another. The mundane mind connected words together in mundane ways to create a familiar reality. The superior ego of the poet created new meaning for the world by weaving words together in new symbolic combinations. Successive poets added to the tapestry of creation by extending their egos into the realm of ideas, creating ever-changing permutations of symbolic relationships. This conception of the poet as creator of symbolic meaning does recall Stirner's claim in "Kunst und Religion" that "[w]ithout art and the idealistically creative artist religion would not exist" ("Art and Religion" 331). For Mallarmé, however, the artist's role involved a degree of genuine mysticism that would have seemed an affront to Stirner.

Furthermore, the infinite that Lanson referred to in Mallarmé's poetry was not the modulation and expression of an individual poet's unspeakable self, but a tapestry of individual expressions, formed by the thousands of poets that make up a tradition. Like Proudhon's anarchist philosophy, Mallarmé's aesthetic blended individualism with collectivism and mysticism in a way that resists definitive analysis. Patrick McGuiness suggests that "Symbolism, like anarchism, oscillates between appealing to a new kind of individual and to a new kind of collective, and finds, in that oscillation, the source of some of its most uncomfortable—but also its most invigorating—contradictions" (111). In its appeal to a new kind of individual, Symbolism approached an egoistic conception of the artist. Thierry Roger recognizes that:

> Symbolist individualism undeniably hides an aristocratism. It constitutes the corollary of the hatred of a "leveling socialism" that we encounter in the writings of Mauclair, Mirbeau or Retté at a time when the majority of writers subscribe to the theory of the artist as a "superior man."
>
> (67)

The Symbolist ideal of the poet as a superior man may not have owed an intellectual debt to Stirner or Nietzsche, but it helped assure the positive reception of their ideas.

Perhaps Mallarmé's greatest contribution to the egoistic tradition of avant-garde manifesto writing, however, was the connection he made between writing, theatre, spectacle, and the self. In "Restricted Action," he suggested that the literary act demanded theatrical performance, and that "Action, in the mode we agreed upon—literary action—does not go beyond the theatre" (217). He proposed that in the act of writing:

> a Place presents itself, on the stage, the enlargement in front of everyone of the spectacle of the Self; there, because of the intermediaries of light, flesh, and laughter, the sacrifice the inspirer makes relative to his personality, completes itself; or it's the end, in an uncanny resurrection, of so-and-so: his word henceforth vain and echoing through the exhalations of the orchestral chimera.
>
> (Mallarmé, "Restricted Action" 217)

In literary acts, authors surrender themselves to their own creations. Through writing, writers are reborn as authorial identities within their works. The avant-garde manifesto takes the rebirth of the author within the creative work to its farthest limit. Through the manifesto, an author attempts to rewrite the history of a movement and establish—or at the least imply—that the manifesto writer is the arbiter of the movement's values. The authorial existence within the manifesto becomes the founder and owner of a movement, and the physical author outside of the text uses the manifesto as a demonstration of authority.

Whenever the tenets of a manifesto are followed, even if by mere coincidence, the authority of the writer as self-appointed leader is reiterated.

By observing the way authors realize themselves within their work, Mallarmé unwittingly predicted, perhaps even inspired, the kind of egoistic manifesto writing that followed in the modernist age. Marinetti's manifestos were nothing if not demonstrations of the literary act as a "spectacle of the Self." The idea of writing serving as a "whirlwind—to send a force in some direction, *any* direction" (Mallarmé, "Restricted Action" 215) is as evident in the work of Wyndham Lewis as in the work of Tristan Tzara. Mallarmé's final exhortation in "Restricted Action," to "risk certain conclusions of extreme art that might burst out, glittering like a cut diamond, now or forever, within the integrity of the book" could stand as an epigram for the avant-garde project (219). That it appeared in a work that devotes so much space to the relationship between the self and art is telling.

What appeared to Lanson to be a Stirnerian aspect in Mallarmé's oeuvre could be seen with at least as much justice as a continuation of the French tradition of elitist individualism that included figures crucial to the development of French Symbolism such as Baudelaire and Huysmans. In fact, a long line of French writers dominated the contents of Huneker's *Egoists: A Book of Supermen*, and although his choice of French egoists was at times questionable,[35] it included essays on Stendhal, Baudelaire, Flaubert, Anatole France, Huysmans, Barrès, Ernest Hello, and Francis Poictevin. At the very least, Huneker suggested a broad similarity between French elitist individualism and Stirner's ideas that helped explain the rapid reception of egoism in 1890s Paris. When Lanson identified the similarity between the poetry of Mallarmé and the philosophy of Stirner in 1893, Mallarmé could not have avoided becoming conscious of these similarities as well. Lanson's contention that Mallarmé was an *anarchiste littéraire*, whose ambitions for poetry rivalled the intellectual aspirations of Stirner, implicated Mallarmé in the development of French literary egoism.

Among the French exponents of intellectual aristocratism identified as egoists by Huneker, Baudelaire stands out both because he drew similar conclusions to

---

[35] Of Stendhal, Huneker recalled that "Brunetière saw in him the perfect expression of romantic and anti-social individualism" (4). He went on to propose that "[t]he Egoist is *beylisme* of a superior artistry" (6). Other authors—particularly Flaubert—did not fit as neatly alongside Baudelaire, Barrès, Nietzsche, and Stirner under the appellation of egoist. Huneker's argument regarding Flaubert, for example, rested on the notion that *The Temptation of Saint Anthony* (1874) demonstrated that he was "the artist who shows us apocalyptic visions of all philosophies, all schools, ethical systems, cultures, religions" (135).

Stirner and because he heavily influenced the ideas of Mallarmé. As Roberto Calasso suggests, "[t]he *décadent* is similar to the fetishist: he celebrates the triumph of the idiosyncratic; he opposes the notion that his singularity might be reabsorbed into a whole. In this, Baudelaire is comparable only with Max Stirner" (*La Folie Baudelaire* 275). Baudelaire was a forerunner of what would become French Symbolism, and Daniel Albright suggests that he "was one of the founders of this school, for his sonnet 'Correspondences' (1857) stated its means and hinted at its goals" (11). "Correspondences" became a conceptual model for Symbolist poetry, with its suggestion that "La Nature est un temple où de vivants piliers / Laissent parfois sortir de confuses paroles; / L'homme y passe à travers des forêts de symboles / Qui l'observent avec des regards familiers" (Baudelaire 18).[36] The role of the poet was to investigate the way "perfumes, colours, sounds may correspond," to bring about a state compared to "Singing the senses' rapture, and the soul's" (19).[37] The idea that only the poet can bring together the symbols of the physical world to transcend mundane reality was an important aspect of Mallarmé's poetry. In "Hamlet," for instance, Mallarmé suggested:

> Nature, in Autumn, prepares its sublime and pure Theatre, waiting to illuminate, in solitude, some prestigious significance, whose meaning the unique, lucid eye can penetrate (notorious, it's man's destiny), it's too bad a Poet should be called back to mediocre pleasures and worries.
>
> (124)

The belief that the poet was a superior person capable of overcoming the limitations of the mediocre masses demanded an aristocratic—even egoistic—sense of self, but that was not the full extent of similarities between the thought of Baudelaire and Stirner.

It was in Baudelaire's portrayal of the archetypal dandy in *Le Peintre de la vie moderne* (The Painter of Modern Life, 1863) that he came closest to a corollary with Stirner's egoist and Nietzsche's *Übermensch*. The dandy figures importantly in Baudelaire's criticism because he suggests that "the word 'dandy' implies a quintessence of character and a subtle understanding of the entire moral mechanism of the world" shared by his ideal *flâneur*, Constantin Guys

---

[36] James McGowan renders these lines as "Nature is a temple, where the living / Columns sometimes breathe confusing speech; / Man walks within these groves of symbols, each / Of which regards him as a kindred thing" (19).
[37] Again taken from James McGowan's translation of *Les fleurs du mal* (1857), the original lines read "Les parfums, les couleurs et les sons se répondent" and "Qui chantent les transports de l'esprit et des sens" (18).

("The Painter of Modern Life" 9). Baudelaire described dandyism as "first and foremost the burning need to create for oneself a personal originality, bounded only by the limits of the properties," and as "a kind of cult of the self" (28), but he came even closer to an egoistic depiction of the dandy—without any apparent knowledge of Stirner's book—to conclude:

> Whether these men are nicknamed exquisites, *incroyables*, beaux, lions or dandies, they all spring from the same womb; they all partake of the same characteristic of opposition and revolt; they are all representatives of what is finest in human pride, of that compelling need, alas only too rare today, of combatting and destroying triviality.
>
> (28)

Baudelaire's proud and elegant dandy, driven by an overwhelming desire to rebel against the triviality of the crowd, sits comfortably alongside Stirner's egoist and Nietzsche's *Übermensch* as another example of the elitist individualism that proved popular in nineteenth-century Europe.

The dandy was the enemy of the crowd and the champion of the self. Baudelaire lamented that "the rising tide of democracy, which invades and levels everything, is daily overwhelming these last representatives of human pride and pouring floods of oblivion upon the footprints of these stupendous warriors" ("The Painter of Modern Life" 29). When he described Guys as "an 'I' with an insatiable appetite for the 'non-I,' at every instant rendering and explaining it in pictures more living than life itself" (9), Baudelaire created the Symbolist paradigm of an imperious, individualistic, and insurrectionary artist passionately immersing himself in the crowd. Comparison to Stirner's egoist was inevitable, but Lanson was the first to make the connection, and it was Mallarmé, not Baudelaire, who became the subject of his criticism.

Barrès and the Cult of the Self

Like Mallarmé, Maurice Barrès proved a crucial, if in some ways a problematic, figure in the proliferation of egoism in European literary circles. Barrès's own brand of egoism—*le culte du moi*—drew heavily from the strands of individualism he encountered in the work of Proudhon, Bakunin, and Eduard von Hartmann. Nevertheless, at the time of its inception, he seems to have been ignorant of Stirner's importance to the development of egoism. Huneker devoted a chapter to Barrès in *Egoists*, where he suggested that Barrès "boldly proclaimed the *culte du moi*," and "proclaimed his disdain for the barbarians who impinged upon his *I*" (211). Barrès was at varying stages in his literary career a Decadent, Symbolist, and member of the *école romane*,[38] and as Lucy Hughes-Hallett notes, his "early novels were among those from which D'Annunzio was lifting ideas, images, even whole sentences, in the 1890s" (326). His political ties were equally diverse, and he was by turns a self-proclaimed socialist, Boulangist,[39] anti-Dreyfusard, associate of Charles Maurras, and popularizer of French nationalism. J. S. McClelland suggests that "[i]f Maurras repelled even his supporters, Barrès charmed even his opponents," and that while "[s]ome doubted his sincerity and others his wisdom [...] all seemed to agree that the man who could become a member of the Académie Française at the age of forty-five must be something special" (143). His first trilogy, itself titled *Le culte du moi*, espoused a philosophy of "[e]goism, egotism, Me with a capital letter" (my trans.; Barrès, *Sous l'œil des barbares* 16),[40] and while Barrès claimed his egoism drew overtly on the work of Proudhon, many of his ideas were strikingly similar to those first expressed by Stirner in *Der Einzige und sein Eigentum*.

Barrès's pre-eminence assured the propagation of his intellectual enthusiasm for egoism. A bookish and aloof youth, he "was born in 1862 in Lorraine, in the small provincial town of Charmes-sur-Moselle, the child of a comfortable middle-class family" (Soucy 27). He moved to Paris in 1882 to study law, but quickly set about establishing himself in the Parisian literary scene. Michael Curtis calls Barrès "fiercely ambitious" and suggests that "[s]teadfastly and smoothly, he organized his own success" (56). He was an effective campaigner, and soon achieved a startling list of literary accomplishments. Soucy notes that "[w]ithin a year he had several articles accepted by the literary review *Jeune France*," had "gained entry into some of the leading literary salons of Paris," had "met Mallarmé and Huysmans," and "single-handedly launched his own literary review, *Taches d'encre* [*Ink Stains*], writing all the articles himself" (30–1). By the time that *Sous l'œil des barbares* (Under the Eyes of the Barbarians)—the first

---

[38] A literary movement founded by Jean Moreas, who wrote the Symbolist manifesto *Le Symbolisme* in 1886. Its members included Raymond de la Tailhède; Maurice du Plessys; Ernest Raynaud; and the influential nationalist, Charles Maurras. Disparaging free verse and vagueness of Symbolist poetry, the *école romane* returned to Classical subject matter and techniques.

[39] A French nationalist and revanchist movement led by General Georges Ernest Boulanger. For a time in the 1880s Boulanger was considered popular and powerful enough to stage a coup d'état.

[40] As mentioned earlier, the word *égoïsme* can denote not only philosophical egoism, but also selfishness more broadly. Barrès list of alternative appellations, "[é]goïsme, égotisme, Moi avec une majuscule," is perhaps an effort to distinguish between more base notions of selfishness and the philosophy of his *culte du moi*.

novel of *Le culte du moi*—was published in 1888, he had also visited Bayreuth and Florence, met Henry James, and "written for the Republican newspaper *Voltaire*" (Soucy 31). Despite the apparent skill with which Barrès charmed his way into Parisian salons, *Sous l'œil des barbares* was initially met with indifference by the press. It languished for weeks before "Paul Bourget gave it a laudatory review and overnight it became a literary sensation" (Soucy 31). Bourget's expansive and adulatory review in the *Journal des débats* on April 3, 1888, won Barrès a legion of young supporters, but his literary individualism was already beginning to chafe against his nationalist politics.

Barrès popularized egoism in both literary and political circles, and proposed a kind of egoistic nationalism that contributed to the development of Italian fascism. In 1889 he entered politics formally, successfully contesting a seat in the *Chambre des députés* as a nominally Boulangist candidate. He cared little for ideology, "was never a member of a party or group, and continually changed his electoral nomenclature while deputy for the first *arrondissement* of Paris" (Curtis 58). Soucy goes so far as to suggest that Barrès's "early political activism, like his early *culte du moi*, was essentially a form of sensation-seeking, little more than egoistic, nihilistic adventurism—with a touch of the dandy as spectator thrown in" (64). Barrès used politics as a means of self-fulfillment and, like D'Annunzio and Marinetti, found self-aggrandizement rather than partisanship to be the natural extension of the egoistic artist's vocation. Nevertheless, politics provided an opportunity to win further acolytes to his cult of self and nation. Instead of aligning himself with an existing ideological program, Barrès dedicated himself to the development of his own philosophical frameworks, first in his *culte du moi* and then later a creed of *la terre et les morts* (the earth and the dead). Where *le culte du moi* promoted an individual sense of self, *la terre et les morts* championed rootedness in French tradition.

Efforts to reconcile the tension between individualism and French national identity eventually led Barrès to apply the amoralism and self-interest of the egoist to the nation at large, creating a program of egoistic nationalism that went on to influence D'Annunzio and Mussolini. Soucy suggests that "Barrès taught a different kind of nationalism, which placed national self-interest (or egoism) above all other principles, which was indifferent to the fate of other nations, which called for economic and intellectual protectionism, which glorified the army and military power, and which subordinated individual rights to *raison d'état*" (11). His strain of nationalism applied the tenets of egoism to authoritarian leadership and proposed that, "[w]hat was good for the individual—power, energy, and force—

was good for the State" (Soucy 8). Combining personal identity and national identity to create an egoistic strain of nationalism, Barrès's fed into aspects of Italian Fascism and German National Socialism because he described "a doctrine of psychic rootedness which together with its later racist supplement closely resembled the Nazi concept of *Blut und Boden* [blood and soil]" (Soucy 39). It also naturally lent itself to the view that the authoritarian leader was the physical embodiment of the state, and that his will represented the will of the state to terrifying effect.

Both Barrès's early *culte du moi* and his later notion of *la terre et les morts* were part of the developing tradition of French elitist individualism that retroactively incorporated the ideas of Stirner and Nietzsche. The protagonist of *Le culte du moi*, Philippe, begins the trilogy "in many respects a typical decadent hero" (Soucy 41). A physically weak but intellectually developed dandy, "the whole book is Philippe's struggle to keep himself in the midst of the Barbarians who want to bend him to their image" (my trans.; Barrès, *Sous l'œil des barbares* 21).[41] His intellectual development in *Sous l'œil des barbares* ultimately leads him to an outburst of Stirnerian revolt:

> After which, if I am told: "Prove yourself, testify that you are a god." I indignantly reply: "What! Like the others! Define me, that is to say limit me! Reflect me in intelligences that will deform me according to their curves! And which grounds did you prepare for me? My task, since my pleasure commits me to it, is to preserve myself intact. I hold myself to free my Self from the alluvium that the foul river of the barbarians constantly ejects."
>
> (my trans.; Barrès, *Sous l'œil des barbares* 243–4)[42]

Philippe's recognition of the importance of maintaining his sense of self in the face of society's impositions on his identity marks the beginning of his path out of decadence. As Soucy suggests, Philippe "begins by seizing on the one undeniable reality in a world of possible unreality: *le moi*, the self, the subjective consciousness" (41). In *Le culte du moi*, Barrès proposed that self-ownership provided a means of escaping the decadence of *fin de siècle* culture, and the intellectual stagnation associated with it.

---

[41] "Et tout le livre, c'est la lutte de Philippe pour se maintenir au milieu des Barbares qui veulent le plier à leur image" (21).

[42] "Après quoi si l'on me dit: 'Prouvez-vous donc, témoignez que vous êtes un dieu.' Je m'indigne et je réponds: 'Quoi! comme les autres! me définir, c'est-à-dire me limiter! me refléter dans des intelligences qui me déformeront selon leurs courbes! Et quel parterre m'avez-vous préparé? Ma tâche, puisque mon plaisir m'y engage, est de me conserver intact. Je m'en tiens à dégager mon Moi des alluvions qu'y rejette sans cesse le fleuve immonde des Barbares'" (243–4).

Barrès discussed the influences on *Le culte du moi* in his introduction to the 1911 edition of *Sous l'œil des barbares*. While he did not mention Stirner, many of the figures that he cited as important to his ideas had strong connections to Stirner's work. Furthermore, Barrès attributed a number of conclusions to these individuals that rightly belonged to Stirner. He suggested that the final book in the trilogy, *Jardin de Bérénice*, provided "a theory of love, where the French writers, who rioted against Schopenhauer and did not know how to recognize in him the spirit of our eighteenth century, will be able to vary their developments, if they distinguish that *here we put* [Eduard von] Hartmann *in action*" (my trans.; my emphasis; *Sous l'œil des barbares* 28).[43] As suggested earlier, Hartmann's work on the ego involved numerous discussions of Stirner's egoism, and *Der Einzige und sein Eigentum* had already described an egoistic foundation for love. As with Nietzsche, Barrès would certainly have encountered the name Stirner and his ideas if he read either Hartmann's *Philosophie des Unbewussten* or his *Phänomenologie des sittlichen Bewusstseins* with any degree of rigor. Barrès also mentioned reading Fichte in his introduction to *Sous l'œil des barbares* which, if nothing else, suggests the breadth of his reading on the subject of the ego and a shared influence with Stirner.

One of the most significant figures in the formulation of Barrès's *culte du moi* was Proudhon. Marx argued in 1852 that the egoistic aspects of Proudhon's philosophy were the product of Stirner's influence, and it was these very ideas that Barrès drew upon most heavily in developing his cult of the self. Barrès cited Proudhon's assertion that "I [...] was all that I could touch with my hand, reach for with my gaze, and that was good for something; not-I was all that could harm or resist me" (my trans.; *Sous l'œil des barbares* 23).[44] Barrès concluded that "[a]pply to the spiritual aspect of things what [Proudhon] says of the physical order and you have the state of Philippe in *Sous l'œil des barbares*. The barbarians are the not-I, that is to say, all that can harm or resist the ego" (my trans.; *Sous l'œil des barbares* 23).[45] Proudhon's conception of expansive self-ownership, taken

---

[43] "De là ce troisième volume, le Jardin de Bérénice, une théorie de l'amour, où les producteurs français qui tapageaient contre Schopenhauer et ne savaient pas reconnaître en lui l'esprit de notre dix-huitième siècle, pourront varier leurs développements, s'ils distinguent qu'ici l'on a mis Hartmann en action" (28).

[44] "Moi, disait Proudhon, se souvenant de son enfance, c'était tout ce que je pouvais toucher de la main, atteindre du regard et qui m'était bon à quelque chose; non-moi était tout ce qui pouvait nuire ou résister à moi" (23).

[45] "Appliquez à l'aspect spirituel des choses ce qu'il dit de l'ordre physique, vous avez l'état de Philippe dans *Sous l'œil des Barbares*. Les Barbares, voilà le non-moi, c'est-à-dire tout ce qui peut nuire ou résister au Moi" (23). It is worth pointing out that this is another instance in which egoism takes on a dialectical character by allowing for the existence of a non-I which Stirnerian egoism identified as an alienated property of the unique individual.

from *De la justice dans la révolution et dans l'église* (On Justice in the Revolution and in the Church, 1858), is a typical example of the line of argument that Marx accused him of lifting directly from Stirner.

Even the language Barrès used to describe his *culte du moi* bore marked resemblances to Stirner's egoism. He proposed—as Stirner had in 1844—that "[o]ur morals, our religion, our national sentiments are crumbling things [...] from which we cannot draw rules for life, and, until our professors have remade our certainties, we should stick to the only reality, the self" (my trans.; Barrès, *Sous l'œil des barbares* 15).[46] He clarified that "[t]he cult of the self is not to accept all of one's self," but "demands from its servants a constant effort. It is an education that is achieved by pruning and by increments: we first have to purify our ego from all the foreign fragments that life continually introduces to it, and then add to it" (my trans.; 22).[47] Even if Barrès was not, as he had suggested elsewhere, directly familiar with the content of Stirner's philosophy, *Le culte du moi* developed a program of radical individualism that drew extensively from thinkers who were. By acknowledging Stirner's importance to theories of the ego, Barrès tacitly recognized Stirner's importance to his own developments in this field. Like Stirner, he proposed that the subjective experience of the ego was the only sure foundation for creating moral values and that the self-development of the individual demanded the conscious rejection of all external influences on the ego.

In 1894, Barrès acknowledged the importance of Stirner to the development of egoism and anarchism. In *De Hegel aux cantines du Nord* (From Hegel to the Workmen's Canteens of the North, 1894) he also demonstrated the extent of his knowledge of the Hegelian tradition. He suggested that the "Hegelian method [...] has kept alive collectivism and Karl Marx in Germany, Proudhon in France, and Bakunin and anarchist terrorism in Russia" (McClelland 150). He noted that "[i]t is said that Bakunin's anarchism owes a great deal to Stirner, who set out the sacred law of egoism," but added "I do not know enough about Stirner to talk about him properly, but at least can see how in Bakunin's mind Hegelianism justifies anarchism" (McClelland 152). This acknowledgment seems to suggest that Barrès's knowledge of Stirner had indeed come indirectly, through books

---

[46] "Notre morale, notre religion, notre sentiment des nationalités sont choses écroulées, constatais-je, auxquelles nous ne pouvons emprunter de règles de vie, et, en attendant que nos maîtres nous aient refait des certitudes, il convient que nous nous en tenions à la seule réalité, au Moi" (15).
[47] "Le culte du Moi n'est pas de s'accepter tout entier [...] réclame de ses servants un constant effort. C'est une culture qui se fait par élaguements et par accroissements: nous avons d'abord à épurer notre Moi de toutes les parcelles étrangères que la vie continuellement y introduit, et puis à lui ajouter" (22).

such as Hartmann's and recent articles on Stirner's place in the anarchist tradition, but is remarkable, considering that *Der Einzige und sein Eigentum* had only become widely available in Germany in the previous year. Even six years before the first complete translation of *Der Einzige und sein Eigentum* into French, intellectuals in France were already beginning to recognize Stirner's importance to their own insurrectionary ideas.

If Barrès had any reservations about connecting his *culte du moi* to the ideas of Stirner, others did not share them. In his article on Stirner, "*Nouvelles modes en philosophie: Max Stirner et Frédéric Nietzsche*," Bourdeau directly compared the egoism of the newly rediscovered Stirner to that of Barrès. He described Stirner as a figure "who demolishes in turn the idol Humanity, and replaces it with *le culte du moi*" (my trans.; Bourdeau 1).[48] Furthermore, he observed "a sinister omen in this resurrection of a forgotten book, as in this new flowering of the antisocial paradox, that expresses itself in works such as *Anarchistes*, by John Henry Mackay, and with originality and grace in *l'Ennemi des lois*, by Maurice Barrès" (my trans.; Bourdeau 2).[49] Even if Barrès was not familiar with the content of *Der Einzige und sein Eigentum* at the time of writing his most influential works, Bordeau immediately identified key similitudes between the philosophies of Barrès and Stirner. For Bordeau, Barrès's most recent novel, *l'Ennemi des lois* (1893), was a clear demonstration that Barrès was popularizing the cause of Stirnerian egoism in Parisian literary circles.

L'Ennemi des lois is best described as a philosophical novel, depicting the revolutionary philosophy of a professor named André Maltère. The nature of this philosophical outlook is perhaps best reflected in the novel's explicitly anarchist title. It begins with Maltère on trial for the publication of a scandalous article that advocates the emancipation of the individual and criticizes both the military and the law. Like Carrard Auban in *Die Anarchisten*, Maltère transforms his opponents' accusations of selfishness into an apologia for egoism. He acknowledges that he is:

> Egoistic, however, I am not so in a way that I deny to others the benefit of my clairvoyance; it is even from this liberality that I answer before you.

---

[48] "Vient alors Max Stirner qui démolit à son tour l'idole Humanité, et la remplace par le culte du moi" (1).

[49] "Faut-il chercher, de même, un sinistre présage dans cette résurrection d'un livre oublié, dans cette floraison nouvelle du paradoxe antisocial; qui s'exprime dans des ouvrages tels que les *Anarchistes*, de John Henry Mackay, et avec originalité, avec grâce dans *l'Ennemi des lois*, de M. Maurice Barrès" (2).

The Prosecutor has reproached me for using my intelligence and the instruction I received from it against society. (my trans.; 24)[50]

Despite frequent references to thinkers including Saint-Simon and Fourier, Stirner is never mentioned as an influence on Maltère's egoistic philosophy. Nevertheless, *égoïsme* is consistently depicted as a liberating force, used against the intellectual shackles of the law and the state.[51] For Bordeau, the egoism of Auban in *Die Anarchisten* and the *égoïsme* of Maltère in *l'Ennemi des lois* reflected a broader resurgence of Stirner's insurrectionary individualism, regardless of whether or not the resemblance was directly acknowledged. Indeed, the final lines of the novel are highly evocative of Stirner's depictions of egoistic love. Barrès describes revolutionaries who "do not break the flowers they love to breathe; that they suffer, that would diminish their pleasure; their refined sensibility removes all immorality" (294).[52] The passage recalls Stirner's suggestion in *Der Einzige und sein Eigentum* that "because I cannot bear the troubled crease on the beloved forehead, for that reason, and therefore for my sake, I kiss it away" (*The Ego and Its Own* 259). In both cases, the notion of moral altruism is challenged by depicting the supposedly altruistic act as the product of a refined egoistic desire for pleasure.

According to Bordeau, Barrès was a crucial popularizer of Stirner's ideas in France in the 1890s. The full extent of his significance was, however, much broader. Through his varying influences on manifesto writers ranging from D'Annunzio to Breton,[53] Barrès was also a key figure in the realization of an egoistic avant-garde manifesto. D'Annunzio reproduced many of Barrès's ideas adapted to fit the context of an Italian audience in the 1890s. In this way Barrès's conception of an egoistic strain of nationalism evidently prefigured aspects of Italian fascism. The fact that his early work has been largely ignored by the

---

50 "Égoïste, toutefois je ne le suis pas d'une façon que je refuse aux autres le bénéfice de ma clairvoyance; c'est même de cette libéralité que je réponds devant vous. M. le Procureur m'a reproché d'utiliser contre la société mon intelligence et l'instruction que j'en ai reçue" (24).
51 Given the context of the work and Barrès's philosophical outlook, there is a strong case to suggest that his use of *égoïsme* here should be translated as "egoism" rather than "selfishness."
52 "Ils ne cassent pas les fleurs qu'ils aiment à respirer; qu'elles souffriraient, cela diminuerait leur plaisir; leur sensibilité affinée supprime toute immoralité" (294).
53 In *Anarchism and the Advent of Paris Dada* (2010), Theresa Papanikolas suggested that "Barrès's early novels [...] reflected the Stirnerian egoism that dominated the prewar anarcho-individualist movement, and they profoundly influenced Breton's generation in their celebration of individual genius" (148). Although it is perhaps more accurate to suggest that anarcho-individualists capitalized on the success of Symbolist efforts to popularize egoism in France, *Anarchism and the Advent of Paris Dada* is—like David Ashford's *Autarchies* (2017)—a landmark study in the reappraisal of Stirner's influence on the European avant-garde.

English-speaking world—neither *le culte du moi* nor *l'Ennemi des lois* has yet been translated into English—obscures the career of a writer whose ideas were comparable with Sorel and Maurras, at least in terms of their influence. The development of Barrès's ideas is emblematic of the way egoism fused with the French tradition of elitist individualism to produce new strains of literary and political thought.

Egoism and the Manifesto in Symbolist Paris

Egoism continued to find fertile ground in the aristocratic individualism of French Symbolism while the avant-garde manifesto proceeded with its own burgeoning development. A translation of the opening section of *Der Einzige und sein Eigentum*, titled "Je n'ai mis ma cause en personne,"[54] appeared in the *Mercure de France* in May 1894, translated by Henri Albert. This translation appeared alongside works by Tailhade and the influential Symbolist writer and critic, Remy de Gourmont. Albert later provided the translation for the first French edition of *Also Sprach Zarathustra* (*Ainsi parlait Zarathoustra: un livre pour tous et pour personne*) published by *Mercure de France* in 1898. By the end of May 1895, a total of five sections taken from the first half of *Der Einzige und sein Eigentum* had appeared in the pages of the *Mercure de France* alongside contributions by prominent figures such as Jean Moréas; Émile Raynaud; Charles Maurras; Alfred Jarry; and, of course, Mallarmé and Barrès. The first full translation of the book into French was published in 1899 and was the work of yet another translator, Robert L. Reclaire. Roberto Calasso notes that by the end of 1900:

> two translations, one by Reclaire, the other by [Henri] Lasvignes, were published, respectively, by Stock and Éditions de *la Revue Blanche*, the latter being another centre—together with the *Mercure*—where the best literature of those years came together.
>
> (*The Forty-Nine Steps* 168)

---

[54] This is a French rendering of the opening line of Goethe's *Vanitas! Vanitatum Vanitas!*, which was quoted by Stirner at both ends of his book. The original German is "Ich hab' Mein Sach' auf Nichts gestellt" (I have set my affair on nothing), and Byington translated it in the first English edition of Stirner's book as "All things are nothing to me" (*The Ego and His Own* 5).

It was Symbolists then—rather than illegalists like Bonnot—who did the most to spread Stirner's ideas among intellectual circles in the 1890s, and these same Symbolists provided a firm foundation for the manifesto-writing practices of the avant-garde in the years that followed.

Critics continue to dispute the exact point at which nineteenth-century declarations of aesthetic principles gave way to recognizable examples of the avant-garde manifesto. The definition of manifesto remains contentious, and the history of literary pamphleteering is long. Regardless of whether or not they were true manifestos—or if such a distinction is even meaningful—the polemics of the Symbolist movement contributed to the development of the strident declarations of Futurism, Vorticism, and Dada, among others. One of the earliest and perhaps most important of these Symbolist programs was "Le Symbolisme" (1886) by Jean Moréas. Appearing in September, in the literary supplement of *Le Figaro*, "Le Symbolisme" represented an effort to defend and control current trends in French poetry. Above its title, the editor added the heading "Un manifeste littéraire," a title that arguably marked the beginning of the avant-garde's preoccupation with the word "manifesto."[55] Martin Puchner contests this starting point, arguing that "it was another twenty-three years before programmatic art manifestos would announce themselves as such and thus openly embrace the foundational and revolutionary inheritance of the genre" (72). If he is correct, the popularity of Stirnerian egoism was at its height at the birth of the modern manifesto. In any case, the manifesto developed in tandem with the reception of Stirner's ideas. By 1891 the concept of a literary manifesto was widespread enough for Moréas to suggest in an article promoting the *école romane* that "[a]ll those who understand that French genius must be pure and not smeared with Northern obscurities, will join me! [...] For details, refer to my prefaces, *manifestos* and interviews" (my trans.; my emphasis; "Une Nouvelle École" 1).[56] If in name only, avant-garde manifesto writing was already underway.

With the benefit of hindsight it is important to recognize the differences between nineteenth-century Symbolist proclamations such as those of Moréas,

---

[55] In *Legitimizing the Artist: Manifesto Writing and European Modernism 1885-1915*, Luca Somigli observes that the label manifesto "was in fact the result of an editorial decision on the part of Auguste Marcade, the editor of the newspaper, who had invited the poet to write a contribution to the debate on 'decadent' poetry" (25).

[56] "Tous ceux qui comprennent que le génie français doit être pur et non barbouillé d'obscurités septentrionales, me rejoindront! [...] Pour le détail, reportez-vous à mes préfaces, manifestes et interviews" (1).

and the twentieth-century manifestos of Futurism, Dada, and Vorticism. Most obviously, Moréas' proclamations—for both Symbolism and the *école romane*—lacked the succinct, numbered pronouncements typical of twentieth-century iterations of the manifesto. Perhaps with the exception of Mallarmé's critical poems, Symbolist programs also lacked the dynamic typography demonstrated by the works of Marinetti, Lewis, and Tzara. Furthermore, compared to works such as Marinetti's "Fondation et manifeste du Futurisme" (1909), "Le Symbolisme" was almost conservative in its aspirations. Mary Ann Caws goes so far as to call Moréas's manifesto "a pale thing, particularly in juxtaposition with James Abbott McNeill Whistler's 'Ten o'Clock' lecture of the previous year" (2). Instead, she notes the importance of Mallarmé's "great antilinear manifesto with its remarkable typographic experimentation: '*Un coup de Dés jamais n'abolira le Hasard*' ('A Throw of Dice Not Ever Will Abolish Chance')[57] of 1897, whose reverberations were felt in the worlds of art as well as poetics" (2). Moréas called for "a rejuvenation of the old metrics; a cleverly ordered disorder; with gleaming rhyme hammered like a shield of gold and bronze next to a rhyme fluid and abstruse; the alexandrine with its multiple and mobile caesuras; the use of uneven numbers" (Moréas, "The Symbolist Manifesto" 51).[58] In contrast, the manifesto became a conduit for vital energy in the hands of Marinetti when he declared that "[c]ourage, boldness, and rebellion will be the essential elements in our poetry" ("Foundation and Manifesto of Futurism" 13). As Puchner suggests, "[e]ven though Moréas wants to break with the past to propel himself into the future, he cannot quite let go of the past entirely" (70). Symbolist *manifestes* tended to share Moréas' ambiguous relationship with tradition and, where they called most fervently for a break with tradition, were more concerned with liberating art from realism, naturalism, and moral instruction.

Still, Anatole France certainly recognized the swagger associated with calling a literary treatise a manifesto. In his immediate response to "Le Symbolisme," he observed that "[a] newspaper, which usually receives the manifestos of

---

[57] Caws chooses this awkward translation of the title in response to the way in which the French title is broken across several pages of the poem. Each part of the title is also a line of the poem and, due to unconventional typography and layout, the piece can be read in a variety of non-linear ways. Reflecting this fact, an even more accurate translation of the title might be: A Throw of Dice / Not Ever / Will Abolish / Chance.

[58] This translation is taken from *Manifesto: A Century of Isms*, but the original text varies a little toward the end: "[…] la rime illucescente et martelée comme un bouclier d'or et d'airain, auprès de la rime aux fluidités absconses; l'alexandrin à arrêts multiples et mobiles; l'emploi de certains nombres premiers—sept, neuf, onze, treize—résolus en les diverses combinaisons rythmiques dont ils sont les sommes" (Moréas, "Le Symbolisme" 180).

princes, has just published the profession of faith of the Symbolists" (my trans.; France 2).⁵⁹ Indeed, the word "manifesto" was still an appellation more closely associated with the official pronouncements of royalty than the maneuvering of political and literary insurgents. Puchner proposes that "the first occurrences of the word 'manifesto' as a title are in many ways the opposite of the [*Communist*] *Manifesto*: instead of a collective, revolutionary, and subversive voice, 'manifesto' here designates a declaration of the will of a sovereign" (12). In some respects, the princely decree, *The Communist Manifesto*, and "Le Symbolisme" had much more in common than Puchner recognizes. All three texts are produced by a single author working largely alone; all three are calls for specific action, and all three claim the right of the author to speak for an entire community. These shared aspects represent the egoistic qualities that are implicit in the manifesto. Machiavelli provided the pre-eminent example of the egoistic concerns of the prince, the tensions between Marx and Stirner underscored the egoistic elements of the *Theses on Feuerbach*, and Baudelaire contributed a great deal of the elitist individualism on show in "Le Symbolisme." Anatole France's response to "Le Symbolisme" suggests that he, too, perceived Moréas' manifesto as a *palace coup* rather than a *jacquerie*. Through its use by the Italian avant-garde—in particular Marinetti—what had until then been an implicit strain of egoism became the driving force of the avant-garde manifesto.

Despite lively competition between the various Symbolist and Decadent circles of *fin de siècle* Paris, Mallarmé, Barrès, and Moréas all shared points of contact that helped to propel the reception of egoism both in Paris and abroad. All three were in correspondence with each other, and Mallarmé referred to the work of Moréas and Barrès in glowing terms.⁶⁰ In turn, Moréas and Barrès were strongly influenced by Mallarmé. Barrès later joined the *école romane*, the neo-classical movement founded by Moréas and Charles Maurras in 1891. Although these poets may have had peripheral connections to the ideas of Stirner, the effect was cumulative. Mallarmé's refiguring of abstract ideals had

---

⁵⁹ "Un journal, qui recoit d'ordinaire les manifestes des princes, vient de publier la profession de foi des symbolists" (2).
⁶⁰ Mallarmé wrote to Barrès that "I feel for you a very special friendship, illuminated by your letter: what conversations I foresee for winter's evenings this year, if you're willing to spend some of them with me!" ("Maurice Barrès" 141). To Moréas he was even more effusive: "The page, which distills, in such a rarity of voice and coloration your written melody, appears to me immaculate, around the words, even the modern ones, which give the impression that you alone have spoken them; and isn't that the greatest charm, to give Poetry the appearance of being foreign, eternally, to the true territory!" (Mallarmé, "Jean Moréas" 173).

been publicly connected to Stirner. Barrès had linked an undeniably egoistic strain of anarchism to the development of French nationalism. Moréas also contributed to the development of French nationalism but, more importantly, he had helped to unite French avant-garde aesthetics and nationalist politics under the banner of the manifesto. Elsewhere, interest in Stirner was gathering momentum in the Parisian literary scene in large part owing to the ongoing role of Symbolist publications like the *Revue Bleue* and *Revue Blanche* in publishing translations of Stirner's writing. In 1904 Gustave Kahn would join the ranks of Symbolists expressing open support for Stirner's thought.[61] All the while *Der Einzige und sein Eigentum* continued to be diversely appropriated and read out of context. Parisians had encountered Stirner as a father of anarchism—itself an anachronistic misreading of his assault on German idealism—but he was now also associated with reactionary politics and developing trends in nationalism. The image of Stirner the anarchist was already being replaced by the idea that he was a founding philosopher of fascism.

---

[61] Kahn was an important and influential member of the Symbolist movement. His role in the transmission of Stirnerian egoism will be discussed in the following chapter in the context of his influence on Marinetti's intellectual development.

3

Italy: The Ascent of the Poet Tyrant

When Gaetano Bresci fatally shot King Umberto I of Italy on July 29, 1900, the murder was the culmination of a decade of brazen political assassinations committed by Italian anarchists across Europe. Two years later *Der Einzige und sein Eigentum* was translated into Italian for the first time, as *L'Unico* (1902), published by the Bocca brothers in Turin. It began with a cautionary introduction by the translator, Ettore Zoccoli, expressing his misgivings about the task he had just completed. Indeed, Zoccoli bluntly asserted that "[i]f I had seen the obvious, or even simply tacit, intent in the publisher of the present translation to make, as they say, *popular* the work of Stirner, I would never have agreed to the question of writing this introduction" (ix).[1] Roberto Calasso suggests that Zoccoli was "[w]orried about the favorable reception that Stirner's 'criminal individualism' was encountering," and "outlines the vicissitudes of *Der Einzige* in some detail, and in particular, in accordance with the tendency of the time, he draws a comparison between Stirner's ideas and those of other anarchist leaders" (*The Forty-Nine Steps* 168). In Italy as in France Stirner was broadly portrayed as one of the fathers of anarchism and the intellectual forebear of Nietzsche. By exposing Stirner's reliance on an "endless chain of fallacious arguments" (Zoccoli xxviii),[2] Zoccoli sought to confront the spread of anarchist terrorism, but it was a futile effort. Following his posthumous successes in Germany and France, Stirner was already on the way to becoming a transnational phenomenon.

By the time that Stirner's ideas reached Italian intellectuals much had been lost in translation and the passage of time. His powerful critique of abstract ideals was all but lost from the anarchist interpretation of egoism that was perpetuated in Paris and transmitted to Italy. Anarchists advanced a version of Stirnerian

---

[1] "Se nell'editore della presente traduzione io avessi veduto l'intento palese, o anche semplicemente tacito, di rendere, come si dice, *popolare* l'opera dello Stirner, non avrei assolutamente aderito alla domanda di scrivere questa introduzione" (ix).
[2] "Attraverso questa interminabile catena di argomentazioni fallaci lo Stirner arriva all'individuo, cui impone gl'imperativi della sua disciplina egoistica" (xxviii).

egoism that focused on the power of criminal acts to bring about revolutionary change. Once again, Stirner was read in the context of Marx and Nietzsche rather than Hegel and Feuerbach. The influence of Barrès's nationalism further polluted the stream of Stirnerian egoism. Egoism was quickly becoming all things to all people, but the first casualty was Stirner's powerful warning about the dangers of unchecked ideals.

The reputation of French literature abroad and the appeal of egoism among French intellectuals all but ensured the eventual popularization of Stirner's ideas in Italy. Continued discussions of his putative influence on Nietzsche were also instrumental in introducing Italians to *Der Einzige und sein Eigentum*. Calasso suggests that "Stirner was received in Italy in much the same way that Nietzsche had once been: with a total inability to grasp the kernel of his thought and with conspicuous effects instead on the attitudes, customs, and language gestures of a provincial mind set that still flourishes today" (*The Forty-Nine Steps* 168). Importantly, several key intellectuals read Stirner's book in German or French rather than the Italian translation with its openly hostile introduction. Among them were Benito Mussolini, who read Stirner while in Switzerland in 1902, and Gabriele D'Annunzio, who acquired a copy of the French translation that had been published by *Éditions de la Revue Blanche* two years earlier. Similarly, Italian Symbolists living in Paris, such as Filippo Tommaso Marinetti, regularly encountered translations and discussions of Stirner's thought in the pages of the *Mercure de France*, the *Revue Blanche*, and other influential French literary journals. Finally, whereas Zoccoli sought to counter the potential of *Der Einzige und sein Eigentum* to serve the cause of anarchist terrorism, he seemed ignorant of the dangers presented by the nationalist strain of egoism developed by Maurice Barrès in France and advanced in Italy by reactionaries such as D'Annunzio, Marinetti, and Mussolini.

In contrast to anarchist readings of Stirner, egoistic nationalism championed the autocratic leader as a patriarch and Stirnerian owner of the state, uniting Italian reactionaries and revolutionaries under the banner of an idealized national identity. In the hands of the D'Annunzians, Futurists, and fascists, Stirner's thought served as a stimulus for revolutionary approaches to Italian literature, art, and politics. In 1909, egoism contributed to the shape and tone of "Le futurisme," Marinetti's first literary manifesto. When his polemic appeared on the front page of *Le Figaro*, he created the standard by which avant-garde manifestos have been judged ever since. Martin Puchner goes so far as to call Marinetti's first Futurist manifesto "the first avant-garde manifesto" (73) and suggests that it was "charged with the socialism of Marx and Lenin" (76). With its glorification of "the destructive act of the libertarian" (Marinetti, "The Foundation and Manifesto of Futurism" 14), it was also charged with Stirnerian egoism. A decade after Marinetti's first manifesto, a similar cocktail of egoism and nationalism—laced with revolutionary calls to action lifted from the writings of Marx—proved influential to both D'Annunzio's *Carta del Carnaro* (The Charter of Carnaro, 1920) and Marinetti's *Il manifesto dei fasci italiani di combattimento* (The Manifesto of the Italian Fighting Leagues, 1919).[3] These proclamations were part of a body of writing that had direct implications for the development of Italian Fascism and German National Socialism.

Egoism in the Age of Anarchist Terror

Back in 1902, however, Zoccoli had good reason to focus on Stirner's role in the development of anarchist theory. Acts of insurrectionary violence, rather than aesthetic revolt, had marred the reception of egoism in Italy. Notions of illegalism and criminal individualism arrived before Symbolism's intellectual and aesthetic interpretation of *Der Einzige und sein Eigentum*. In Germany, Stirner had been championed by the poet, John Henry Mackay, and the composer, Hans von Bülow, while his most vocal French supporters wrote for literary magazines such as the *Mercure de France* and the *Revue Blanche*. In contrast, Italian proponents of egoism were far more likely to be political dissidents. Under the direct influence of Bakunin, a brand of insurrectionary anarchism flourished in Italy that hailed the bandit and the assassin as revolutionary heroes. Well before the illegalist Bonnot gang began their Parisian crime spree in 1911, Italian anarchists had already concluded that bold crimes could do more to challenge the might of the state than literary pamphleteering. Recent interest in *Der Einzige und sein Eigentum* in Germany and France merely reinforced the perception among Italian opponents of anarchism that it was the creed of the nihilist and the criminal.

In truth, Italian anarchism accommodated all manner of philosophical dispositions, including various strains of individualism, socialism, and nationalism. Given the importance of the *Risorgimento* to Italy's revolutionary

---

[3] When D'Annunzio took control of Fiume he renamed the city the Italian Regency of Carnaro. Written with the assistance of the syndicalist, Alceste De Ambris, the *Charter* was the political manifesto of the Fiume experiment. Marinetti's *Manifesto of the Italian Fighting Leagues*, better known as the *Fascist Manifesto*, was also written with the assistance of De Ambris.

tradition, it is unsurprising that many Italian anarchists shared distinctly chauvinistic tendencies.[4] Peter Marshall suggests that Carlo Pisacane, the Duke of San Giovanni in Naples, stood out as "a transitional figure between the old nationalists and the anarchist movement, acting as a chief of staff in Mazzini's army and spreading Proudhon's and Fourier's ideas" (446). Insurrection, revolution, and civil war had all been important aspects of the unification effort, and in Italy nationalism and anarchism were not the diametrically opposed philosophies they elsewhere appeared to be. When Bakunin arrived in Italy in 1864 the fifty-year-old Russian was already "an ardent disciple of Italian nationalism," and "[f]or a brief moment Garibaldi seemed to fill to perfection the role of Bakunin's ideal revolutionary hero" (Carr 315). And while Bakunin's time in Italy represented a "transition from the revolutionary nationalism of his middle years to the revolutionary anarchism of his last period" (Carr 335), Italians themselves were not so easily dissuaded from the insurrectionary potential of patriotism. In France egoism had provided Barrès with a conceptual bridge between the self and the nation, and in Italy it served a similar purpose. For some, like D'Annunzio, it also helped resolve a lingering desire to connect the classical past to the revolutionary future.

Bakunin only lived in Italy for three years, but his time was spent sowing the seeds of—if not actively contributing to—the cause of insurrection. He dabbled in Freemasonry, traveled to Stockholm and London, and met with Marx for the last time. Upon returning to Florence he established the first of several secret revolutionary brotherhoods. In October 1865 he moved to Naples and "founded a new secret society which he boldly styled an International brotherhood" (Carr 330). Like the Carbonari, the Illuminati, and the Freemasons, Bakunin's revolutionary brotherhoods were, at times, more inclined to melodrama and dithering than tangible forms of political insurrection.[5] Their membership "was composed mainly or exclusively of disgruntled Italian intellectuals," and to at

---

[4] In 1859 and 1860 war between Sardinia and Austria, revolutions in central Italy, and an insurrection led by Giuseppe Garibaldi resulted in a largely unified Italy under the rule of King Victor Emanuel II. Derek Beales and Eugenio Biagini suggest that "[f]or most historians and for nearly all Italians, unification was not the sudden and accidental upshot of war and diplomacy. It was a result or a stage of their national revival, known as the Risorgimento, which originated in the eighteenth century and has lasted, according to many writers, into the twentieth" (2).

[5] Discussing Byron's membership in the Ravenna branch of the Carbonari in 1821, Richard Lansdown suggests that the group's "greatest weakness, as Byron saw, lay in their lacking any basis in real proletarian discontent (of the kind that helped to fire the Neapolitan revolution). One of their sections was called 'The Mob [*turba*],' but there was no mob" (24). The same accusation could certainly be leveled at Bakunin's revolutionary brotherhoods, whose membership consisted almost entirely of disaffected young bourgeois.

least one member "the ideas of Bakunin seemed limited to the childish game of inventing every week a new cypher in which the brothers might correspond with one another" (Carr 324–5). Nevertheless, Bakunin brought with him an intimate knowledge of anarchist theory—along with Stirner's conception of insurrectionary will. By 1866, however, Bakunin concluded that "nationalism could as easily become the ally of counterrevolution as of revolution" (Carr 335), and he spurned the insurrectionary potential of the *Risorgimento*. In August 1867 he abandoned Italy and made for Switzerland but left behind a curious melange of insurrectionary anarchism, nationalism, and communism that persisted into the twentieth century.

The instability of Italian anarchism in the wake of Bakunin's departure contributed to the wave of individualist terrorism that occurred in the 1890s. In Bakunin's absence, Italian anarchism had devolved into a series of chaotically shifting allegiances between Bakuninite collectivism, communism, nationalism, and parliamentary socialism. One prominent anarchist, Andrea Costa, "became a deputy, and played an important part in forming the Italian Socialist Party" (Marshall 448). Another, Carlo Cafiero, "suddenly went over to the parliamentary socialists" before going insane, "obsessed by the idea that he was enjoying more than his fair share of the sun" (449). In the 1880s Italy's foremost theorist of anarchism, Errico Malatesta, began an attempt "to form a new nationalist anarchist 'party' but it failed to get off the ground" (449). Where meaningful solidarity became a practical impossibility, individualism thrived, and the failures of anarchism opened possibilities for egoism. Marshall suggests that "[i]t was not long before anarchism in Italy became the preserve of constantly changing, largely autonomous groups in the small towns" (449), and it was this new generation of independent rebels who soon commanded the attention of the international community. In 1898 the Italian government was forced to respond.

Zoccoli's criticism of *Der Einzige und sein Eigentum* was part of an ongoing campaign against individualist anarchist terrorism. When he suggested that all forms of anarchism "find the near or remote germ of the vitality which has brought them to the attention of today's public in Stirner's doctrine" (Zoccoli xv),[6] he was undoubtedly considering criminal individualism's role in a series of assassinations that scandalized the whole of Europe. On June 24, 1894, Sante

---

[6] "—tutte queste dottrine, insomma, trovano il germe prossimo o remoto di quella vitalità che le ha imposte all'attenzione odierna del pubblico nella dottrina dello Stirner" (xv).

Geronimo Caserio murdered the French president, Marie François Carnot. Then, on August 8, 1897, another Italian, Michele Angiolillo, shot dead the Spanish prime minister, Antonio Cánovas del Castillo. Events reached a climax in 1898, when "Luigi Lucheni, a young Italian anarchist, rushed up to" Empress Elisabeth of Austria and "plunged a three-edged file, its tip honed needle-sharp, into the Empress's heart, soon causing a fatal haemorrhage" (Jensen 325). The murder of the Empress, "a popular figure who had been famous in her younger days for her charm and beauty," outraged Austrians (325). Her death sparked "[a]nti-Italian riots [...] in the German and Austro-Hungarian Empires, and in towns along the Austrian side of the Italian border, Slavic mobs sacked Italian homes, forcing hundreds to flee the country" (325). There had never been such a sequence of high-profile killings, and governments struggled with the fact that the murderers were only loosely connected by nationality and political disposition. The Italian government finally bowed to international pressure and proposed "a pan-European conference to deal with anarchist plots and propaganda" (325). The highly secretive International Conference of Rome for the Social Defence against Anarchists convened on November 24, 1898, just two months after Empress Elisabeth's death.

Within two years of that conference the King of Italy was dead. Within a few months, so too was the President of the United States.[7] This was the political context in which Zoccoli declared the danger of Stirner's ideas. He saw in his assault on morality the germ of anarchism's most violent impulses. Still, "not all anarchist agitators, who found in Stirner's criminal individualism the gold mine of their arguments, wanted to demonstrate" their "mindful devotion to the master" (Zoccoli xiv).[8] Like Marx, Zoccoli suggested that anarchist theorists such as Bakunin and Proudhon had pillaged Stirner's most important—and dangerous—conclusions without giving him due credit. He added other anarchists of note to Marx's list of plagiarists, proposing that Stirner influenced the "utopian optimism" of Kropotkin, the "libertarian egoism" of Benjamin

---

[7] Unlike the other assassins, the man who shot President McKinley, Leon Czolgosz, was not an Italian. Czolgosz became radicalized after hearing about the murder of King Umberto I and meeting Emma Goldman in 1901. Goldman was perhaps the most famous anarchist intellectual to publicly endorse Stirner's ideas.

[8] "Ma non tutti gli agitatori anarchici, che trovarono nell'individualismo criminale dello Stirner la miniera aurifera delle loro argomentazioni, vollero dimostrare altrettanta memore devozione per il maestro. Non lo contraddissero mai, lo saccheggiarono senza fine e lo ricordarono poco. Ecco la posizione quasi costante di tutti i teorici dell'anarchia che sono oggi più in vista, rispetto allo Stirner" (xiv).

Tucker and even the "revolutionary pietism" of Tolstoy (xiv–v).⁹ "[T]he almost constant position of all the anarchist theorists who are more prominent today than Stirner," Zoccoli claimed, was that "[t]hey never contradicted him, they sacked him endlessly and remembered him little" (xiv). While it was an exaggeration to suggest that Stirner's total rejection of all notions of external authority was compatible with Tolstoy's spiritual basis for radicalism, Zoccoli's line of argument indicates that French discussions of Stirner's place in the history of anarchist theory had reached Italy as early as 1902.

Zoccoli's approach to refuting *Der Einzige und sein Eigentum* had several similarities to the one taken by Marx in *Die deutsche Ideologie*. Like Marx, Zoccoli's most reliable rhetorical tool was a mischaracterization of Stirner's line of argument. In contrast to the interminable prolixity of *Die deutsche Ideologie*, however, Zoccoli's summary in *L'Unico* was mercifully short. Placing Stirner within a tradition that included David Strauss, Bruno Bauer, and Feuerbach, Zoccoli suggested that "the rationalistic atheism of Feuerbach, which benefited socialism, became the dogmatic atheism of Stirner, which would have benefited anarchist doctrine" (xx). He ignored Stirner's criticism of Proudhon, his opposition to all forms of dogmatism, and the fact that anarchism was not an organized movement when Stirner was writing in 1844.

Nevertheless, while assassins and political rebels arrived at egoism through illegalist interpretations of Stirner's writings, and the Italian public encountered Stirner through Zoccoli's criticism, other groups were exposed to the aesthetic brand of egoism that had developed and flourished in the Parisian literary scene. While those terrorists using egoism to justify theft and murder may never have heard of Stirner, Italian Symbolists were far more likely to be acquainted with *Der Einzige und sein Eigentum* at first hand. D'Annunzio, Marinetti, and Mussolini emerged as crucial not only to the popularization of Stirner's ideas in Italy, but also to the development of the manifesto's avant-garde iteration. Culturally, and ultimately politically through their various contributions to fascist ideology, D'Annunzio, Marinetti, and Mussolini provided models for the manifesto-writing tyrant of modernity.

Italy is also an important location in the history of Stirner's reception because it was in Italy that anarchist and nationalist interpretations of egoism began to come into clear opposition. On the one hand, egoism was distinctly libertarian in

---

⁹ For his part, Tucker made no secret of the influence that Stirner exercised on his own thought. Along with Emma Goldman, Steven T. Byington, and Dora Marsden, Tucker was a crucial figure in the promotion of *Der Einzige und sein Eigentum* in the United States and Britain.

character; on the other, it became distinctly fascist. One group sought a society comprised of a multitude of egoists; the other sought to enthrone the supreme egoist. Marinetti and D'Annunzio frequently found themselves on both sides of the conflict, struggling to reconcile personal desires for radical individual liberty with their advocacy of strident and warlike nationalism. The tensions between anarchist and nationalist interpretations of Stirner go some way to explaining the sympathy libertarians have frequently expressed for certain aspects of fascist ideology—in both the early twentieth century and beyond. Ezra Pound's effort to liken Mussolini to Thomas Jefferson in *Jefferson and/or Mussolini* (1935) is a pertinent example of this trend. The wildly differing political views between—and even within—twentieth-century avant-garde movements such as Futurism and Dada were partly the result of differing interpretations of a radical individualism that originated in the work of Stirner. The manifesto was the perfect medium to advance the cause of either perspective, but Marinetti was the first to take full advantage of it to advocate the nationalistic strain of egoism.

Marinetti and the Birth of Futurism

Filippo Tommaso Marinetti was chief among the Italian manifesto writers who encountered Stirnerian egoism through connections to French Symbolism. He founded Italian Futurism, co-wrote the manifesto of Italian Fascism, and was perhaps the most prolific polemicist of the twentieth century. There is no doubt that his views were informed by Stirner's ideas. Ernest Ialongo proposes that "during Marinetti's most radical political period, 1918–1920, his views of a libertarian society of self-regulating individuals owed much to Stirner's influence" (5). Still, it is difficult to determine precisely when Marinetti first encountered Stirner's magnum opus, and to what extent he was conscious of its importance to his own aesthetic and political positions. Marinetti never seems to have directly referred to Stirner in his writings, instead suggesting the importance of anarchic individualism and libertarianism—movements variously influenced by Stirner's thought—to Futurism's rebellious impulses. Nevertheless, his involvement with literary journals that published translations of Stirner, his close association with the Symbolist leader, the poet and critic Gustave Kahn, and his connections to anarchism all suggest that Marinetti was acquainted with Stirner's ideas before the foundation of the Futurist movement in 1909. Having been part of the aristocratic, individualistic, and revolutionary milieu of Parisian Symbolism, Marinetti was well placed to introduce Italians to its aesthetic reading of Stirner.

Marinetti's colonial and cosmopolitan upbringing was somewhat at odds with his later role as anti-clerical Italian nationalist and arch-Futurist. He was born in Alexandria in 1876 and spent his formative years in Egypt, a childhood he later described as having "started off with rose and black, a blossoming, healthy little tot in the arms and between the carbon-coke breasts, of [his] Sudanese nurse" (Marinetti, "Self-Portrait" 5). He "received a French education at a Jesuit Lycée" in Alexandria before being sent "to Paris to take his baccalauréat at the Sorbonne" in 1894 (Berghaus 15). Günter Berghaus suggests that Marinetti "spent more time in the cafés than in the lecture halls, frequented the cabarets and music halls of Montmartre, and gained access to the salons of Parisian literary society, thereby becoming well-informed on the latest trends in French art and literature" (15). After graduating that same year, Marinetti moved to Italy to study law at the University of Pavia before transferring to the University of Genoa. Importantly, he "commuted regularly between France and Italy in order to keep in contact with his friends and acquaintances of the Parisian art scene" (Berghaus 16). Through his participation in the Symbolist circles of Paris, and particularly through his close friendship with Kahn, Marinetti encountered Stirner's insurrectionary writings for perhaps the first time.

Kahn was central to Marinetti's intellectual development in *fin de siècle* Paris. Berghaus calls him "Marinetti's discoverer and mentor," and suggests that he "introduced his young disciple to many political artists and activists, who subsequently exercised considerable influence on his early poetic and dramatic output and who served as animating spirits for his Futurist vision of a new art and society" (34). Indeed, Kahn was among the first to formally recognize the young Marinetti's poetry. Writing in 1920, Marinetti recalled that his poem, "Les Vieux Marins" (The Old Sailors, 1898), was "awarded a prize by Catulle Mendès and Gustave Kahn, the directors of Sarah Bernhardt's *Samedis populaires*, and was then gloriously recited by the great actress herself, in her own theatre" (Marinetti, "Self-Portrait" 7). In many ways this prize marked Marinetti's arrival in Parisian literary circles. It was also the beginning of Kahn's support and patronage of the young poet, which continued into the twentieth century.[10] An influential proponent of *Der Einzige und sein Eigentum*, if Kahn did not introduce Marinetti

---

[10] In "We Renounce Our Symbolist Masters, the Last of All Lovers of the Moonlight" (1911), Marinetti demonstrated his continued allegiance to Kahn by suggesting that "[w]e accept none but the enlightened work of four or five great precursors of Futurism" (45). The following list of authors included "Émile Zola; Walt Whitman; Rosny-Aîné, the author of *Bilateral* and *The Red Wave*; Paul Adam, the author of *Trust*; Gustave Kahn, the creator of Free Verse; and Verhaeren, the glorifier of machines and of tentacular cities" (45).

to the ideas of Max Stirner, it was only because the younger man was already familiar with them.

In his 1904 review of Victor Basch's *l'Individualisme anarchiste: Max Stirner* for the *Nouvelle revue*,[11] Kahn emerged as another advocate for Stirnerian egoism. Kahn's work had already appeared alongside writing by and about Stirner in volumes of the *Revue Blanche* in 1899 and 1900 but, in this review, he directly addressed Stirner's importance and ongoing influence, suggesting that:

> Even if Stirner's thought had only literary importance, his great book, *l'Unique et sa propriété*, would nonetheless remain most interesting to study, for they always deserve our attention, and to the highest degree, these books which, like *l'Unique et sa propriété*, were ahead of their time, suffered the insult of obscurity from the day of their publication, only to be reborn later, thanks to the inspection of a clearer critic and better messenger of the contribution of the past.
>
> (my trans.; 131)[12]

Like others, Kahn proposed that Nietzsche owed an intellectual debt to Stirner and that there was a marked similarity between Nietzsche's *Übermensch* and Stirner's egoist. He observed that "the *Übermensch* of Nietzsche, is he not close to Stirner's I? Obviously yes. That in Nietzsche's ideology, in addition to [Arthur de] Gobineau's share, the influence of Stirner is not preponderant, this is hardly contestable" (my trans.; 133).[13] Kahn concluded that "the *Übermensch* of Nietzsche, the egoist or the all-powerful of Stirner, they are the same thing, both come to the cult of strength, of the hero, to the deification of genius. The world is made to prepare the triumph of the individual" (my trans.; 134).[14] Focusing

---

[11] The book that Kahn had reviewed, *Individualisme anarchiste: Max Stirner*, made the case that Stirner's thought continued to prove widely popular in Paris in the first decade of the twentieth century. Basch went as far as to propose: "*La pensée de Stirner est en train de s'insinuer dans la trame des idées contemporaines, est en train de redevenir une force intellectuelle avec laquelle il sera peut-être nécessaire de compter*" ("Stirner's thought is in the process of insinuating itself into the fabric of contemporary ideas, is in the process of becoming again an intellectual force which it will perhaps be necessary to take into consideration"; my trans.; 3).

[12] "La pensée de Stirner n'eût-elle qu'une importance littéraire, son grand livre, *l'Unique et sa propriété*, n'en demeurerait pas moins des plus intéressants à étudier, car ils méritent toujours, et au plus haut degré, l'attention, ces livres qui comme *l'Unique et sa propriété*, ont devancé leur temps, ont subi dès le lendemain de leur publication, l'injure de l'oubli, pour renaître par la suite, grâce à l'inspection d'une critique plus clairvoyante et meilleure messagère de l'apport du passé; comme son livre, Max Stirner est curieux, et l'indifférence de ses contemporains incite la critique à mieux faire tomber du médaillon qu'il s'est obtenu dans la galerie des grands philosophes, la poussière d'oubli qui s'y était accumulée" (131).

[13] "Maîtres et esclaves, ce sont les mots de Nietzsche; le surhomme de Nietzsche, n'est-il pas bien près du *Moi* de Stirner? Evidemment oui. Que dans l'idéologie de Nietzsche, outre la part de Gobineau, l'influence de Stirner ne soit prépondérante, cela n'est guère contestable" (133).

[14] "Donc le surhomme de Nietzsche, l'égoïste ou le multipuissant de Stirner, c'est la même chose tous deux en arrivent au culte de la force, du héros, à la divinisation du génie. Le monde est fait pour préparer le triomphe de l'individu" (102).

on the similarly insurrectionary attitudes of the egoist and the *Übermensch* to traditional morality, Kahn glossed over the marked differences that have been observed between the two concepts. Still, the review confirmed Kahn's awareness of Stirner's historical and philosophical importance. The review's enthusiasm for Stirner's book also suggested that Kahn had read *Der Einzige und sein Eigentum* himself, likely in the form of the widely available translation published by Éditions de la *Revue Blanche* in 1900.

Kahn's review was printed at a time when Marinetti had already demonstrated his own interest in Nietzsche. Two years earlier he had published "his first book, a cycle of nineteen poems, called *La Conquête des étoiles* (The Conquest of the Stars, 1902), dedicated to his friend and mentor, Gustave Kahn" (Berghaus 19). The anthology depicted "the revolt of the sea against the stars" (19), and Berghaus proposes that "[t]here is a Promethean courage behind this revolt, and the Dionysian vitality of Nietzsche's *Übermensch* is clearly alluded to" (20). In one section the stars are equated with the realm of the ideal, and Marinetti describes "the suicides, those whose courage / has failed, under the weight of their hearts," and who have "died / from having stirred up in their blood the fire of the Ideal, / the great enveloping flame of the Absolute! / They died of believing in the promises of the Stars" (my trans.; *La Conquête des étoiles* 23–4).[15] The ocean's revolt against the heavens has been read as an incipient example of Futurism's revolt against Symbolist idealism, but it also illustrates Marinetti's broader interest in the struggle between the conquering will and the institutionalized ideal. Whereas it is unclear if Marinetti knew of *Der Einzige und sein Eigentum* prior to writing this collection, he certainly would have found Kahn's reading of Stirner's book entirely congruent with his own aesthetic reading of Nietzsche.

In Marinetti's narrative, the sovereign sea rises up against the idealism of the heavens, and while Berghaus remarks on the clear influence of Nietzsche, it is worth noting that the conquest of the stars is a motif employed to similar effect by Stirner in *Der Einzige und sein Eigentum*.[16] Under the heading "My Self-Enjoyment," Stirner proposed:

> Without doubt culture has made me *powerful*. It has given me power over all *motives*, over the impulses of my nature as well as over the exactions and

---

[15] "Ce sont les suicidés, ceux dont le courage / a defailli, sous le poids de leur cœur, / fournaise d'étoiles! Ils sont morts / d'avoir attisé dans leur sang le feu de l'Idéal, / la grand flamme enveloppante de l'Absolu! / Ils sont morts d'avoir cru aux promesses des Étoiles" (23–4).

[16] The conquest of the stars is a theme that returns once more in Wyndham Lewis's *Enemy of the Stars*, the only work in which Lewis directly mentions Stirner by name.

violences of the world. [...] I become, through the sciences and arts, the *master* of the refractory world, whom sea and earth obey, and to whom even the stars must give an account of themselves. The spirit has made me *master*.—But I have no power over the spirit itself.

(*The Ego and Its Own* 294)

Culture enabled the conquest of the natural world, but both Stirner and Marinetti suggested that it was necessary to rebel against the limitations that culture and tradition imposed on individual will. Just as Marinetti's sovereign sea revolts against the astral ideal, Stirner's egoist confronts the strictures of moral idealism. Such similarities were likely the product of Marinetti's reading of Nietzsche but, after Kahn's review of *Individualisme anarchiste* in 1904, such similarities surely informed Marinetti's perception of a kinship between Stirner, Nietzsche, Kahn, and himself.

The extent of Marinetti's preoccupation with the ideas of Nietzsche, as well as other forms of radical philosophy is well documented. Berghaus suggests that "the young Marinetti of pre-Futurist days was attracted to all those movements that could be called 'revolutionary,' whatever their colours might be" (38). As far as Nietzsche was concerned, "[i]t was probably in Paris that Marinetti began to imbibe Nietzschean thought, either directly or through reading the first translations that began to appear in France from 1893 onwards" (Berghaus 24). Ialongo concurs, proposing that Marinetti "went out of his way to insist that the Futurists were not simply neo-Nietzscheans, but the influence of Nietzsche's ideas on Marinetti's thinking are undeniable" (19). Nietzsche was, however, just one of the radical thinkers Marinetti became acquainted with while part of the Parisian literary scene. The young poet "was an admirer of Nietzsche's radical individualism and Bergson's dynamic concept of the universe, but he also studied Marx and Engels, Bakunin and Sorel" (Berghaus 25). Such intellectual pursuits would have naturally led an engaged reader such as Marinetti to discussions of Stirner that appeared alongside—and at times within—contemporary essays devoted to Nietzsche, Marx, and Bakunin.

Moreover, Marinetti demonstrated an interest in various aspects of anarchist theory. Marja Härmänmaa suggests that "Marinetti, like many other futurists, had personal connections with the anarchistic circles" (858), and goes on to note that he "regularly visited the Abbaye de Créteil, a utopian community in the vicinity of Paris, founded by Georges Duhamel and Charles Vildrac in 1906, and known as a base for artists and writers cultivating anarchistic theories" (858). While its founders called the collective "a 'Communistic' and a 'Bolshevik' experiment," Berghaus proposes that "[t]he socialist vision that inspired the members of this 'artists' commune' was principally derived from Proudhon and Tolstoy" (36). The Abbaye de Créteil may have declared itself a communist collective but the theories that underpinned its positions were undeniably anarchist in orientation. Like his friendship with Kahn, an association with this commune afforded Marinetti a greater insight into the various trends in anarchist thought. In such an environment, and with interests in individualism, Nietzsche, Bakunin, and Sorel, it can be assumed with confidence that Marinetti was conscious of Stirner's importance to individualist anarchism when he founded the Futurist movement. Marinetti's fictionalized account of the birth of Futurism in *The Untameables* (1922) certainly described an egoistic approach to leadership: "The great book of Futurism teaches us to make everything up, even God! We've got to make up a leader for that crowd. I am that leader! Come with me!" (Marinetti, *The Untameables* 180). When he suggested in 1910 that "[i]f a Latin *idea* (and by this we don't mean a *word*) has circled the earth, it is a sign […] the eternal, dynamic phenomenon of rebellion has found recruits even in the magnificent antithesis of its opposing idealistic currents" ("Our Common Enemies" 51), he was well aware that he was referring to a Stirnerian conception of rebellion.

In 1908, Marinetti's mounting aspirations and growing dissatisfaction with the Symbolist movement led him to plan his own literary coup d'état. Rather than attempting to seize ownership of Symbolism as others, like Moréas, had done, Marinetti instead prepared to announce the formation of his own—entirely new—aesthetic movement. By October he had completed a draft manifesto but had not yet settled on a name for the new group. Marinetti later suggested that "[f]or a moment, I hesitated between the words 'Dynamism' and 'Futurism.' My Italian blood, however, surged the more strongly when my lips proclaimed aloud the freshly invented word 'Futurism'" ("Futurism's First Battles" 151).[17] In February 1909, versions of what was now the first manifesto of *Futurismo* began appearing in the pages of French and Italian newspapers and journals, most notably when Marinetti paid a considerable sum to have a slightly abridged version of his polemic printed on the front page of *Le Figaro* on the twentieth of that month.

---

[17] Berghaus also suggests that Marinetti had originally "attempted to set up a new artistic movement, which he intended to name Elettricismo or Dinamismo" (*Critical Writings* xviii).

The Futurist Manifestos

Titled "Le Futurisme," the version of the first Futurist manifesto that appeared in *Le Figaro* was among several to begin with a fantastical account of the movement's birth. Marinetti takes a central role in his story, inspiring his friends to chase death through the streets in their motorcars after a night of frenetic writing. He crashes his car, emerges from the vehicle, and dictates the Futurist program. The narrative itself operates as an example of Futurist writing, and is more concerned with conveying a sense of speed than establishing the logical coherence of the new movement. This fictionalized retelling of the events that lead to the foundation of Futurism serves as an introduction to the manifesto itself, which then appears under the subtitle "Manifeste du Futurisme." These tenets are, in turn, followed by another example of Marinetti's bellicose prose, in which he takes an opportunity to attack his prospective opponents. Marinetti is listed as the sole author of "Le Futurisme," and there are no signatories to the manifesto. In its entirety, the piece expounds both the foundation and program of Futurism, and this dual purpose underpins the title, *Fondation et manifeste du Futurisme*, which Marinetti ascribed to subsequent versions of the work. These later publications included a short pamphlet that could be freely obtained by mailing "a corporate address, 'Direzione del Movimento Futurista, Corso Venezia, 61 Milano'" (Puchner 72), as well as an unabridged version of the manifesto published in Marinetti's own journal, *Poesia* (1905–20), in March 1909. The *Poesia* edition remains the closest thing to a standard version of the first Futurist manifesto, which continued to be translated, altered, adapted, and republished many times over the course of more than a century.

The fictionalized account which begins *Fondation et manifeste du Futurisme* was the final part of the text to be written, and it served to both mythologize the birth of Futurism and take control of the history of the movement. With this introduction, Marinetti created an official version of Futurism's beginnings, and established himself as the movement's founder, leader, and owner. No other writers or artists are mentioned by name in the work, and Marinetti only alludes to the involvement of others by referring to "My friends and I" or by adopting plural pronouns ("The Foundation and Manifesto of Futurism" 11). In this regard, Marinetti emerges as the sole proponent of Futurism, while other Futurists are characterized as nameless troops to be commanded in his assaults on tradition. By writing an account of Futurism's birth, Marinetti not only took ownership of his movement, but also attempted to rewrite history as well. In *The Communist Manifesto*, Marx had famously claimed that "[t]he history of all hitherto existing society is the history of class struggles" (57), and Marinetti assessed the contribution of the past in similar fashion. Centuries of writing are reduced to a torpid past which must be overcome by the vital energy of the machine age. History is equated with "the tedious, mumbled prayers of an ancient canal and the creaking bones of dilapidated palaces on their tiresome stretches of soggy lawn" (Marinetti, "The Foundation and Manifesto of Futurism" 11). The future is filled with "black spectres that rake through the red-hot bellies of locomotives, hurtling along at breakneck speed" (11).[18] Marinetti's imagined history later reinforces the third point of his manifesto when he claims that "[u]p to now, literature has extolled a contemplative stillness, rapture and reverie" and the Futurists are the first to "glorify aggressive action, a restive wakefulness, life at the double, the slap and the punching fist" (13). It is an entirely subjective account, but Marinetti paraded it as historical fact. The intention was not to record Futurism's place in history, but to create a history that served Futurism. Futurism, in turn, served Marinetti, as its original and only owner.

Of course, Marinetti's introduction also provided him with an opportunity to demonstrate the aesthetics of his new movement. His exploits are described in the same overwrought style that is used later that year in *Mafarka le Futuriste*. In both cases, Marinetti's writing is characterized by its literary excesses and frenetic pacing. At times, endless clauses run together in oblique metaphorical descriptions. He describes the shock of trams hurtling past is just such a fashion by comparing them to hamlets being swept away by the River Po: "Et nous, voilà brusquement distraits par le roulement des énormes tramways à double étage, qui passent sursautants, bariolés de lumières, tels les hameaux en fête que le Pô débordé ébranle tout à coup et déracine, pour les entraîner, sur les cascades et les

---

[18] It should be noted that the word specter appears both here and in Marx's *Communist Manifesto*. In "The Enemy of the Stars" (1914), Wyndham Lewis similarly referred to the "ghost, Humanity" (61). In *Specters of Marx* (1993), Derrida certainly suggested a connection between Marx's use of specter (*Gespenst*) and Stirner's use of spook (*Spuk*). He proposed that "[w]hat Stirner and Marx seem to have in common is the critique of the ghostly. Both of them want to have done with the revenant, both of them hope to get there. Both of them aim at some reappropriation of life in a body proper" (Derrida 161). Marx, Marinetti, and Lewis were all familiar with Stirner's thought at the time they referred to specters and ghosts in these works.

remous d'un déluge, jusqu'à la mer" (Marinetti, "Le Futurisme" 1).[19] The violent spectacle of modern technology is amplified by the rapidly shifting sequence of images. Elsewhere, ellipses and exclamation points abound. The result intentionally verges on becoming turgid and, at times, almost incomprehensible. At one point, Marinetti declares that "we, like young lions, chased after Death, whose black pelt was dotted with pale crosses, as he sped away across the vast, violet-tinted sky, vital and throbbing" ("The Foundation and Manifesto of Futurism" 12). The figurative language frequently alludes to Marinetti's childhood in Egypt and here, as elsewhere, the nascent Futurists are praised for their reckless pursuit of death.

The introduction, like the rest of *Fondation et manifeste du Futurisme*, is a panegyric to masculinity and the vital powers of technology, violence, and will. It also contrasts the enervated decadence of *fin de siècle* literature with the vital energy of the bourgeoning Futurist movement. In the story, Marinetti and a group of unnamed friends are seated "beneath the lamps of a mosque, whose star-studded, filigreed brass domes resembled our souls, all aglow with the concentrated brilliance of an electric heart" (Marinetti, "The Foundation and Manifesto of Futurism" 11). The men are surrounded by decadence but respond with frenetic energy rather than the ennui that is commonly associated with late nineteenth-century French literature. Marinetti describes the soon-to-be Futurists "trailing our age-old indolence back and forth over richly adorned, oriental carpets, debating at the uttermost boundaries of logic and filling up masses of paper with our frenetic writings" (11). Like the sea in *La Conquête des étoiles*, Marinetti places the Futurists in opposition to an astral ideal, and he compares his friends to "magnificent beacons or guards in forward positions, facing an army of hostile stars, which watched us closely from their celestial encampments" (11). The men are poised for battle with the Symbolist ideal but are caught in a stalemate between the stultifying forces of culture and their own vital energies. Through two sudden interventions, the industrial age soon provides a stimulus for Futurist revolt.

---

[19] Günter Berghaus translated the passage as "Suddenly we were startled by the terrifying clatter of huge, double-decker trams jolting by, all ablaze with different colored lights, as if they were villages in festive celebration, which the River Po, in full spate, suddenly shakes and uproots to sweep them away down to the sea, over the falls and through the whirlpools of a mighty flood" (Marinetti, "The Foundation and Manifesto of Futurism" 11).

Importantly, it is Marinetti's words and not modernity's interventions that rouse the other incipient Futurists from their deadlock. Indeed, it is Marinetti alone who is afforded the privilege of direct speech in *Fondation et manifeste du Futurisme*. The group is "startled by the terrifying clatter of huge, double-decker trams jolting by," but soon lapses into a state of somber silence ("The Foundation and Manifesto of Futurism" 11). Once again modernity interjects, this time in the form of the "sudden roar of ravening motorcars" in the street outside (11). Marinetti is inspired to rise and act. Assuming the role of Futurist prophet, he repeatedly implores the men to take to the streets:

> "Come on! Let's go!" I said. "Come on, my lads, let's get out of here! At long last all the myths and mystical ideals are behind us. We're about to witness the birth of a Centaur and soon we shall witness the flight of the very first Angels! … We shall have to shake the gates of life itself to test their locks and hinges! … Let's be off! See there, the Earth's very first dawn! Nothing can equal the splendour of the Sun's red sword slicing through our millennial darkness, for the very first time!
> (12)

The passage suggests the dawning of a new age, and the group take to motorcars and hurl themselves along the roads, driven by an urge to live themselves out in spectacular fashion. Marinetti declares that there is "[n]othing at all worth dying for, other than the desire to divest ourselves finally of the courage that weighed us down!" (12). Stirner similarly proposed in 1844 that "[h]enceforth, the question runs, not how one can acquire life, but how one can squander, enjoy it; or, not how one is to produce the true self in himself, but how one is to dissolve himself, to live himself out" (*The Ego and Its Own* 284). In this spirit, Marinetti incites his friends to "become food for the unknown" ("The Foundation and Manifesto of Futurism" 12), before he rounds a corner, brakes for two cyclists and crashes into a ditch.

Far from being an inglorious end to Marinetti's campaign, the accident is portrayed as a defining moment for Futurism's birth. The cyclists are described by Marinetti as "gesticulating that I was on the wrong side, dithering about in front of me like two different lines of thought, both persuasive but for all that, quite contradictory" ("The Foundation and Manifesto of Futurism" 12).[20] There will

---

[20] There are several possible candidates for the different lines of thought Marinetti refers to. Among these are competing notions of individualism and collectivism, anarchism and nationalism, as well as liberty and authority. Later in this chapter it will be seen that Marinetti conceived of Futurism as a movement that could reconcile individualism and collectivism through the domination of powerful individuals.

be no tolerance for such uncertainty or dithering in Futurism, and it is with "disgust" that Marinetti recalls that his motorcar's "wheels left the ground and I flew into a ditch" (13). Nevertheless, he emerges from the "[f]ine repair shop of a ditch!" triumphant (13). Marinetti suggests that "[w]hen I got myself up—soaked, filthy, foul-smelling rag that I was—from beneath my overturned car, I had a wonderful sense of my heart being pierced by the red-hot sword of joy!" (13). The brush with death symbolically demonstrates the extent of Marinetti's irrepressible vitality. His motorcar, too, is transformed. A group of fishermen and naturalists retrieve the wreck using "huge iron-mesh nets" and "the car's frame emerged, leaving its heavy, sober bodywork at the bottom of the ditch as well as its soft, comfortable upholstery, as though they were merely scales" (13). What remains of the car is the essential: the bone, sinew, and beating heart of the machine. It has been stripped of all unnecessary material and distilled into an embodiment of speed and power.

Christ-like, Marinetti resurrects his motorcar in front of an audience of fishermen. He claims that "[t]hey thought it was dead, that gorgeous shark of mine, but a caress was all it needed to revive it, and there it was, back from the dead, darting along with its powerful fins!" ("The Foundation and Manifesto of Futurism" 13). Through his pursuit of death, Marinetti has transcended mortal limitations. Like his motorcar, he has tested his limits and shed all extraneous material. The scene verges on a pastiche of Nietzschean overcoming, but "covered in repair-shop grime—a fine mixture of metallic flakes, profuse sweat, and pale-blue soot—with [his] arms all bruised and bandaged, yet quite undaunted" (13), Marinetti announces the Futurist manifesto to the world. It is a testament to conquering will rather than collective solidarity, and Marinetti claims to have "dictated our foremost desires to all men on Earth who are truly alive" (13). The manifesto that follows purports to be a record of this declaration.

The first Futurist manifesto is the archetypal example of the avant-garde manifesto. It consists of a series of numbered declarations that are largely concerned with posturing and rhetorical flair rather than establishing the aesthetic values of the movement it announces. Stirner helps us understand that we as readers frequently misunderstand manifestos because we misunderstand their purpose, which is ownership as an end in itself. Here, far more space is devoted to attacking traditional positions than proposing alternative ones, and, at one point, Marinetti goes so far as to suggest that "[w]e wish to destroy museums, libraries, academies of any sort, and fight against moralism, feminism, and every kind of materialistic, self-serving cowardice" ("The Foundation and Manifesto of Futurism" 14). Traditions, institutions, and quintessential abstractions such as moralism and feminism, are singled out for destruction. Where the manifesto purports to describe Futurist art, it is in the broadest of terms. Marinetti obliquely suggests that "any work of art that lacks a sense of aggression can never be a masterpiece" (14). While the subject matter of Futurist art is clear in Marinetti's claim that "[a] racing car, its bonnet decked out with exhaust pipes like serpents with galvanic breath [...] is more beautiful than the Winged Victory of Samothrace" (13), its style is never addressed in concrete terms. Ultimately, the manifesto itself is forced to serve as a practical example of the Futurist writing it is supposed to describe. Its tenets are instead devoted to the more important task of insurrection against traditional ideals.

Just as Stirner demanded the subordination of all ideals to the egoist, Marinetti used the "Foundation and Manifesto of Futurism" to render the aesthetic values of Futurism subject to his own will. In each instance of the manifesto's publication, Marinetti lists himself as the sole author, and when he pivots between singular and plural pronouns in the manifesto it is not just to place himself within the Futurist movement but above it. Marinetti speaks for the entire movement when he declares that "[w]e wish to glorify war—the sole cleanser of the world—militarism, patriotism, the destructive act of the libertarian, beautiful ideas worth dying for, and scorn for women" ("The Foundation and Manifesto of Futurism" 14). It is Marinetti alone, however, who commands that "what I won't allow is that all our miseries, our fragile courage, or our sickly anxieties get marched daily around these museums" (15). Likewise, it is not the Futurists but Marinetti who emerges from his crash, coaxes his car back to life, and dictates the manifesto of Futurism to the world. Futurists were those whom Marinetti called Futurist, and all "men who are truly alive" are implicated in his manifesto (13). As the sole exponent of Futurist values, Marinetti granted himself the capacity to define—and redefine—what it meant to be Futurist. The only person not subject to this manifesto is Marinetti himself. Like much of his writing, this first manifesto orchestrates and negotiates a complicated tension between promoting the insurrectionary will of the individual on the one hand and the revolutionary might of the collective on the other.

In fact, Marinetti openly declared his commitment to reconciling individual will and collective action. He attempted to fuse Stirnerian rebellion and Marxist revolution. His first manifesto simultaneously proposed to "sing the praises of the man behind the steering wheel," and "sing of the great multitudes who are roused up by work, by pleasure, or by rebellion" (Marinetti, "The Foundation and Manifesto of Futurism" 13–14). Like Barrès, Marinetti developed an ideology of egoistic nationalism that championed both the superior individual's rejection of tradition and society's rootedness in national identity. In an interview appearing in *Comœdia* in March 1909, he observed that "there has been little or no comprehension of how, in our thinking, we can reconcile the glorification of patriotism and the exaltation of the anarchist's acts of destruction" (Marinetti, "Futurism: An Interview" 18). He went on to propose that

> Without getting bogged down in long, tedious digressions of a more or less philosophical nature, you will acknowledge, as I do, that these two apparently contradictory ideas, the collective and the individual, are, in fact, closely related. Does not the development of the collective depend on the exertions and initiatives of individuals?
>
> (18)

On one level, Marinetti was suggesting that all crowds are composed of individual wills operating in unison to achieve some shared end, but this logic—particularly when read in the context of the introduction to the first Futurist manifesto—also justified the kind of nationalistic autarchy that later typified Italian fascism. After all, Marinetti had gone to great lengths to convey his singular importance to Futurism, and the extent to which his exertions and initiatives were responsible for the realization of the movement at large. Futurism was a collectivist movement led by the iron will of its leader and creator.

While Marinetti's understanding of collectivism relied heavily on his reading of Georges Sorel and Gustave le Bon, his portrayal of elite individuals rebelling against tradition borrowed from the ideas of Stirner and Nietzsche. Like Stirner, Marinetti declared his desire for the "[g]lorification of instinct and flair in the human animal, the cultivation of divining intuition, wild, ruthless individualism, contempt for ancient, exploitative wisdom, giving free rein to our emotional and physical impulses, daily heroism of body and spirit" ("Futurism: An Interview" 20). Stirner, too, desired an individualism that championed instinct, intuition, the untrammeled fulfilment of impulses and scorn for tradition. Härmänmaa argues that "the importance given to action at the cost of thought, due to which the movement was labeled a 'mystique of action,' was not the only point of similarity with Stirner's theory," but that "the glorification of individualism [...] should be considered a fundamental element of Futurism's social utopia at the expense of economic and political questions" (860). Ialongo also suggests that "Marinetti was certainly an anarchic individualist in his denunciations of the church, the state, bourgeois and Christian morality, and traditionalism as shackles on individual freedom" (5). Like Malatesta and Barrès, Marinetti attempted to weld aspects of anarchism and nationalism together into a cohesive ideology. And like Barrès, Marinetti eventually discovered that the only way to reconcile individual will and collective action was through a fascistic dogmatism that allowed for the total liberty of a narrow elite—in Marinetti's case, artists—at the expense of all others.

It is worth noting that, unlike Barrès, Marinetti was never entirely comfortable with the compromise that underpinned his egoistic nationalism. In this regard, Ialongo draws a sharp distinction between the nationalisms of Barrès and Marinetti. He suggests that Marinetti "was perpetually struggling throughout his political life to find a means to advance *both* the needs of the individual *and* the needs of the nation" (Ialongo 6). In contrast, he proposes that "[s]uch an intellectual and political struggle was never countenanced in the nationalism of Enrico Corradini or Maurice Barrès, or ultimately, in the politics of Benito Mussolini" (6). There is, however, cold comfort in Ialongo's suggestion that although Marinetti "consistently compromised his defense of individual rights in politics [it] does not alter the fact that he attempted to formulate a politics that reconciled the needs of the one and the many" (6). The sacrifice of individual liberties was as much an inevitable product of logic for Marinetti as it was in the contest between Barrès's notion of *le culte du moi* and *la terre et les morts*. Even Mussolini variously expressed his support for Stirner's egoism while espousing the tenets of fascism. In each instance it was far easier to confer the liberties associated with radical individualism on a nation's leader than it was to reconcile a single national identity with a multitude of competing egos. It appeared that the cultish worship of an authoritarian leader was perhaps the only practical way to merge nationalist ideology and the insurrectionary impulses of egoism. The fact that Marinetti was never entirely happy with this marriage does not excuse his role in promoting it.

Marinetti's affiliation with anarchism was sometimes tenuous, but he consistently used the manifesto in an egoistic fashion, as a means of expressing his will in artistic and political spheres. The introduction to the Futurist novel *Mafarka le futuriste* (1910) is a significant example of the Stirnerian and Nietzschean tenor of Marinetti's literary pamphleteering. In it he declared that

"I am the only one who has dared to write this masterpiece, and it is by my hands that it will someday die, when the world's growing splendour has equalled and superseded it" (*Mafarka the Futurist* 1). Nietzsche's concept of the *Übermensch* figures strongly in *Mafarka le futuriste*, a surreal story which culminates with the titular hero-king building a mechanical superman named Gazourmah. But Marinetti's declaration that he will destroy his novel also has distinctly Stirnerian implications. In "Kunst und Religion" Stirner had already described the way in which inspired artists retook ownership of their exhausted works in order to create new ideals to inspire the masses. At the end of the introduction, Marinetti assumes the role of an egoistic prophet. He declares:

> In the name of the human Pride that we adore, I tell you that the hour is near when men with broad foreheads and chins of steel will give birth prodigiously, by one effort of flaring will, to giants infallible in action … I tell you that the mind of man is an unpractised ovary … It is we who are the first to impregnate it!
>
> (3)

There are many obvious parallels between Marinetti and his conquering hero-king Mafarka. Both men are obsessed with war, violence, technology, and the power of will; and like Mafarka, Marinetti uses the manifesto in a kingly fashion, in order to rally and command.

Although Marinetti never ceased to praise the destructive act of the libertarian, his estimation of anarchism itself waxed and waned over the course of his manifesto writing. In a lecture on "The Necessity and Beauty of Violence" (1910) he had suggested that "individual freedoms, which proliferate as they develop toward a possible and desirable anarchy, must coexist with the principle of authority" (Marinetti 65). A year later, however, in "War, the Sole Cleanser of the World" ("Guerra sola igiene delmondo," 1911), he proposed that "[a]narchy, turning its back on the infinite principle of human evolution, suspends its curving leap only at the absolute ideal of universal peace, at a ludicrous paradise composed of warm embraces, under rustling palm leaves, out in the country" (Marinetti 53). The utopianism advanced by Proudhon, Tolstoy, Kropotkin, and members of the Abbaye de Créteil was clearly the target of this rebuke, but it is a criticism that is not relevant to the insurrectionary programs of the illegalists, libertarians, and other, more Stirnerian factions within anarchism. In fact, Marinetti went on to describe Futurism in terms that brought it even closer to Stirner's ideas. He proposed that "the anarchists are content to attack the political, legal, and economic branches of the social tree," while the Futurists "want to dig out its deepest roots and burn them, those which are planted in the mind of man" (Marinetti, "War, the Sole Cleanser of the World" 53). Stirner too had desired to rid humanity of the "'sense of right' and 'law-abiding mind'" that had been "so firmly planted in people's heads that the most revolutionary persons of our days want to subject us to a new 'sacred law,' the 'law of society,' the law of mankind, the 'right of all,' and the like" (Stirner, *The Ego and Its Own* 167). Marinetti condemned a string of vices that included a "desire for minimum effort; cowardly quietism; love of whatever is ancient and old, of whatever is sickly and corrupted; horror of the new; scorn for youth; veneration of time, of accumulated years; for the dead and the dying" (53). Like Stirner, he criticized the "instinctive need for restricted order, for laws, chains, obstacles, for police stations, for morality, for chastity; fear of unrestricted freedom" (53). It is a list that bears a striking similarity to Stirner's list of fixed ideas in *Der Einzige und sein Eigentum*, although Marinetti obviously did not share in Stirner's animosity toward notions of a fatherland. While Futurist ideology was an assortment of ideas taken from the writings of Nietzsche, Sorel, Bergson, and many others, Marinetti's conception of a Futurist revolt against law, tradition, and morality also owed a clear debt to Stirner's thought.

In the manifesto, "Contro i professori" (Against Academic Teachers, 1910),[21] Marinetti made a similar attempt to distinguish Futurism from the ideas of Nietzsche. He declared that "I have no choice but to show how utterly mistaken the critics are in labelling us Neo-Nietzscheans" (81). Marinetti argued that Nietzsche's philosophies relied on classical mythology to such an extent that they were entirely incompatible with Futurist values. He suggested that Nietzsche's "Superman is a product of the Greek imagination, spawned from the three great stinking corpses of Apollo, Mars, and Bacchus," and declared on behalf of all Futurists:

> We are opposed to this Greek Superman, begat from the dust of libraries, and against him we set the Man who is extended by his own labours, the enemy of books, friend of personal experience, pupil of the Machine, relentless cultivator of his own will, clear in the flash of his own inspiration, endowed with the feline power of scenting out, with the ability to make split-second judgements, possessing those instincts typical of the wild—intuition, cunning, and boldness.
> (81)

---

[21] Berghaus suggests this translation of the manifesto's title.

Marinetti decried Nietzsche's traditionalism and intellectualism but, in some respects, this brought his position closer to that of Stirner. Importantly, Marinetti's glorification of instinct and condemnation of ancient wisdom demonstrated his common ground with Stirner's insurrectionary egoism, which radically opposed all forms of conventional education, including the abstract values of antiquity.[22]

When Marinetti spoke to English audiences in 1910 he, too, played a role in spreading interest in egoism abroad. Paul Edwards suggests that "[a]lthough Lewis does not discuss Futurism in his writings until 1913, his direction as a writer as well as a painter was at least in part determined by Marinetti's ideas as early as 1910" (103). In a lecture delivered to the Lyceum Club that year, Marinetti declared:[23]

> Well, I want you to know that we admire the unremitting, warlike patriotism that sets you apart. We admire your national pride that guides your great muscular race with courage. We admire your powerful individualism which yet does not prevent you from opening your arms wide to welcome individualists from other countries, whether they be libertarians or anarchists.
>
> ("Lecture to the English on Futurism" 89)

Marinetti delivered several such speeches to English audiences in the years preceding the War. It was no accident that—despite his injunction to scorn women—the first of these lectures took place at a women's club. An egoistic strain of feminism had already developed in England and the United States. Indeed, if Marinetti's presence marked the arrival of Futurism, Stirnerian egoism had already arrived through the work of feminists, anarchists, pederasts, and libertarians.

Beginning from apparently incompatible interpretations of egoism advanced by anarchists and nationalists, Marinetti had reconciled the two in the form of the insurrectionary Futurist tyrant. This figure was equal parts autocrat and rebel, shaping the world into a personal utopia of vitalism and force. Futurist revolt clearly owed a debt to Stirner's conception of insurrection—as opposed to the leveling force of Marxist revolution—but it paid no heed to Stirner's warnings

---

[22] Stirner called Socrates "a fool that he concedes to the Athenians a right to condemn him" and chided that "[i]t was with hair-splitting and intrigues that Greek liberty ended. Why? Because the ordinary Greeks could still less attain that logical conclusion which not even their hero of thought, Socrates, was able to draw" (*The Ego and Its Own* 190–1). The Greek, Stirner argued, had never realized that "[t]here was no *judge over him*" (191).

[23] Constance Smedley founded London's Lyceum Club in 1904, an organization dedicated to the intellectual and professional advancement of women. The organization continues this work today, with branches in many countries.

about the power of untrammeled ideas. The Futurist was only committed to rising above ideals and morals that were not Futurist, and abstract notions of nationalism, violence, speed, and technology were allowed to run rampant. Once again, Stirner's greatest insight, that ideas must continually be challenged by the individual who conceives of them, was the first aspect of his thought to be cast aside. For Futurists like Marinetti, egoistic ownership amounted to the use of personal ideas to exert control over others. Other Italians would use egoism in much the same way, including D'Annunzio and Mussolini. Unable to assimilate Stirner's ideas into their own thought, these men nevertheless took advantage of his conclusions to manipulate others through the use of manifesto writing in much the same way that they utilized Gustave Le Bon's crowd psychology to brutal effect. Whereas anarchists had used egoism to break free of moral constraints, the forebears of Italian fascism used Stirner's ideas in the same way that Marx had, to take personal ownership of a movement's beliefs and dominate the will of the crowd.

From Egoistic Nationalism to Italian Fascism

Gabriele D'Annunzio was another Italian proponent of egoism and nationalism who influenced contemporary trends in Italian, French, and English literary circles. Before the turn of the century, at University College, Dublin, James Joyce was introduced to his writing and "was convinced that his *Il Fuoco* (The Flame, 1900) was the most important achievement in the novel since Flaubert, and an advance upon Flaubert" (Ellmann 60). Tellingly, Joyce was also among the writers to later cite the importance of Stirner's ideas.[24] Other authors, including Arthur Symons, D. H. Lawrence, Hemingway, and Pound, while not always as enamored with the Italian impresario's writing, certainly acknowledged his importance to developments in European literature. D'Annunzio—inspired partly by the work of Barrès—espoused his own strain of egoistic nationalism, which had dramatic implications for art and politics

---

[24] In *James Joyce and the Politics of Egoism* (2001), Jean-Michel Rabaté observes that Joyce "insisted in a note for his biographer, Herbert Gorman, that he was well read in the anarchist tradition, quoting among the writers he read, 'Most, Malatesta, Stirner, Bakunin, Kropotkin, Elisée Reclus, Spencer, and Benjamin Tucker, whose *Instead of a Book* proclaimed the liberty of the non-invasive individual'" (27).

alike. Indeed, D'Annunzio was a significant influence on his contemporaries, including Marinetti and Mussolini.

On September 12, 1919, Gabriele D'Annunzio and almost 200 Italian Grenadiers set out from Ronchi dei Legionari, northwest of Trieste, bound for the city of Fiume, now Rijeka in Croatia. That morning the poet had publicly declared his intent to seize the contested city on behalf of Italy. Allied and Italian forces had been mobilized to halt his advance.[25] By the time D'Annunzio reached Fiume, however, he had convinced more than 2000 Italian soldiers to join his cause and he was received into the city as a conquering hero. John Woodhouse suggests that "Fiume fell, without a blow being struck, and bells, sirens, and cheering crowds made it clear that the 'invasion' was welcome to the more boisterous Italian section of the populace" (331). D'Annunzio claimed the city as the Italian Regency of Carnaro and appointed himself its Commandant. He ruled the port city as a dictator for a little over a year, until the Italian government finally dislodged him in December 1920. D'Annunzio's coup was a disaster for Italy's international reputation, and served to "divide the Italian people, help bring down at least three Italian governments (weakening for ever traditional party structures and alliances), set regiment against regiment, defer the signing of the European peace treaty, and create long-lasting distrust between Italy and her wartime allies" (Woodhouse 315). The entire affair was the realization of D'Annunzio's egoistic and nationalistic aspirations, which were, in turn, the product of a long career spent imbibing the ideas of Barrès; Nietzsche; Sorel; and, of course, Max Stirner.

Today, D'Annunzio does not usually rank among the influential manifesto writers of the avant-garde. Nevertheless, his literary experiments were certainly considered innovative by his contemporaries in Europe and the United Kingdom. Moreover, the Fiume incident demonstrated the extent—albeit politically motivated—of a D'Annunzian movement, and the need to consider his harangues and polemics in the light of an emerging avant-garde manifesto-writing tradition. During the First World War he was certainly an influential polemicist, and he released tens of thousands of eloquently worded pamphlets

---

[25] Woodhouse provides a detailed account of the complicated political circumstances that led to D'Annunzio's takeover of Fiume in *Gabriele D'Annunzio: Defiant Archangel* (1998). The heart of the matter was that "[a]t the peace negotiations in Versailles President Wilson refused to accept the well-known Allied promises of territorial concessions to Italy, which France, Britain, and Italy had secretly negotiated over four years earlier in the absence of isolationist America" (Woodhouse 316). D'Annunzio—along with many others in Italy and the disputed territories—took umbrage with this perceived betrayal, setting off a series of events that culminated in D'Annunzio's irredentist march.

from planes over Trieste and Vienna in grandiose acts of wartime propaganda.[26] Similarly, Lucy Hughes-Hallett suggests that D'Annunzio's *Carta del Carnaro* (1920) "was a product, not of practical thinking, but of the artistic imagination" (525), before observing that "D'Annunzio had promised a 'politics of poetry,'" and that, with the charter, "he and [Alceste] de Ambris would produce its manifesto" (Hughes-Hallett 526).[27] A year earlier, de Ambris had assisted Marinetti with the drafting of the Fascist manifesto in another confluence of political and literary rhetoric, and Marinetti's wildly shifting opinions about D'Annunzio provide another example of the latter's role in the development of egoistic nationalism and, later, the literary manifesto.

Despite his flamboyance and excess, D'Annunzio's privileged persona was largely the product of shameless self-aggrandizement and copious personal debt. He was born in Pescara on March 12, 1863, and was the third of Francesco Paolo Rapagnetta's five children. Nevertheless, the aristocratic surname, D'Annunzio, was not entirely an affectation.[28] Francesco "had been adopted at the age of 13 by a childless uncle, Antonio D'Annunzio, and had been brought up with the surname Rapagnetta-D'Annunzio" (Woodhouse 12). When his first son "Gabriele came to be baptized, the Rapagnetta element had been allowed to drop from the family name," providing D'Annunzio with a name that not only suggested nobility, but later "enabled Gabriele to make high-sounding play of his own name, Gabriel of the Annunciation" (12). There are many accounts of D'Annunzio's childhood—of varying reliability—but they consistently suggest that although he was a successful student, many of the transgressive behaviors that marred his later life and career were already on display. Woodhouse, for example, describes a litany of bad behavior that includes plagiarism, insubordination, and fighting, all underpinned by the fact that "D'Annunzio's sole concern was self-gratification and glory: to make his existence as interesting and preferably as joyful as possible for himself, whatever the consequences for others; to create a work of art from

---

[26] One of D'Annunzio's leaflets was printed in the colors of the Italian flag and declared, in German, that the Italians could be dropping bombs, but chose to drop greetings instead. In it, D'Annunzio questioned the lauded intelligence of the Viennese, given the fact that they were willing to wear Prussian uniforms, and likened their participation in the war to suicide. A copy of the pamphlet is held in the British Library.

[27] Alceste De Ambris was an Italian nationalist and syndicalist who played a part in the early development of fascism, but later expressed his opposition to Mussolini's regime.

[28] Gabriele made a point of beginning his surname with a lowercase letter. As Woodhouse suggests, "D'Annunzio always signed himself 'Gabriele d'Annunzio,' the form which implied a noble origin" (12-13). Though still a point of contention, most contemporary scholarship capitalizes the preposition in D'Annunzio.

his life and to immortalize it in words" (4). In this regard, little changed with age and experience. Vainglorious, willful, rebellious, and manipulative, it is easy to see how D'Annunzio later found Stirner's insurrectionary egoism compatible with his own approach to art and intellectual life.

By the time that *l'Unique et sa propriété* was published by the *Revue Blanche* in 1900, D'Annunzio was already a conscious example of the writer as egoist. The young poet had moved to Rome in 1881, where he worked as a journalist and then as a gossip columnist. Anthony Rhodes suggested that "[h]is early articles on Rome, and the exciting discoveries he was making, of its beauty, architecture and history, contain the best of his prose, which had not yet become inflated and baroque" (29–30). As he imbibed the cosmopolitan atmosphere of Rome in the 1880s, however, D'Annunzio increasingly attracted a reputation for being a decadent and self-aggrandizing dandy. Woodhouse observes that "[t]he lascivious nature of his life in Rome found expression in the largely pornographic poems of *Intermezzo di rime* (Poetic Intermezzo) which D'Annunzio began to publish sporadically in *Cronaca bizantina* before collecting together twenty-six of them in a single volume in 1883" (44). His profligacy and immorality gained a philosophical aspect when he encountered Nietzsche's ideas in the 1890s, and the figure of the *Übermensch* became central to his writing. Rhodes suggests that "[i]t was when he visited Greece for the first time, in 1895, that this feeling of the Superman (and the possibilities of a *Mediterranean* Superman) was born in the Abruzzese peasant poet" (50). Thus informed by Nietzsche's ideas—as well as Barrès's notions of *le culte du moi* and *la terre et la morts*—D'Annunzio went on to produce a staggering array of fictional egoists.

Among the many examples of D'Annunzio's interpretation of the *Übermensch* are Giorgio Aurispa in *Il trionfo della morte* (The Triumph of Death, 1894), Claudio Cantelmo in *Le vergini delle rocce* (The Virgins of the Rocks, 1895), Ruggero Flamma in *La gloria* (Glory, 1899), and Stelio Effrena in *Il fuoco* (The Flame, 1900). Each of these men is driven by a desire to impose his will on others that is, in most cases, compromised by an equally strong desire for sensual gratification. In *Il trionfo della morte*, for example, Giorgio is locked in an intense struggle for control with his lover, Ippolita, but his passion prevents him from maintaining the dominance he desires in the relationship. Power shifts between the two, culminating with Giorgio's decision to hurl Ippolita off a precipice as a final and permanent demonstration of his might. The novel ends with "a brief but savage struggle, as between two mortal foes who had nourished a secret and implacable hatred in their souls" before both crash "headlong into death, locked in that fierce embrace" (D'Annunzio, *The Triumph of Death* 315). These men are certainly egoistic in their aspirations for total ownership, but it is an egoism originating from the influence of Barrès and Nietzsche, rather than Stirner's critique of abstraction. There is nothing of Stirner's self-gratifying, egoistic love in this depiction of a desire to completely possess another person, but it is easy to understand how D'Annunzio's interpretation of Nietzsche led him to encounter Stirner's thought in the early twentieth century.

Although it is generally considered to be one of D'Annunzio's weakest plays, *La Gloria* clearly demonstrates the influence of Barrès's *le culte du moi* and *la terre et les morts* on his nationalism, and the role of egoism in D'Annunzian politics. The play draws heavily from the thought of Nietzsche but, by incorporating aspects of Barrès's egoistic nationalism, it also espouses an elitism which is close to Stirner's concept of the unique individual. Woodhouse effectively summarizes the play's plot when he suggests that it "describes the competition for power between the old conservative politician Cesare Bronte and the bright new political orator Ruggero Flamma, eager to reconstruct the city, the fatherland, and a Latin vitality or 'force'" (185). After conspiring with Bronte's mistress Comnena to poison Bronte, Flamma stages a coup d'état. Another political rival, Claudio Messala, inspires an angry mob to march on Rome, and the Machiavellian Comnena assassinates Flamma before surrendering his body to the crowd. Like Bronte, Flamma becomes consumed by a decadent desire for self-destruction after recognizing the limitations of his will and power. In comparison, Comnena exhibits a devious egoism that enables her to seduce, manipulate, and ultimately dominate successive tyrants.

Like much of D'Annunzio's oeuvre, *La Gloria* is a tragedy depicting the rise and subsequent fall of a Latin *Übermensch* who is unable to overcome his own self-destructive decadence. As Bronte's lover, Comnena symbolizes the empire that successive would-be tyrants struggle for possession of, but it is actually Comnena who asserts ownership over each man who claims her. Throughout the play, Flamma's supporters describe him in terms that resemble Nietzsche's *Übermensch*, but Comnena demonstrates—and demands—even greater expressions of self-will. One supporter in particular, Giordano Fauro, repeatedly observes Flamma's domineering pride and desire to exert control over the crowd. Fauro recalls "[a]ll the pride of Ruggero Flamma (don't we know him and don't we love him for this too?), all that greedy pride was there throbbing nakedly" (my trans.; D'Annunzio, *La Gloria* 25).²⁹ Furthermore, Fauro suggests that Flamma is the realization of Bronte's desire for a successor who is "a true man, fit for the great emergency, a vast and free human heart, a child of the earth, rooted in the depths of our soil" (my trans.; 26).³⁰ The notion of a proud and domineering leader whose sense of identity is rooted in national soil is borrowed directly from Barrès's concept of *la terre et les morts* and his desire for psychic rootedness in national identity. Flamma's supporters also recognize their leader's ambivalent relationship with the masses, and his will to own and control the public as his property. Another of Flamma's supporters, Sigismondo Leoni, suggests that Flamma "has never been able to overcome the physical horror of the crowd," and that "[t]o control and to dominate, he needs to be physically higher, to breathe freely" (my trans.; 32).³¹ Like Philippe in Barrès's *Sous l'œil des barbares* (1888), Flamma must isolate himself from the barbarians who seek to impose their will on his sense of self. For Flamma, however, the ultimate goal is to bend the will of the mob to his own ends.

While Flamma is certainly a Nietzschean figure, Comnena expresses opinions that reveal a greater kinship with the newly rediscovered egoism of Stirner. When Flamma proposes to rebuild the nation with faith "[i]n the truth and in the power of my idea" (my trans.; D'Annunzio, *La Gloria* 164),³² Comnena mocks him in typically Stirnerian fashion:

> "In myself," you had to answer. You must have faith in yourself: in your nerves, in your bones, in your arteries, in your courage, in your passion, in your hardness, in your greed, in all your substance, in all the weapons that nature has given you to fight, to surpass others, to have no equal, to be the first, the master, the only one.
>
> (my trans.; 165)³³

Power does not come from faith in a personal ideal, but from unwavering demonstrations of self-confidence and will. Flamma's desire to surpass all

---

²⁹ "Tutto l'orgoglio di Ruggero Flamma (non lo conosciamo e non l'amiamo anche per questo?), tutto quell'avido orgoglio era là nudo palpitante" (25).
³⁰ "Io mi coricherei anzi tempo silenziosamente nella fossa che voi mi aprite, se vedessi tra voi un vero uomo, atto alla gran bisogna, un vasto e libero cuore umano, un figlio della terra, radicato nelle profondità del nostro suolo" (26).
³¹ "È strano: egli non ha mai potuto vincere l'orrore fisico della folla, il raccapriccio istintivo che gli dà il contatto col mostro. Per dominarsi e per dominare egli ha bisogno di essere materialmente più in alto, di avere il respiro libero" (32).
³² "Nella verità e nella potenza della mia idea" (164).
³³ "'In me stesso' dovevi rispondere. In te devi aver fede: nei tuoi nervi, nelle tue ossa, nelle tue arterie, nel tuo coraggio, nella tua passione, nella tua durezza, nella tua avidità, in tutta la tua sostanza, in tutte le armi che ti ha dato la natura per combattere, per superare gli altri, per non avere eguali, per essere il primo, il padrone, il solo" (165).

others is undeniably Nietzschean, but Comnena's suggestion that this is only possible if he rises above his own ideals to become "il solo" is much closer to Stirner's concept of the singular egoist. Comnena argues that strength does not come from an idea, but that "[t]he forces with which you must play and fight are none other than the human passions, which you made free by destroying the device that compressed them" (my trans.; 169).[34] Power and ownership demand the rejection of ideals and morals as a means of liberating instinct and will, and it is these later qualities which enable the domination of the crowd. Because he falls back on ideals as a source of authority, Flamma loses control of the mob to his rival.

Whereas Nietzsche's influence on D'Annunzio is well documented, less attention has been paid to his familiarity with Stirner's ideas. D'Annunzio's knowledge of Stirner's thought is not mere conjecture. His copy of the 1900 edition of *l'Unique et sa propriété* can still be found in his private library at the Vittoriale degli italiani, the villa where he lived from 1922 until his death in 1938. The book contains a label from Alfonso Dori's bookshop in Florence, which suggests D'Annunzio purchased it between 1900 and 1911. Like many of the books in his library, D'Annunzio's copy of *l'Unique et sa propriété* contains blue pencil marks that indicate his reading, but there are also two pages of Henri Lasvignes' introduction that are marked with the brown ink D'Annunzio reserved for passages of greater importance. The first of these discusses Stirner's interpretation of the state. Lasvignes suggests that "[t]he tension of human instincts is calculated mathematically and these instincts are all funneled in the direction of society's benefit" (my trans.; xiv).[35] He goes on to conclude that "[t]he basis of a flourishing nation is therefore slavery" (my trans.; xiv).[36] Both pages equate the concept of freedom with personal ownership. Lasvignes' proposition that an individual egoist might achieve liberty through personal gratification and property is remarkably close to the attitude that D'Annunzio had already expressed in *La Gloria*. For D'Annunzio, Lasvignes, and Stirner alike, freedom was not something that could be granted, but something that had to be taken by force.

D'Annunzio's decadent lifestyle and peculiar place in the political history of Italy have meant that far more time has been dedicated to writing about his

---

[34] "Le forze con cui tu devi giocare e batterti non sono se non le passioni umane, che tu hai fatte libere distruggendo l'ordegno che le comprimeva" (169).
[35] "La tension des instincts humains est calculée mathématiquement et ces instincts sont canalisés tous dans le sens du profit de la société" (xiv).
[36] "La base d'une nation florissante est donc l'esclavage" (xiv).

exploits than accurately translating his body of work. Even in Italy there has been a concerted effort to downplay D'Annunzio's literary legacy due to his role in the development of fascist ideology and aesthetics. In 1992, Paolo Valesio declared that "[t]he literary injustice committed with regard to Gabriele D'Annunzio is the most flagrant of the twentieth century in Italy and perhaps in all of Europe" (1). For Valesio, a conspiracy of silence regarding D'Annunzio represented "the most pernicious negative trend in Italian literary criticism since World War II: the tendency to subordinate literary judgements to moralistic and political criteria, even while defending the autonomy of art and literature" (1). Despite what Valesio saw as a "current, and welcome, flowering of D'Annunzian scholarship in America" (ix), the situation remains largely unchanged in the English-speaking world. If D'Annunzio is better known today, it is primarily as a historical curio—the flamboyant and cruel profligate who managed to commandeer a city—viewed from the relative safety of the twenty-first century.

The fact that much of D'Annunzio's oeuvre remains unavailable in English—or exists only in the form of bowdlerized translations—has disguised his importance to contemporaries in avant-garde and modernist circles.[37] Woodhouse suggests that "[i]n Britain, at least during the early part of the twentieth century, and amongst the literate and upper-middle classes, D'Annunzio was read and more or less appreciated by such as Arthur Symons, Ouida, Henry James, James Joyce, Osbert Sitwell, W. B. Yeats, Harold Nicholson, D. H. Lawrence, and Marguerite Radclyffe Hall" (2). In many cases, admiration and disdain were doled out in similar measure. Joyce remarked that "the three writers of the nineteenth century who had the greatest natural talents were D'Annunzio, Kipling, and Tolstoy—it's strange that all three had semi-fanatic ideas about religion or about patriotism" (Ellman 673). In *Across the River and into the Trees* (1950), Hemingway's Colonel Cantwell describes D'Annunzio as a "great writer" before adding, to himself, "poet, national hero, [...] the great, lovely writer of *Notturno* whom we respect, and jerk" (45). Such ambivalence was a common response to both D'Annunzio's writing and his behavior. Those who encountered his novels

---

[37] Woodhouse points out that "the heavily bowdlerized version of *Il piacere* [1889], translated as *The Child of Pleasure* by Georgina Harding in 1898, omits any kind of intellectual reflection on serious subjects" in addition to excising sexually explicit material (85). More recently, "[f]ollowing the expiration of copyright in 1988, Daedalus unloaded upon an unsuspecting Anglophone public the very translations which Miss Harding had bowdlerized in the late 1890s, without any open reference to the original date of publication or to the omissions and changes which she made and which scholars have pointed out over the past century" (86).

in Italian or in French translation found them to be a disconcerting combination of elaborate prose, Nietzschean themes, and scandalous subject matter.

Some readers, such as D. H. Lawrence, noted the egoism that underpinned D'Annunzio's characters. William Blissett suggested that "[t]he evidence of Lawrence's familiarity with D'Annunzio dates from after *The Trespasser*" was published in 1912, but that he may have encountered D'Annunzio's writing earlier (27). In 1914, Lawrence proposed in a letter to George Campbell that "Russia, and Germany, and Sweden, and Italy, have done nothing but glory in the suicide of the egoist" (Lawrence, *The Letters of D. H. Lawrence* 247). He continued that "the Egoist as a divine figure on the Cross, held up to tears and love and veneration, is to me a bit nauseating now, after Artzibasheff and D'Annunzio, and the Strindberg set, and the Manns in Germany" (247).[38] Although Lawrence was a harsh critic of D'Annunzio's prose, he recognized the fact that "D'Annunzio is a god in Italy," who "can control the current of the blood with his words, and although much of what he says is bosh, yet the hearer is satisfied, fulfilled" (Lawrence, *Twilight in Italy* 112). Through his repeated depictions of egoists and *Übermenschen* in his fiction and own demonstrations of tyrannical self-will in Fiume, D'Annunzio played a similar role to Maurice Barrès in the popularization of nationalistic egoism and, indirectly, the thought of Stirner.

With D'Annunzio's march on Fiume the world was introduced to a new kind of tyrant, schooled in the egoistic philosophies of Stirner and Nietzsche. As dictator of the newly declared Regency of Carnaro, he was certainly driven by a Stirnerian sense of personal importance and a desire for ownership. In his autobiography Mussolini recalled a letter that D'Annunzio had purportedly sent on the eve of his march on Fiume:

> Gabriel D'Annunzio, before starting from Ronchi, wrote me the following letter:
> "Dear Companion,
>   The dice are on the table. To-morrow I shall take Fiume with force of arms. The God of Italy assist us!
>   I arise from bed with fever. But it is impossible to delay. Once more the spirit dominates the miserable flesh."
>
>   (Mussolini, *My Autobiography* 82)

---

[38] Lawrence also mentioned D'Annunzio in *Kangaroo* (1923): "*L'anatomia presuppone il cadavere*: anatomy presupposes a corpse, says D'Annunzio. You can establish an exact science on a corpse, supposing you start with the corpse, and don't try to derive it from a living creature. But upon life itself, or any instance of life, you cannot establish a science" (330).

As Commandant of Fiume he would, with the assistance of Alceste De Ambris, produce his great political manifesto, the *Carta del Carnaro*, in 1920. De Ambris provided the ideological program of the charter and, as in the case of his earlier contribution to the fascist manifesto, he incorporated progressive values such as direct democracy, gender equality, and religious freedom. De Ambris also established the separation of powers between executive, legislative, and judicial functions. Nevertheless, the manifesto allowed D'Annunzio, as Commandant, unrestrained authority over every facet of government during periods of national emergency. The charter suggested that "[w]hen the Regency comes in extreme danger and sees its health in the devoted will of an individual who knows how to excite and lead all the forces of the people to struggle and victory," a Commandant can be appointed, possessing "supreme power without appeal" (my trans.; D'Annunzio, *La Reggenza Italiana Del Carnaro* 45).[39] Article 44 of the charter proposed that "[t]he Commandant, for the duration of his rule, combines all the political and military, legislative and executive powers," while "[t]he members of the executive assume the office of secretaries and commissioners with him" (my trans.; 45).[40] For the entirety of the Fiume experiment, the Regency of Carnaro remained a dictatorship, under the absolute rule of D'Annunzio. In 1848 Stirner had provided Marx with a justification for writing *The Communist Manifesto* and seventy years later the same ideas about the ownership of ideals helped to justify manifestos of proto fascists like D'Annunzio and Marinetti.

By the time that D'Annunzio had installed himself as the Commandant of Fiume in 1919, Mussolini was also well aware of Stirner's importance to a new brand of revolutionary politics. In 1908 Mussolini—still at that time a socialist—contributed a series of articles to the republican newspaper *Il Pensiero Romagnolo* (1894–1910) which demonstrated his familiarity with the ideas of Stirner and Nietzsche alike. He suggested that "[f]or some time, artists from all over the world, from Ibsen to D'Annunzio, followed in Nietzsche's footsteps" and that "individualists, a little sated by the rigidity of the Stirnerian gospel, turned anxiously to Zarathustra and in the philosophy of the Enlightened one they find the germ and reason for every revolt and every moral and political

---

[39] "Quando la Reggenza venga in pericolo estremo e veda la sua salute nella devota volontà d'un solo, che sappia raccogliere eccitare e condurre tutte le forze del popolo alla lotta e alla vittoria, il Consiglio nazionale solennemente adunato nell'Arengo può nominare a viva voce per vóto il Comandante e a lui rimettere la potestà suprema senza appellazione" (45).
[40] "Il Comandante, per la durata dell' imperio, assomma tutti i poteri politici e militari, legislativi ed esecutivi. I partecipi del Potere esecutivo assumono presso di lui officio di segretarii e commissarii" (45).

attitude." (my trans.; Mussolini, "*La filosofia della forza*" 174).[41] Still, Mussolini expressed a degree of skepticism about the current popularity of the "*Antisofi dell'egoismo*" (174). He observed that "[i]t is not enough to create new tables of moral values, it is also necessary to humbly produce bread, so the unique can never be 'unique' in the Stirnerian sense of the word, because the fatal law of solidarity bends him and overcomes him," to the extent that "[a]n individual cannot be conceived of who can live detached from the infinite chain of beings" (my trans.; 175).[42] It was the inevitability of social life, Mussolini suggested, that led Nietzsche to express his will to power. Mussolini proposed that Nietzsche's philosophy directed Stirner's concept of self-ownership outward as a need to exert power over others. In reality, Stirner had demonstrated the importance of exerting power over abstract ideas, but Mussolini's reading of Stirner and Nietzsche had important implications for the development of fascism.

Even if Mussolini believed that the unique individuality that Stirner described was unobtainable, he still considered him a crucial thinker in the history of Western philosophy. In 1911 Mussolini wrote to his friend, Cesare Berti, from prison and suggested that in his reading he had been ascending the "Dolomites" of thought "called Stirner, Nietzsche, Goethe, Schiller, Montaigne, Cervantes, etc." (my trans.; "Letter to Berti" 258).[43] In 1914 he mused that although the possibility of attaining Stirner's unique was "absurd," it was nonetheless a "wonderful" notion (Mussolini, "In tema di neutralità: Al nostro posto!" 331). Then, in 1919, he described Stirner's thought in his most enthusiastic terms to date, declaring: "Leave the way free for the elemental power of the individual; for there is no other human reality than the individual! Why shouldn't Stirner become significant again?" (Mussolini, "Vecchie Usanze" 194).[44] In the introduction to his abridged edition of *The Ego and His Own*, John Carroll

---

[41] "Per qualche tempo gli artisti di tutti i paesi, da Ibsen a D'Annunzio, hanno seguito le orme Nietzschiane. Gli individualisti un po' sazi della rigidità dell'evangelio stirneriano si sono volti ansiosi a Zarathustra e nella filosofia dell'Illuminato trovano il germe e la ragione di ogni rivolta e di ogni atteggiamento morale e politico" (174).
[42] "Non basta creare delle nuove tavole di valori morali, bisogna anche umilmente produrre il pane, L'unico non può dunque mai essere 'unico' nel senso stirneriano della parola, ché la fatale legge della solidarietà lo piega e lo vince. [...] Non si concepisce un individuo che possa vivere avulso dall'infinita catena degli esseri" (175).
[43] "E queste dolomiti del pensiero si chiamano Stirner, Nietzsche, Goethe, Schiller, Montaigne, Cervantes, etc." (258).
[44] The translation here is from Carroll's introduction to *The Ego and His Own* (14). The original Italian is: "Lasciate sgombro il camino alle forza elementari degli individui, perché altra realtà umana, all'infuori dell'individuo, non esiste! Perché Stirner non tornerebbe d'attualità" (194).

suggests that although "Mussolini's notorious exhibitionism made him less a passionate follower of ideas than an intellectual opportunist," Stirnerian egoism "would have fed his ambition" (13). Moreover, Mussolini's opportunistic use of ideas that furthered his own egoistic aspirations was itself entirely congruent with Stirner's thought. There can be no doubt that the Mussolini of 1922 was an egoist, and a conscious one at that. At the very least, the ideological malleability of fascism found a convenient justification in the form of Stirnerian egoism. Nevertheless, the horrors of the First World War stood between Stirner's Italian reception and the marches on Fiume and Rome. And in the years before war ravaged Europe Stirner's thought was to find yet another willing readership, this time among the ranks of English modernism.

Between them, Marinetti, D'Annunzio, and Mussolini advanced a drastically altered form of Stirnerian egoism in the early twentieth century. They portrayed egoism as a philosophy founded on the domination of others through the cynical use of ideology, morality, and belief. These Italian egoists were no longer concerned with esoteric notions of "ownness" or the individual's power over abstractions; they sought instead to instrumentalize ideals as a source of authority and self-glorification. Through this refiguring of his philosophy within the context of political and socio-economic ideas Stirner came to be considered as a foundational figure in the development of fascism and German National Socialism. Indeed, political allegiances began to shift due to the influence of Stirner's thought. Under the sway of a brutish and oppressive interpretation of egoism Marinetti's anarchism tipped over into authoritarian nationalism; Mussolini's socialism into fascist rhetoric; and D'Annunzio's decadent bohemianism into a cult of self-aggrandizement. For those with only a cursory familiarity with *Der Einzige und sein Eigentum* the similarities between Mussolini, Hitler, and Stirner could seem obvious.[45] Barrès pioneered this nationalistic reading of Stirner in Paris, but in America, and in due course in England, new anarchist and libertarian interpretations of egoism were also beginning to take shape.

---

[45] As far afield as Australia connections were frequently drawn between the ideas of Stirner and Hitler, as demonstrated by an article by C. R. Bradish that was published in the Melbourne *Age* on July 4, 1942, titled "Nietzsche, Hitler and Stirner: Pathological Studies." Indeed, British and Australian journalists drew connections between Stirner's ideas and German militarism during both World Wars—without any real evidence to support such conclusions.

4

The Transatlantic Shift: Beyond Anarchism and Nationalism

Stirner's ideas arrived in the United States in 1886, in the context of a sustained flourishing of radical thought inspired by the likes of Herbert Spencer; Ralph Waldo Emerson; and the anarchist, Lysander Spooner. Compared to the situation on the European continent, the English language reception of Stirner led to the development of two, far more distinct, forms. In America Stirner's ideas were largely developed along libertarian lines. In England, elitist and reactionary readings of Stirner were more predominant. By the early twentieth century both European and American interpretations of egoism were infiltrating British intellectual circles, but the situation in England was complicated by pre-existing discussions of philosophical egoism that were not directly connected to Stirner. In fact, encounters with Stirner's name and work in England were part of a broader engagement with philosophical egoism that began in the work and reading habits of a list of Victorian intellectuals that included Spencer and George Eliot. Egoism entered English philosophy through an interest in the writings of Kant and Feuerbach but, as in Germany, this line of enquiry inevitably led to the thought of Stirner. It was almost three decades before European, American, and English enquiries into egoism would eventually meet in the manifestos of the Vorticist movement.

   Accounting for the spread of Stirner's ideas in the English-speaking world is a task complicated by the wide variety of ways in which readers could encounter the concept of egoism by the beginning of the twentieth century. Between 1900 and 1920 it was not unusual for young intellectuals to stumble upon references to Stirner within a few years of each other, but through entirely different means. Many paths led to Stirner's book: Wyndham Lewis may have first heard mention of it while visiting Munich in 1906; T. S. Eliot read about Stirner when he reviewed James Huneker's *Egoists* for the *Harvard Review* in 1909; "[i]t is likely that [Herbert] Read's first encounter with egoism occurred at the Leeds Art

Club, in around 1911" (Quincey-Jones 391); James Joyce encountered Stirner through his reading of anarchist theory; and Rebecca West probably learned about Stirner while attending *The Freewoman* discussion circle in 1912. Through a combination of strategy and circumstance, a diverse list of intellectuals with connections to egoism eventually began to coalesce around Dora Marsden's radical feminist journal, *The New Freewoman*, in 1913. Even before it rebranded itself as *The Egoist* in 1914, that magazine had become an important junction between Stirnerian egoism and English modernism. Marsden's own conversion to egoism in August 1912, and *The Egoist*'s contribution to England's manifesto moment were, however, part of a campaign that began more than twenty years earlier, on the other side of the Atlantic, in the pages of Benjamin Tucker's individualist journal *Liberty* (1881–1908).

Feuerbach and Egoism in Victorian England

Stirner's English reception involved the transmission of ideas back and forth between the England, Europe, and the United States. Renewed European interest in Stirner in the 1880s had begun with John Henry Mackay's research into the history of materialism at the British Museum Library while staying in London in 1887. Many English intellectuals at that time were also reading about developments in German philosophy, part of a trend that Rosemary Ashton suggests began with Coleridge's interest in the work of Kant, Schelling, and Schlegel in the 1820s, and which was stridently continued in the writings of Carlyle. Through them, according to Ashton, "Victorians like George Eliot, [George Henry] Lewes, [John Stuart] Mill, [Matthew] Arnold, Richard Holt Hutton, and the philosopher J. H. Stirling absorbed a culture which could no longer be simply English" (2). In one sense, Victorian interest in German philosophy laid the foundations for Stirner's eventual popularity by ensuring the translation of his predecessors and contemporaries. George Eliot translated works by Strauss, Spinoza, and Feuerbach in the 1840s and 1850s, and her de-facto husband George Henry Lewes introduced the reading public to a much wider array of German intellectuals through *The Biographical History of Philosophy* (1846). By 1870 English readers were familiar with a list of German thinkers that included Bruno Bauer, Fichte, Heine, Reinhold, Jean Paul, Goethe, and Hegel—but not Stirner. They had, however, been introduced to the philosophical concept of *Egoismus* (egoism) as it appeared in the thought of Kant, Fichte, and Feuerbach. By 1880, therefore, general references to "egoism" were common in the writings of Eliot, Herbert Spencer, and George Meredith.

References to *Egoismus* in the work of German intellectuals—most importantly Feuerbach—contributed to the rediscovery of Stirner's thought in England, but also led to a persistent ambiguity in the meaning of the term. Herbert Spencer, for instance, developed evolutionary theories relating to egoism and altruism, and while his ideas proved popular with the libertarians who promoted Stirnerian egoism in the early twentieth century, his thought had no direct connection to Stirner's. By the time that *Der Einzige und sein Eigentum* was translated into English in 1907, "egoism" could suggest the kind of self-involvement portrayed by Feuerbach, the evolutionary self-interest described by Spencer, or the rebellion of the unique individual delineated by Stirner—to mention but three understandings of the concept. Frequently the term referred to an impracticable mix of all these meanings, combined with elements of Proudhon's anarchism and Nietzsche's aristocracy of the intellect. Such was the case for Stirner's earliest English translators, a group of American individualist anarchists associated with *Liberty*.

The English reception of philosophical egoism in the 1870s and the American revival of Stirner's thought in the 1880s combined to produce even more adulterated interpretations of Stirnerian egoism than those developed in France and Italy. In England as in Europe, Stirnerian egoism was associated with aristocratism, nationalism, and anarchist crime, but now it was further diluted by tenuous connections to social Darwinism, contractual rights, theosophy, and mysticism. By 1913 self-described proponents of Stirner's thought regularly berated each other for failing to understand the full implications of egoism while themselves ignoring aspects of his work that they found incompatible with their own views. Egoism increasingly described an incoherent jumble of contradictory ideas advanced by mutually hostile groups. The consequence was further confusion about what Stirner's ideas actually entailed, and an increasing disconnect between the use of the word egoism and Stirner's thought.

Nevertheless, it is important to recognize that the popularity of egoism among American libertarians in the 1880s owed a great deal to earlier English conceptions of egoism associated with Feuerbach. If mid-nineteenth-century intellectuals in England had not become interested in Feuerbach's interpretation of egoism there would have been little opportunity for libertarians to pursue egoism's development through to Stirner. Eliot, Spencer, and Meredith all helped to popularize the concept of egoism in English circles.[1] Rosemary Ashton suggests that Eliot "widened the influence of Feuerbach's [...] religion of humanity during twenty years of novel writing, as well as by direct transmission in her translation" (161). Feuerbach's humanism provided Eliot with a more hopeful vision and "pointed to a more agreeable post-Christian future" (Cunningham 16). Indeed, she observed to Sara Hennell in 1854 that "[w]ith the ideas of Feuerbach I everywhere agree, but of course I should, of myself, alter the phraseology considerably" (Eliot, "GE to Sara Sophia Hennell" 153). The idea of egoism—no doubt influenced by Feuerbach's thought—later became a ubiquitous feature of Eliot's novels.

By popularizing the word "egoism" in its philosophical sense, Eliot provided the impetus for further English investigations into the delineation of *Egoismus* in German philosophy. In the nineteenth century, a distinction emerged between egotism and egoism, where one referred to mere selfishness and the other to more complicated—and potentially beneficial—forms of self-concern. Unlike Stirner, however, Feuerbach associated egoism with a tendency to confuse personal shortcomings with the shortcomings of the species. He suggested that if a person "makes his own limitations the limitations of the species, this arises from the mistake that he identifies himself immediately with the species—a mistake which is intimately connected with the individual's love of ease, sloth, vanity, and egoism" (Feuerbach, *The Essence of Christianity* 7).[2] According to Eliot's translation, egoism was responsible for blinding individuals to the nature of the world by causing them to see reality as a reflection of the self. Stirner's egoism was a direct refutation of Feuerbach's depiction of the blindly self-interested ego. He proposed that egoism was the truth which subdued the illusory rule of ideals, but even after his rediscovery English and American readers suggested the existence of a dialectical relationship between altruism and egoism which

---

[1] After translating Strauss's *Das Leben Jesu* (The Life of Jesus, 1835) into English in 1846 Eliot completed an unpublished translation of Spinoza's *Ethica, ordine geometrico demonstrata* (Ethics, Demonstrated in Geometrical Order, 1677) and turned to Feuerbach's most important work. Eliot's translation of *Das Wesen des Christentums* (The Essence of Christianity, 1841) was completed in 1854 and it was one of her few works to be published under the name of Marian Evans.

[2] All quotations are taken from Eliot's translation. Feuerbach's own word here is *Selbstsucht* (selfishness) rather than *Egoismus* (egoism), but it is one of several instances where Eliot instead chose to translate a variety of similar words as egoism. Feuerbach's use of *Egoismus* was largely confined to the chapter discussing "The Significance of the Creation in Judaism" (Feuerbach, *Das Wesen des Christentums* 142).

had its origins in the quintessentially Victorian moral outlook of Eliot and her contemporaries.

The writings of Eliot, Spencer, and Meredith all suggest the extent to which Feuerbach influenced the meaning of the word egoism in the decades preceding the rediscovery of *Der Einzige und sein Eigentum*.[3] As Ashton points out, "George Eliot owed a lot to Feuerbach for his stimulating humanism, and as a novelist she reaped benefits particularly from his emphasis on the use of the senses and the faculty of imagination as central to religious myth and the exercise of moral duty alike" (166). Drawn from the work of Feuerbach, the word egoism appears in *Adam Bede* (1859), *Middlemarch* (1871–2), and *Daniel Deronda* (1876). In *Middlemarch* the narrator describes the nature of egoism through a now famous parable:

> Your pier-glass or extensive surface of polished steel made to be rubbed by a housemaid, will be minutely and multitudinously scratched in all directions; but place now against it a lighted candle as a centre of illumination, and lo! the scratches will seem to arrange themselves in a fine series of concentric circles round that little sun.
>
> (Eliot 264)

Through a process of "exclusive optical selection" (264), the candle creates the illusion that it is at the center of an ordered reality. For Eliot egoism operated in a similar way, to impose a false order on the random events that occur around the individual. The narrator suggests that "[t]he scratches are events, and the candle is the egoism of any person now absent—of Miss Vincy, for example" (264). This parable has strong implications for Eliot's aesthetic realism, but it is also important because it is not egotism, vanity, or selfishness which is used to describe Rosamund Vincy's self-concern but "egoism," adapted directly from her translation of Feuerbach.

In *Middlemarch*, as elsewhere in Eliot's work, egoism is often associated with common vanity, but it also conveys the more profound and perhaps unavoidable tendency of individuals to (mistakenly) perceive themselves to be at the center

---

[3] Eliot seems unaware of *Der Einzige und sein Eigentum* as neither she nor Lewes referred to it in their writings. In Lewes' *A Biographical History of Philosophy* (1845–6) he revealed the extent of his familiarity with the *Junghegelianer*: "Strauss has turned the history of Christ into a myth; Feuerbach and Bruno Bauer have carried this 'historical scepticism' to the utmost limit of speculative infidelity. And to make the anarchy complete, every small professor sets up as a prophet, and either promulgates a doctrine of his own, or throws himself back upon Kant, or Fichte, or Reinhold" (235). Whether Lewes knew of Stirner to be one such "small professor" must remain a matter of speculation, but he evidently did not consider the author of *Der Einzige und sein Eigentum* to be worthy of note if he did.

of events. Eliot's parable recalls Feuerbach's suggestion that when "man places himself only on the practical stand-point and looks at the world from thence, making the practical stand-point the theoretical one also, he is in disunion with nature; he makes Nature the abject vassal of his selfish interest, of his practical egoism" (*The Essence of Christianity* 112).[4] Eliot's depiction of egoism as a kind of self-deception was drawn from the ideas of Feuerbach and put her writing at odds with the interpretation of egoism found in *Der Einzige und sein Eigentum*. Repeated references to egoism also helped popularize the word's philosophical sense, and invited the interest of others.

An English understanding of egoism shifted with the contribution of Spencer, who focused on it primarily as the antithesis of altruism. Spencer provided a more generous assessment of egoism than Eliot in his ten-volume *System of Synthetic Philosophy* (1862–92). An early reference to egoism appeared in the second volume of the work, *The Principles of Psychology* (1872), in a note defending Spencer's borrowing of Comte's use of altruism:

> Altruism and altruistic, suggesting by their forms as well as by their meanings the antitheses of egoism and egoistic, bring quickly and clearly into thought the opposition, in a way that benevolence or beneficence and its derivatives do not, because the antitheses are not directly implied by them.
>
> (Spencer, *The Principles of Psychology* 607)

A more rigorous discussion of egoism then appeared in *The Data of Ethics* (1879), where Spencer devoted four chapters to establishing the relationship between egoism and altruism. Working forward from a contemporary interpretation of egoism as self-interest and incorporating Charles Darwin's theory of evolution—without any apparent knowledge of *Der Einzige und sein Eigentum*—Spencer concluded that egoism preceded apparently altruistic behaviors. He proposed that "[e]thics has to recognise the truth, recognised in unethical thought, that egoism comes before altruism" (Spencer, *The Data of Ethics* 187). According to Spencer, egoism was enshrined by evolutionary theory because "[u]nless each duly cares for himself, his care for all others is ended by death; and if each thus dies, there remain no others to be cared for" (187). Nevertheless, Spencer did not reduce all altruism to an egoistic desire for self-satisfaction as Stirner had in *Der Einzige und sein Eigentum*.

If George Eliot popularized the philosophical usage of egoism through her novels, George Meredith similarly introduced English readers to the figure of the

---

[4] Feuerbach actually used the word *Egoismus* here (Feuerbach, *Das Wesen des Christentums* 143).

ego*ist*. Like Spencer, he suggested a connection between egoism and evolutionary theory, and in *The Egoist* he provided an example of nature's power to humble the absolute egoist.[5] He interpreted egoism as a characteristic that was once evolutionarily useful but now hampered human progress. Egoism was found in the brutish will of the feudal lord, which may have been necessary for building an empire, but was detrimental to humane civilization. In Meredith's novel comedy serves as a corrective by humbling the over-developed ego. Its prelude suggests that "[t]he remedy of your frightful affliction is here, through the stillatory of Comedy, and not in Science" (Meredith 3). Through comedy, the arrogance and conceit of the egoist bring about his own downfall. Like Eliot and Spencer, Meredith employed egoism as the dialectical opposite of altruism and as a lack of awareness of an individual's place in a wider world. Discussions of the novel later appeared in *The Freewoman* just before Marsden's introduction to Stirner's book.

Meredith's novel depicts the dramatic humiliation of an unequivocal egoist as well as the dramatic awakening of egoistic motivations in otherwise altruistic characters. As in Spencer's evolutionary theory, neither unrestrained egoism nor reckless altruism are desirable qualities, and nature plays a role in moderating such impulses. The titular egoist of Meredith's comedy is Sir Willoughby Patterne, a handsome but tyrannical young man whose efforts to find a worthy bride are repeatedly frustrated by his vanity and duplicity. After traveling the world to avoid an initial romantic disgrace, Willoughby returns to his home, Patterne Hall, where he pursues Clara Middleton while simultaneously inviting the attentions of Laetitia Dale. Meredith's depiction of the egoist as a petty tyrant blinded by self-interest had no apparent connection to Stirnerian egoism but became the stereotypical example of the egoist in English literature prior to the translation of *Der Einzige und sein Eigentum* into English. An extreme example of Feuerbach's sense of egoism, Willoughby is unable to see beyond himself and, as a result, he has no measure of his own character. He goes so far as to warn Clara to "[b]eware of marrying an Egoist, my dear" (96–7), and the advice awakens Clara to her situation:

> None of them saw the man in the word, none noticed the word; yet this word was her medical herb, her illuminating lamp, the key of him (and, alas, but she thought

---

[5] Meredith occupies a contentious place in the history of Stirner's English reception. Although *The Egoist* pillories absolute egoism, the book's fixation on the figure of the egoist has invited several comparisons to Stirner's thought. Jean-Michel Rabaté, for example, suggests in *James Joyce and the Politics of Egoism* (2001) that "[o]ne should include George Meredith […] within the circle of the writers directly or indirectly influenced by Stirner's conception of radical egoism" (24). While not beyond the realm of possibility, there is little reason to suggest that Stirner's ideas had any bearing on the novel. Meredith was, however, familiar with the use of egoism by both Eliot and Spencer.

it by feeling her need of one), the advocate pleading in apology for her. Egoist! She beheld him—unfortunate, self-designated man that he was!—in his good qualities as well as bad under the implacable lamp, and his good were drenched in his first person singular. His generosity roared of *I* louder than the rest.

(97)

Over the course of the novel Clara, Laetitia, and even Vernon all accuse themselves of being egoists, while Willoughby alone fails to acknowledge that egoism is his defining characteristic. This self-knowledge is only possible because their egoism is not absolute, and in the case of Clara this self-awareness frees her from Willoughby's grasp.

Though probably unfamiliar with Stirner's thought, Eliot, Meredith, and Spencer all contributed to its rediscovery by popularizing the concept of egoism. By the end of the nineteenth century, Spencer's fame was at its height, particularly among radical liberals and libertarians opposed to the power of the state. There were numerous discussions of Spencer's thought in the pages of *Liberty*, and in Mackay's novel, *The Anarchists*, Carrard Auban's library "contained, first, the philosophical and politico-economical works of the great thinkers of France, from Helvetius and Say to Proudhon and Bastiat; less complete in number, but in the best editions, those of the English, from Smith to Spencer" (51). Similarly, the fiction of Eliot and Meredith proved popular in both radical and literary circles. English conceptions of egoism, from their starting point in Feuerbach, broadened to embrace the history of philosophical egoism and led to references to *Der Einzige und sein Eigentum* in books by Friedrich Albert Lange and Eduard von Hartmann. James L. Walker and John Henry Mackay were simply the first to be sufficiently struck by the acuity of Stirner's arguments to become the standard-bearers of his thought in particular.

An American Interlude

In the United States the picture was very different. There was of course a transatlantic influence exerted by the English writers just discussed. In addition, however, early interest in philosophical egoism in the United States was directly related to the ideas of Max Stirner—although American libertarians and anarchists incorporated Stirner's thought selectively, ignoring, borrowing, and adapting it to their own positions as they saw fit. James L. Walker, the first proponent of Stirnerian egoism to emerge in the United States, retained Stirner's immoralism, his concept of a union of egoists, and his depiction of the unique individual, but abandoned (or ignored) his related criticism of idealized liberty. He used Stirner's ideas to undermine support for natural rights in favor of unrestrained liberty and the defense of contractual rights. In reality, his branch of radicalism—which he called philosophical anarchism—blended the often incompatible ideas of Stirner and Proudhon with pre-existing notions of American libertarianism. It was a movement that did little service to the complexity of Stirner's thought, but it did bring his ideas about the tyrannizing power of language and the rejection of conventional morality before a wider English-language readership, and so laid the basis for his later impact on manifesto writing.

In 1886 Walker introduced Americans to Stirner's ideas through a series of articles he wrote for *Liberty*.[6] Within a year, he had converted several important anarchists and libertarians to an offshoot of Stirnerian egoism he variously described as "egoistic anarchism" and "philosophic anarchism." As a result of his efforts, Americans were writing about Stirner years before Barrès, Marinetti, and D'Annunzio began incorporating aspects of egoism into their personal visions of an artistic elite. According to some American intellectuals, including those associated with the periodicals *Liberty* and *Egoism* (1890–7), Stirner espoused a radical extension of the laissez-faire capitalism to which they subscribed. Once again, anarchists proved instrumental in the dissemination of Stirner's ideas, but these were anarchists of a different color to the syndicalists and communists associated with terrorist violence in the United States. Stirner's American proponents were individualistic and idealistic freethinkers who championed the thought of Josiah Warren, Lysander Spooner, and Herbert Spencer, among others, and in 1887 they began a campaign to translate Stirner's book into English for the first time. It took twenty years for the translation to make it into print in 1907, but copies of the book accordingly began to appear in England just as European interest in egoism was reaching its height. British artists, writers, and thinkers who encountered references to Stirner through European sources could conveniently access Stirner's thought in the form of a second edition of *The Ego and His Own*, published in London by A. C. Fifield in the middle of 1912.

---

[6] A biographical note in Walker's posthumously published *The Philosophy of Egoism* (1905) observes that "Dr. Walker was born in June 1845, at Manchester, England, of wealthy parents, who gave him a liberal education," and suggests he had graduated from "institutions of learning in England, France, and Germany" (70). He moved to the United States during the 1860s, and worked for newspapers including the *Chicago Times*, the *San Antonio Herald*, the *Galveston-Dallas News*, the *Austin Statesman*, and the *State Gazette of Austin*.

When Mackay emerged as the champion of Stirnerian egoism in Europe, Walker had already spent a year popularizing Stirner's ideas in the United States. Mackay first encountered references to Stirner in Lange's writings on the history of materialism, but Walker appears to have been introduced to Stirner's ideas by Eduard von Hartmann's *Philosophie des Unbewussten* (Philosophy of the Unconscious 1869) more than a decade earlier.[7] In fact, Walker claimed he arrived at many of egoism's conclusions before he learned about Stirner. He asserted that "in the first half of the sixties I was an Atheist and self-conscious Egoist," but knew nothing about Stirner's writings "until the spring of 1872" (Walker, *The Philosophy of Egoism* 65–7). Mid-nineteenth-century discussions of egoism in the writings of Spencer and Eliot may account for this early conversion. Upon reading *Der Einzige und sein Eigentum*, Walker recalled that "[t]here for the first time I saw most plainly stated, my own thought, borne out by illustrations that will test the nerve of every professed Egoist" (67). Dora Marsden would express similar sentiments twenty-five years later.

The articles that Walker contributed to *Liberty* throughout the 1880s testify to the profound influence Stirner's book exerted on his subsequent thought. On March 6, 1886, two short articles by Walker—using the pseudonym *Tak Kak*[8]—introduced many of *Liberty*'s readers to egoism's capacity to challenge idealized notions of justice. The first, "What is Justice?," did not mention Stirner's name, but was grounded in his proposition that "[m]y concern is neither the divine nor the human, not the true, good, just, free, etc., but solely what is *mine*, and it is not a general one, but is—unique, as I am unique" (Walker 7). Walker described justice as "an idea presupposing a power that lays down a rule or law to which the individual owes respect and obedience" ("What is Justice?" 8) and proposed that for Christians justice was embodied by God. He characterized society as an "egoist," because "society's justice" demands "I must sacrifice my wishes to the family, to the State, to humanity" (8). Refusing to accept the justice imposed by church or state, Walker contended:

> When [a man] comes to full consciousness, he sets up as his own master, and thereafter, if there is to be any use for the word justice, it must mean the rules

---

[7] In his introduction to *The Ego and His Own* (1907), Walker suggested that "[w]e owe to Dr. Eduard von Hartmann the unquestionable service which he rendered by directing attention to this book in his *Philosophie des Unbewussten*, the first edition of which was published in 1869, and in other writings" (Introduction xiii).

[8] Russian for "because" or "since."

of a union of egoists with benefits to at least balance duties; and these duties are simply matter of contract.

(8)

Walker's advocacy for a union of egoists and his suggestion that justice should be considered a matter of contract were also borrowed directly from Stirner's book. In *Der Einzige und sein Eigentum*, Stirner suggested that "I, the egoist, have not at heart the welfare of this 'human society,'" but "transform it rather into my property and my creature; that is, I annihilate it, and form in its place the *Union of Egoists* [Verein von Egoisten]" (161).

Walker modified Stirner's egoism to correspond with the values of *Liberty*'s editor, Benjamin Tucker, and this resulted in a mischaracterization of Stirnerian egoism that persisted well into the twentieth century. Tucker was a vocal proponent of Proudhon, and Walker was careful to excise any aspect of Stirner's thought that challenged Tucker's views.[9] He avoided Stirner's suggestion that "Proudhon, like the communists, fights against *egoism*" (*The Ego and Its Own* 222). He also expunged Stirner's repudiation of idealized notions of freedom:

> Freedom teaches only: Get yourselves rid, relieve yourselves of everything burdensome; it does not teach you who you yourselves are. Rid, rid! That is its battlecry, get rid even of yourselves, "deny yourselves." But ownness calls you back to yourselves, it says "come to yourself!"

(148)

When he paraphrased Stirner's defense of contract Walker similarly avoided related assaults on political liberty. In reality, Stirner had suggested that it did not matter "if I myself deprive myself of this and that liberty (such as by any contract)," because "I have to let my liberty be limited by all sorts of powers and by every one who is stronger" (271). Walker, however, went on to associate egoism with the position that "liberty is a good in itself and the means of all other good" ("The Rational Utilitarian Philosophy" 8). Elsewhere, he simply ignored any aspect of Stirner's writing that he found too difficult to reconcile with the tenets of anarchism.

The attenuated form of Stirner's egoism that Walker advocated in *Liberty* resembled illegalism insofar as it rejected the rules imposed by society and the

---

[9] Tucker translated Proudhon's most famous work, *Qu'est ce que la propriété?* (*What Is Property?* 1840) into English in 1876, and his continued support of Proudhon's anarchism eventually contributed to his rejection of Stirnerian egoism in 1914.

state, but Walker's focus was on political and economic freedom rather than the liberating power of crime. His interpretation of egoism dominated the reception of Stirner's thought in the United States, and in England it was the first point of contact most readers had with Stirner's ideas.[10] Walker proposed:

> the laws of society, and the State, one of its forms, are tyrannies or disagreeable impediments to me [...] and I see no difficulty in discarding them but your respect for ideas such as "right," "wrong," "justice," etc., I would have you consider that these are merely words with vague, chimerical meanings.
>
> ("What is Justice?" 8)

Nevertheless, Walker shared the illegalist view that egoism justified all manner of crime, including murder. He went so far as to assert that there was "nothing wrong" with a mistreated wife "putting six inches of steel into the bosom of her liege lord" (8). At this early stage, Tucker rejected such arguments and condemned murder, suggesting that he "will continue to do all that we can to prevent the killing of any men, white or yellow, who propose to mind their own business" (8). Within a year, however, Tucker shifted his position to become one of Walker's staunchest supporters, and many influential contributors to *Liberty*—including Gertrude B. Kelly and her brother John—abandoned the publication in disgust.[11]

In an increasingly bitter dispute about egoism in *Liberty*, the Kelly siblings took Walker to task, and their criticisms revealed inconsistencies in the prevailing interpretation of Stirner's position. Despite the valid objections put forward by John and Gertrude, Walker secured majority support from the journal.[12] John aimed a parting shot at Walker in July, and it provided an insightful critique of the way in which Walker had misrepresented Stirner's thought. He noted the tautology that was implicit in Walker's arguments and suggested that "it is impossible to base a society upon contract unless we consider a contract as having some binding effect, and that the binding effect of a particular contract cannot be due to the contract itself" (Kelly, "A Final Statement" 7). Walker's interpretation

---

[10] Walker wrote the introduction for the 1907 edition of *The Ego and His Own*, and this introduction also appeared in the second edition that was published in London in 1912.

[11] Gertrude Bride Kelly was an Irish-born surgeon and activist who moved to the United States as a child in 1868. A feminist, Irish nationalist, and individualist anarchist, Kelly was an influential—if now largely forgotten—figure in the radical politics of New York in the 1880s. Her brother, John Forrest Kelly was an electrical engineer who at one stage worked for Thomas Edison. Like his sister, he was an active Irish nationalist and individualist anarchist.

[12] Wendy McElroy provides a detailed discussion of *Liberty*'s egoism debate in *The Debates of Liberty: An Overview of Individualist Anarchism, 1881–1908* (2003).

of egoism demanded the existence of an objective morality because it attributed inherent value to contractual relations.[13] Kelly further mocked Walker's attempts to reconcile the thought of Stirner and Proudhon, rightly pointed out that "Stirner expressly attacked Proudhon" (7), and used quotations to demonstrate the latter's support for an objective concept of justice. Nevertheless, Kelly agreed to "step aside, Mr. Editor, and await the glorious results promised as the result of the crusade against morality" (7). He ended his assault by bitterly asking "why not use the plain term selfishness instead of egoism?" (7). The article marked the end of the intellectual debate. Walker's version of Stirner's egoism had won the day.

The departure of the Kelly siblings cemented *Liberty*'s conversion to egoism, but the incompatibility of Proudhon's anarchism and Stirner's egoism proved to be a persistent weakness in this branch of American radical thought. In August Gertrude Kelly submitted a final protest about the recent developments. She called the authenticity of Tucker's anarchism into doubt:

> Without this being the age of "preternatural suspicion" we might well be led to suppose that you had been "hired by the enemy" to bring disgrace upon the cause of agnosticism and Anarchism by allowing such distortions of their principles as Tak Kak has presented to appear in the columns of *Liberty* with little or no comment from you.
>
> (Kelly, "A Letter of Protest" 7)

The protest was immediately followed by a comment from the editor, in which he observed that "the tone of Miss. Kelly's article, when placed in contrast with the dignity and evident self-command which she has shown in almost everything else she has written, is sufficient indication of the weakness of her present position" (7). History shows that Tucker was mistaken, and more than twenty years later Dora Marsden would capitalize on the contradiction between anarchism and egoism to argue for a more logically consistent interpretation of Stirner's thought.

The most important—though not immediate—outcome of *Liberty*'s conversion to egoism was the publication of the first complete translation of *Der Einzige und sein Eigentum* into English. Despite Walker's success with winning support for

---

[13] Of course, Stirner made no such claim about any kind of obligation. In contrast to Walker, he suggested: "In the very act of joining them and entering their circle one forms a *union* with them that lasts as long as party and I pursue one and the same goal. But today I still share the party's tendency, as by tomorrow I can do so no longer and I become 'untrue' to it. The party has nothing *binding* (obligatory) for me, and I do not have respect for it; if it no longer pleases me, I become its foe" (*The Ego and Its Own* 211).

Stirner's ideas, it took two decades for his efforts to result in an English edition of Stirner's book; nor did he see it in print, dying in 1904 as he did. David Ashford observes that "[i]n collaboration with Emma Heller and Steven T. Byington, Walker produced a translation into English that would appear, four years after his death, in an edition published by Tucker in New York in 1907, with a second edition published in London and New York in 1913" (56).[14] This translation arrived fortuitously, just as European interest in Stirner was reaching the English literary scene. When British intellectuals began to demonstrate their own interest in Stirner's ideas, Tucker was quick to capitalize on the situation by inserting himself into the discussion. From June 1913, both he and Byington became regular contributors to *The New Freewoman*, a journal that, along with *The Eagle and the Serpent* (1898–1927) and *The New Age* (1894–1938), helped popularize *The Ego and His Own* in England. As it had in *Liberty*, discussion of egoism in *The New Freewoman* quickly descended into heated argument. This time, however, Tucker found himself on the losing side of a debate that pitted egoism against anarchism.

Divergent Egoisms

The first two decades of the twentieth century marked the height of Stirner's influence in Europe and the United States. After tortuous journeys back and forth across the Continent and the Atlantic, distinct interpretations of Stirner's thought began to reach Britain in the 1900s. Illegalist and nationalist streams of egoism filtered into England from across the Channel, while Tucker worked to export his philosophical anarchism to England. Marinetti continued to harangue English audiences about an Italian Futurism which was demonstrably influenced by both Stirner's assaults on morality and his own insurrectionary impulses. Illegalists, philosophical anarchists, and Futurists each adopted select aspects of Stirner's thought and abandoned what was incompatible with their beliefs. Stirner's rejection of traditional morality and advocacy of a union of egoists proved popular, while his criticism of idealized liberty and national identity were frequently ignored. In many cases members of these groups were not aware of Stirner's direct influence on their ideas.

---

[14] It is worth pointing out that the 1907 edition of the book was certainly available in the United Kingdom, and that the second edition was published in 1912. An advertisement in the August 1912 number of Emma Goldman's journal, *Mother Earth*, read: "Just out. The long expected new edition of Max Stirner's *The Ego and His Own*. A classic of original revolutionary thought" (vol. 7, no. 6).

When English readers of *The Freewoman* were introduced to Stirner's ideas in 1912, French illegalism was at the peak of its notoriety. The Bonnot Gang began their crime spree in France and Belgium at the end of 1911, and many of their ideas had developed out of the French individualist journal *l'Anarchie* (1906–14), founded by Albert Libertad. After his death in 1908, editorship of the journal had passed to Émile Armand, "a thirty-six-year-old Parisian who had progressed from the Salvation Army, through Tolstoyanism, to individualist anarchism, having read Max Stirner the previous year" (Parry 42). In Europe, Stirner continued to be connected to Nietzsche, and this led many Europeans to perceive the aristocratic qualities of the *Übermensch* in Stirner's egoist. Illegalists, like other groups, generally emphasized what suited them. Ignoring the more complicated aspects of Stirner's thought, they used egoism to characterize crimes as acts of political insurrection, and criminal gangs as unions of egoists.

Stirnerian egoism also proved attractive to a diverse range of intellectuals and artists who desired to free themselves from conventional standards of morality and taste. Using the pseudonym *Saggita*, Mackay continued to campaign for free-love and pederasty, and Stirner's ideas apparently provided a philosophical justification for both. J. Edgar Bauer suggests Mackay's "connections to the intellectuals who gathered around the journal *Der Eigene* (*The Self-Owner*) and later, in 1903, founded *Die Gemeinschaft der Eigenen* ('*The Community of the Self-Owners*')" (7).[15] Taking its name from Stirner's concept of "ownness," *Der Eigene* (1896–1932) was founded as an individualist anarchist journal, but "in 1898, was changed into the first international cultural-homoerotic journal" (Bauer 7).[16] At the same time, Stirner's opposition to convention was taken up by artists soon associated with Paris Dada. Both Francis Picabia and Marcel Duchamp were drawn to Stirner because of his repudiation of objective values. Theresa Papanikolas suggests that in New York in 1913:

> Duchamp had just arrived from Munich, where he had spent months studying Stirner's writings, and his enthusiasm for *The Ego and His Own* and its promise of a world liberated from guiding principles [...] fatefully motivated his friend Picabia to challenge contemporary political and sexual codes, and to abandon his Cubist style for the free personal expressiveness of pure abstraction.
>
> (8)

---

[15] The translations of these titles are Bauer's.
[16] Peter Morgan notes that the name *Der Eigene* "would have been generally recognized among the intellectual circles of social-democratic and left-wing politics as hailing from the early anarchist thinking of Max Stirner, whose take on anarchism had gained a new relevance for those advocating radical change to the norms of sex and sexuality from the 1890s onward" (123).

Stirner's association with individualism, rebellion, and the free-love movement already put him in good standing with revolutionary European artists and bohemians.

By the turn of the twentieth century, authoritarian interpretations of Stirner that emphasized the egoistic leader's absolute ownership of society were also gathering momentum. Barrès had abandoned the egoism inherent in *le culte du moi* for the cause of French national identity.[17] D'Annunzio, Marinetti, and Mussolini further developed this trend, which placed more focus on Stirner's appeals for total ownership than the coexistence of a community of self-interested individuals. Theirs was a Stirner who declared: "Let us not seek the most comprehensive commune 'human society,' but let us seek in others only means and organs which we may use as our property!" (Stirner, *The Ego and Its Own* 275). Marinetti certainly brought this interpretation of egoism with him to England in his lectures, but it was already evident in the work of white nationalists such as Arthur Desmond, whose rhetoric borrowed heavily from the work of Stirner and Nietzsche.[18]

Even thinkers who were more closely associated with anarcho-communism began to consider the revolutionary power of egoism. Emma Goldman had met with Mackay in 1893, and in 1910 she decried "the narrow attitude which sees in Max Stirner naught but the apostle of the theory 'each for himself, the devil take the hind one'" (*Anarchism and Other Essays* 50).[19] Unlike many of her friends and allies, the concept of an aristocracy of the intellect appealed to Goldman, and she certainly sympathized with Stirner's connections to free-love and hedonism. She praised both Nietzsche and Stirner, and suggested that "if society is ever to

---

[17] Two decades later André Breton saw this shift as a betrayal of Barrès's earlier position. Theresa Papanikolas observes that "[o]n May 7, 1921, the Dadaists 'formally' charged Barrès with an 'attack on the security of spirit,' and in doing so they applied their characteristically ironic posture to the more serious, moral issue of preserving commitment to one's beliefs" (148). Barrès had not so much betrayed his earlier beliefs as transitioned toward more nationalistic interpretations of egoism associated with authoritarianism.

[18] The pseudonym Ragnar Redbeard most likely belonged to Arthur Desmond, a secretive white-nationalist possibly born in New Zealand. Desmond associated with several influential Australian politicians and authors including Jack Lang and Henry Lawson, and spent time living in New Zealand, Australia, the United States, and England. His *Might Is Right or The Survival of the Fittest* (1896) remains a mainstay of white-supremacist literature. In 1916 John Erwin McCall published a pamphlet by Ragnar Redbeard titled *The Famous Sayings of Max Stirner* which contained a series of passages from Stirner's book, headed with a swastika.

[19] In his review of *The Ego and His Own* for *Mother Earth* in May 1907, Max Baginski was more measured in his support for Stirner's ideas. He suggested that communists "have certain points of contact with Stirner," but took umbrage with Walker's interpretation of *Der Einzige und sein Eigentum*. He asserted that "J. L. Walker entirely misunderstands the very spirit of Stirner when he states in his Introduction: 'In Stirner we have the philosophical foundation for political liberty.' Stirner has nothing but contempt for political liberty" (147). Baginski was correct to observe Stirner's condemnation of the democratic ideal. For Stirner, freedom was something to be taken, not granted.

become free, it will be so through liberated individuals, whose free efforts make society" (50). Interpretations of Stirner's ideas were as many and varied as the movements associated with them and continued to proliferate throughout the first half of the twentieth century.

English Responses to *The Ego and His Own*

English readers were provided with a cursory introduction to Stirner's ideas in 1898 by John Erwin McCall's self-described "Journal of Egoistic Philosophy," *The Eagle and the Serpent*.[20] In England, Stirner's thought was inevitably associated with Nietzsche's aristocratic philosophy, and this was certainly the case in McCall's journal. Perceptions of Stirner in England at that time were largely confined to a general sense that he was an influence on the thought of Nietzsche—albeit an obscure one.[21] Still, the journal attracted several high-profile contributors, including George Bernard Shaw and the notorious proponent of social Darwinism, Ragnar Redbeard, with the latter providing another instance of the nationalistic interpretation of egoism that had proven popular in France and Italy. At its inception *The Eagle and the Serpent*'s masthead suggested it was "Dedicated to the Philosophy of Life Enunciated by Nietzsche, Emerson, Stirner, Thoreau and Goethe." In reality, early issues were largely an assemblage of Nietzschean aphorisms and related commentary. The journal's first "Course of Study for Beginners in Egoism," for example, consisted entirely of a handful of English articles about Nietzsche. A letter from John Henry Mackay that was published in June 1898 described the situation faced by *The Eagle and the Serpent* quite succinctly. Mackay observed that "[i]t seems to me an impossibility, or rather a curiosity to edit a paper on the philosophy of Egoism and not to know Max Stirner, the founder of the philosophy at all, as you seem to do" ("Benedictions and Maledictions" 47). The few contributions that

---

[20] John Erwin McCall was the pseudonym used by the American activist John Basil Barnhill. The iconography of the powerful eagle and the wise serpent is ancient, with origins in near-eastern mythology, but the title of McCall's journal was lifted straight from the first page of *Also Sprach Zarathustra*: "You have come up here to my cave for ten years: you would have grown weary of your light and of this journey, without me, my eagle and my serpent" (Nietzsche 39).
[21] In England, translations of Nietzsche began to appear from around 1895, well before discussions of Stirner. In contrast, Americans were introduced to Stirner before translations of Nietzsche had become widely available, and his work was considered without the same kind of comparison. In the United States some of the earliest translations of Nietzsche's writings were actually published in *Liberty* following its conversion to egoism.

even mentioned Stirner were, for the most part, responses to articles that had already been published in *Liberty* and *Egoism*.

Widespread discussion of Stirner's writing in England began only after the completion of Byington's English translation of *Der Einzige und sein Eigentum*. In July 1907 the co-editor of *The New Age*, Holbrook Jackson, promoted the newly available translation of Stirner's book in the journal's marginalia. He observed that "[n]ow that Nietzsche has entered the sphere of general discussion it is natural that publishers should find a growing demand for works dealing with the philosophy of Egoism, and Mr. Fifield is doing a service by issuing a translation of Max Stirner's *The Ego and His Own*" (Jackson 188). Jackson went on to propose that the publication of this new translation was part of a broader trend in the United States, suggesting that there was "quite a literature of Egoism in the States," even if it was "not always of the best order" (188). In comparison, "England has had but one consciously and deliberately egoistic journal [...] *The Eagle and the Serpent* and it led a chequered and fitful career in the later eighteen-nineties and the early nineteen-hundreds" (188). Indeed, while *The Eagle and the Serpent* played a role in popularizing Stirner's name among English readers of Nietzsche, the journal did little to spread the substance of Stirner's ideas. The task of introducing English audiences to his thought instead fell to the editors of *The New Age*, Alfred Orage and Jackson, when they printed a review of Stirner in translation in August 1907.

Stirner's assault on secular morality was one of several provocative opinions entertained by Orage and Jackson in the columns of *The New Age*. Controversy for them was a means to stoke intellectual debate and to goad famous authors into contributing to the journal by organizing "spectacular controversies which they could not bear to keep out of" (Carswell 36). Under the stewardship of Orage and Jackson—two men united by a shared interest in *Also sprach Zarathustra* and *Bhagavad Gita*—and with funds provided by George Bernard Shaw, the journal became a theatre for wider debates about new trends in art, literature and political thought.[22] John Carswell observed that "*The New Age* was as much a journal of ideas as of comment, and it chimed with the aspirations of

---

[22] A reference to Max Stirner appeared in the very first number of *The New Age*, in a brief note by Jackson promoting Shaw's essay, *John Bull's Other Island*. Jackson suggested that Shaw "repudiates the allegations so carelessly made that his philosophy is derived from Stirner, Nietzsche, and Schopenhauer, by showing that the ideas of these philosophers are all to be found in our native books; and that they have been imported from Germany neither by himself nor by any other English thinkers" ("Book Notes" 13). There was, however, no such mention of Stirner in Shaw's book.

thousands of individuals and small groups throughout the country who were uncommitted, progressive and for the most part young" (35). Still, Shaw would have been unimpressed to find his money being used to promote *The Ego and His Own*, not to mention Tucker's philosophical anarchism.[23] Tucker secured Shaw's acquiescence by offering him a significant publishing deal.

By 1907 Stirner's supporters in Europe, the United States and England were beginning to work together in order to further the spread of Stirnerian egoism. Tucker went to a considerable effort to ensure that Orage and Jackson would publish a positive appraisal of *The Ego and His Own*. Tucker and Mackay had been in correspondence since 1905, and in July 1907 Tucker reached out with a proposition for the editors of *The New Age*. In 1895 he had paid Shaw to write a hostile review of Max Nordau's *Entartung* (Degeneration, 1892–3) for *Liberty* and he now offered to republish Shaw's essay in the form of a book. Both offers were likely to have involved considerable remuneration from Tucker. Shaw recalled that an outrageous commission was associated with the original article:

> Accordingly, said Mr Tucker, I invite you, Shaw, to ascertain the highest price that has ever been paid to any man, even to Gladstone, for a magazine article; and I will pay you that price for a review of *Degeneration* in the columns of *Liberty*.
>
> (*The Sanity of Art* 11)

The resulting essay was titled *The Sanity of Art*, published as a special issue of *Liberty* on July 27, 1895. This was the first time that Shaw had written specifically for an American publication. Regarding the book deal, he suggested that "Mr Tucker wishes to reproduce his editorial success in a more permanent form, and is strongly seconded by Messrs Holbrook Jackson and A. R. Orage in England" (286). *The Sanity of Art* was accordingly republished by Tucker in 1908, and he used the back-matter as another opportunity to advertise *Liberty* and, of course, *The Ego and His Own*.

The New Age's review of *The Ego and His Own* was probably the first considered appraisal of Stirner's work to be written in England. It contained a discussion of an intellectual kinship between Stirner and Nietzsche but ignored the more

---

[23] In a paper delivered to the Fabian Society in 1891, Shaw devoted significant effort to denouncing the economic practicability of Tucker's individualist anarchism. He suggested that "as a candid, clear-headed, and courageous demonstrator of Individualist Anarchism by purely intellectual methods, Mr Tucker may safely be accepted as one of the most capable spokesmen of his party" ("The Impossibilities of Anarchism" 68).

recent anarchist interpretations of *Der Einzige und sein Eigentum*. Instead, the reviewer opined that "[i]n the absence of a complete translation of the work of Nietzsche (for which, by the way, somebody or other deserves to be shot), we may be grateful for this translation of Nietzsche's John the Baptist" ("The Unique Individual" 250). Focused on Stirner's criticism of abstract values, the review suggested that Stirner "began the enormously difficult task of endeavouring to hammer into the minds of his contemporaries the differences, and sometimes the radical antagonisms between words and realities" (250). Stirner remained relevant to the twentieth-century reader precisely because revolutionary thought had not yet progressed from a reliance upon words that were either ill-defined or entirely meaningless.

By pursuing the logic of *The Ego and His Own*, the reviewer came precariously close to agreement with Stirner's dismissal of the inherent value of political liberty and democracy, and expressed qualified support for his indictment of liberalism's hollow terminology. The review suggested that "[a]t this moment we are all employing words without meaning, and talking of things that have no real existence" ("The Unique Individual" 250). Liberty and democracy, for example, were not the goals of reform, but means to more practical ends. Once deprived of practical context, appeals to liberty, egality, and fraternity ran the risk of collapsing into abstraction. Contemporary appeals to liberty as morally good led the reviewer to conclude that Stirner's "principle of uniqueness is really incompatible with a good deal of the modern talk of reform" (251). Comparing Stirner's indictment of political liberty to Ibsen's observation that Norway "was a land of political liberty peopled by slaves," the reviewer suggested that "[t]he curse of politics is that we confound political liberty with freedom." (251). Political rights were not freedoms, but concessions granted by the tyranny of the state. Democracy only granted "the permission to choose one's masters," and the reviewer proposed that:

> Unless it can be shown (as we hold it can) that the change of mastership is for the better, there would be nothing to say for democracy. On the other hand, unless democracy is regarded merely as a means, its modified tyranny is no less a tyranny than any other despotism.
>
> (251)

The review concluded with a ringing endorsement which suggested Stirner's book was "far too important to be missed by anybody in search of ideas" (251). Such high praise was remarkable, given that *The New Age* was published for an ostensibly Fabian readership.

Tucker tried to forge a connection between *The New Age* and Stirnerian egoism in much the same way that Walker had with *Liberty* in 1887, but he failed to receive ongoing Fabian support. There were only a handful of references to Stirner in *The New Age* between 1907 and 1912, and those which appeared after Tucker republished *The Sanity of Art* were almost universally hostile. A review of Paul Eltzbacher's book, *Anarchism*, in June 1908, suggested that "Stirner was not only a very dull German writer, but he was one of the stupidest of the rationalists" (Randall 114). More charitably, a review of Vernon Lee's *Gospels of Anarchy* a month later described Lee's attempt:

> to reconcile, for the benefit of moderate-minded persons, the claims of those two schools which are carrying on the greatest of all modern controversies—the battle between Liberty and Law, between Anarchist and Moralist, between Stirner-Nietzsche-Ibsenism and the traditional philosophy, of Christendom and the East.
> (Randall 335)[24]

None of this helped win converts to egoism, but it did entrench the notion that Stirner was the progenitor of philosophical anarchism and that he was somehow connected to the ideas of Ibsen and Nietzsche. Oscar Levy further reinforced this perception in October 1911, when he referred to "Caspar Schmidt, better known under his pseudonym of Max Stirner, who in 1845 published—as a Hegelian, if you please—his book, *Der Einzige und sein Eigentum*, which has become the gospel of theoretical Anarchy" (4). By the time that the second edition of *The Ego and His Own* was published in 1912, it was clear that Tucker could no longer expect any sympathy from the editor of *The New Age*.

Tucker seems to have abandoned his first attempt to convert an English publication to egoism by the time that Orage published a vitriolic review of the second edition of *The Ego and His Own* in April 1912. In it, A. E. Randall called Stirner "the first who ever burst into that uproar of self-assertion that is really no more than a trumpeting of truisms" (592). In a line of attack that was more appropriately directed at Walker's deficient interpretation of Stirner's

---

[24] In *Gospels of Anarchy* Lee claimed that Stirner and the other intellectual anarchists were, despite their often bitter rhetoric, the staunchest defenders of systemic order. She suggested: "The professed anarchists under examination, Stirner, Ibsen, Whitman, Brewster, and Barrès, nay (I am sorry to have to tell him so!) Bernard Shaw, are by no means more subversive, in their most intentional subversiveness, than the other apostles who did not dream of preaching or practising intellectual anarchy [...] intellectual anarchy, in short, is greatest among upholders of old religious dogmas or ethics, and the framers of carefully thought-out systems" (Lee 28). She considered Stirner to be the earliest of these systematic opponents of systemic thought. It is telling that she also recognized Barrès's place in this tradition of intellectual anarchy.

book than *Der Einzige und sein Eigentum* itself, Randall mocked: "Here are these poor Anarchists giving away free egos, all warranted to work wonders, and only one of these Unique Ones is allowed by Nietzsche to be unique" (592). Walker's egalitarian interpretation of Stirner's book severely undermined its logical consistency when compared to Nietzsche's overtly aristocratic philosophy. Using quotations from Goethe and Théodule-Armand Ribot, Randall took up another line of attack by suggesting that there was no evidence that the individual ego was singular or unique, and he dismissed Stirner's arguments as mere wordplay. The ego was not a creative force, he suggested, but a mere side-effect of lived experience. Randall concluded that "Stirner's philosophy is simply the philosophy of the possessive case, and the Unique One is only a part of speech masquerading as a psychological entity" (593). If Tucker held any hope for a second positive review of *The Ego and His Own* in *The New Age*, it was dashed by Randall's assault. Nevertheless, another opportunity to secure an English organ of egoism was about to present itself.

From *The Freewoman* to *The Egoist*

It is not difficult to see how Stirnerian egoism appealed to Dora Marsden's personal brand of radical feminism. Maroula Joannou suggests that "Marsden was the archetypal New Woman: a university graduate, intellectual, independent, outspoken, and inventive," but notes that her "responsibility to the individual self (that characterised the New Woman) and the commitment to collective action and change to better the lot of all women [...] met, jostled uncomfortably, and were responsible for many of the contradictions that shaped her life and work" (596). As a New Woman, Marsden frequently found herself at odds with the sometimes-puritanical approach of the mainstream suffragist movement. Joannou describes a tension between "suffragettes who were also interested in exploring a new personal morality and the respectable 'public face of suffragism' that had to be maintained through their publications, which were far more interested in upholding the pieties of the Edwardian women's movement" (597). By 1912, Stirnerian egoism was already being espoused by radical individualists, members of the free love movement, and advocates of pederasty. Mackay and Goldman had already indicated the liberating implications of Stirner's approach to traditional values, and it was a simple matter to use egoism to justify the creation of a new morality which ministered to the New Woman's bourgeoning individuality.

In August 1912 Marsden emerged as a vociferous proponent of *The Ego and His Own*. In an editorial for *The Freewoman* (1911–12) titled "The Growing Ego," she declared:

> We have just laid aside one of the profoundest of human documents, Max Stirner's *The Ego and his Own*. A correspondent has asked us to examine Stirner's doctrine, and shortly we intend to do so. Just now we are more concerned to overcome its penetrative influence on our own minds, by pointing out the abrupt and impossible termination of its thesis rather than to point out its profound truth.
>
> (Marsden 221)

Marsden was a driving force behind *The Freewoman*'s subsequent conversion to an egoistic interpretation of feminism, but the journal had showed growing signs of interest in Stirner's ideas even before Marsden first read *The Ego and His Own*. Several of *The Freewoman*'s contributors—including Rebecca West, Selwyn Weston, and perhaps even Marsden's close friend Grace Jardine—had read Stirner's book months earlier. In fact, one of these three authors was probably the correspondent who recommended *The Ego and His Own* to the journal's editor. Furthermore, Marsden had expressed an interest in philosophical anarchism's attitude to egoism and altruism as early as May 1912. Her conversion was not the result of an epiphany brought about by reading Stirner's book but was rather the product of a continued interest in individualist theories. By the time that she read *The Ego and His Own*, Marsden was already familiar with the concept of egoism as it was used by both Spencer and the philosophical anarchists. Stirner's book became the starting point of a new direction in her necessarily idiosyncratic approach to the relationship between the individual and society.

Marsden had founded *The Freewoman* in 1911 as an alternative to papers backed by the Women's Social and Political Union such as *The Vote* (1909–33) and *Votes for Women* (1907–18). In a later article for *Time and Tide*, Rebecca West suggested:

> She conceived the idea of starting *The Freewoman* because she was discontented with the limited scope of the suffragist movement. She felt that it was restricting itself too much to the one point of political enfranchisement and was not bothering about the wider issues of feminism. I think she was wrong in formulating this feeling as an accusation against the Pankhursts and suffragettes

in general [but] there was certainly a need for someone to stand aside and ponder on the profounder aspects of feminism.

(Marcus 4–5)[25]

From the outset on November 23, 1911, *The Freewoman* espoused an individualistic interpretation of feminism. In her first editorial, Marsden contrasted bondwomen with freewomen and suggested that "Bondwomen are the women who are not separate spiritual entities—who are not individuals" ("Bondwomen," 1). In contrast to the freewoman's fully formed individual personality, bondwomen were described as "complements" who, "[b]y habit of thought, by form of activity, and largely by preference, [...] round off the personality of some other individual, rather than create or cultivate their own" (1). Marsden advanced an exclusive, well-nigh Nietzschean, conception of women's liberation that was far less concerned with political liberties than the intellectual sovereignty of individual women. All but rejecting the claim that "woman is an individual, and that because she is an individual she must be set free," Marsden posited that "[i]t would be nearer the truth to say that if she is an individual she is free, and will act like those who are free" (1). Such rhetoric was a significant departure from the attitude of the Women's Social and Political Union, and *The Freewoman*'s distinctly libertarian tone became increasingly strident with each number.

The first explicit reference to egoism in *The Freewoman* appeared in December, 1911, in a Christmas-themed leading article written by Selwyn Weston titled "A Gospel of Goodwill." It began with a reappraisal of the depiction of egoism in Meredith's, *The Egoist*. It was not Willoughby's egoism, Weston suggested, but rather a lack of conscious egoism that led to his downfall. He proposed that "Willoughby Patterne, so conscious of his Nature's needs, was beaten in the contest for Clara Middleton by nothing but his own obtuseness—the utmost, I believe, of which the man was culpable" (81). As a reading of *The Egoist* it left much to be desired, but this was because Meredith and Weston referred to entirely different conceptions of egoism. Meredith's egoism owed a great deal to Feuerbach's notion of vain self-delusion and little—if anything—to Stirner's insurrectionary selfhood. By comparison, Weston regarded egoism as the genuine motivation for ethical behavior, and considered conscious egoism to be the means by which individuals could liberate themselves from idealized

---

[25] Reproduced in Jane Marcus's introduction to *The Young Rebecca: Writings of Rebecca West 1911–17* (1982).

notions of morality. The remainder of Weston's essay was spent endorsing the cause of conscious egoism. He concluded that "[i]f one may urge a plea in this Christmas season, let it be for a more conscious egoism in place of the pseudo-altruism so prevalent to-day; and if by chance we encompass an act of kindness, let us find no overweening virtue in it, for assuredly there is none" (82). It must have proven a peculiar Christmas message for readers of *The Freewoman*.

Weston confirmed that he knew about Stirner's book in an article published on January 11, but the essay also revealed the limits of Weston's understanding. "Millennium" also included the first direct reference to Stirner found in *The Freewoman*. The essay was primarily concerned with criticizing the writer and composer, Francis Grierson, but Weston soon turned to a consideration of Nietzsche's aristocracy of the intellect, and suggested that "Nietzsche's elaboration of Max Stirner's Superman has his place in the scheme of things, but he is not final" (148). While there were similarities between the immoralism of Stirner and Nietzsche—and a likely line of influence between the two— the *Übermensch* was not an elaboration of the egoist. Stirner was far more interested in various interpretations of the *Unmensch*, or non-human, than any transcendent superhuman ideal. In *Der Einzige und sein Eigentum* he suggested that "Christianity knows only one man, and this one—Christ—is at once an un-man again in the reverse sense, namely a superhuman man [*übermenschlicher Mensch*], a 'God'" (159). Any ideal that claimed to supersede the unique experience of the living individual was anathema to Stirner's egoism. For Stirner "man is nothing else than my humanity, my human existence, and everything that I do is human precisely because *I* do it, not because it corresponds to the concept 'man'" (159). Like many philosophical anarchists, Weston advanced a confused amalgam of fundamentally irreconcilable ideas drawn from the work of Stirner, Nietzsche, Proudhon, and others. He proposed that "[i]t is through the conscious lapse into egoism which leads to the slopes of Superman that Socialism strives to gain the heights of final freedom" (149). Weston did little to clarify Stirner's position for his readers, but was nevertheless a crucial figure in *The Freewoman*'s conversion to egoism.

As a leading member of the Freewoman Discussion Circle, Weston potentially introduced several important feminists to *The Ego and His Own*, including Rebecca West, Grace Jardine, and Dora Marsden herself. A letter from West to Marsden in June 1912 noted Weston's active participation in the meetings, suggesting that "[e]veryone behaves beautifully at the Freewoman Discussion

Circle—it's like being in Church—except Miss Robinson, Mr Weston, and myself" (13). Weston started the discussion on June 19 with a speech on "'Ideas of Freedom,' and his opening was followed by a long and heated debate" ("The Freewoman Discussion Circle" 115). By this time West was already aware of Stirner's book and mentioned it approvingly in a review of June as "anarchic" and "a serious thing" ("Minor Poets" 48). West and Weston were close—there were even rumors that they were romantically involved—and it is likely that Stirner had come up in conversation.[26] In fact, it may have been West who introduced Marsden and Jardine to *The Ego and His Own*.[27] Regardless, Marsden showed an interest in the concept of egoism even before she became aware of Stirner's association with it.

Like many English radicals, Marsden was introduced to the concept of egoism by sources other than Stirner's book. Her earliest references to egoism in *The Freewoman* borrowed from Spencer's interpretation of the word or, at the very least, reflected individualist anarchist notions of egoism and altruism drawn from Spencer's philosophy. In May 1912, the third part of Marsden's series of leading articles on "Interpretations of Sex" provided a philosophical account of sexual intercourse. Marsden rejected her earlier assertion that "the begetting of children was not the purpose of sexual love-passion" and—after a complicated diversion into the nature of passion and utilitarianism—concluded that the purpose of sex was "to get the most out of it, and this 'most' is not an ultimate 'most,' but that which is 'most' to us at our particular individual stage of development" ("Interpretations of Sex" 501-2). Far from providing the final word on the matter of sexual relations, she deferred to the preferences of the individual. Her reasoning was founded on an extension of Spencer's conception of altruism and egoism:

> If a man appears to be leading a life of renunciation, looking joyous about it, one may be certain he is receiving his value's worth. He has given up something he values a little for something he values much more. *All altruism is developed egoism*. All of it which is not is either a pose or a pathetic and pitiful mistake.
>
> (502)

---

[26] Bonnie Kime Scott suggests that "Barbara Low, secretary of the Freewoman Discussion Circles [...] told Mrs. Fairfield (apparently inaccurately) that Rebecca was having an affair with Selwyn Weston" (*Selected Letters* 14).

[27] Kathryn Laing uses a reference to Stirner to date a letter from West to Jardine, suggesting that "[o]ne important clue to corroborate this claim is West's reference, in her letter to Jardine, to a reprint of Max Stirner's *The Ego and His Own*" (237).

Those who found joy in idealized love would pursue it; those who found joy in procreation, carnal pleasure, or abstinence could do likewise. It was part of a broader theory of life that Marsden proposed, based on a refusal "to acquiesce in a convention of life which leaves you dull" (502). Marsden was criticizing the moral puritanism of the Women's Social and Political Union and conventional feminist approaches of the time, but the angle which she took brought her closer to Stirner than Spencer. Like Stirner, she now justified the rejection of societal conventions which did not minister to the individual.

Stirner's influence on Rebecca West was less powerful—and ultimately less destabilizing—than it proved to be on Marsden. West was certainly among the philosophical anarchists who drove changes at *The Freewoman*, but she refused to follow Marsden into what was soon to become the impenetrable depths of her metaphysics. In a letter to Jane Lidderdale in 1967, West recalled that Marsden "developed this extraordinary fusion of religion and William Morris socialism and solipsism and anarchism, and there was something else beside" and "I had simply turned my mind away from the inevitable outcome of what she was, and it was a shock" (West, *Selected Letters of Rebecca West* 405). For West, Stirner was an important figure, but one in a long line of such figures. Stirner's influence on her thought was subtler, and best seen in her frequent criticisms of duty and convention. In an essay on Strindberg published in *The Freewoman* that August, for example, West argued against the duty to remain in an unhappy marriage in distinctly Stirnerian terms:

> The happy marriage, which is the only proper nursery, is indissoluble. The unhappy marriage, which perpetually tells the child a bogey-man story about Life, ought to be dissolved. [...] To submit to unhappiness is the essence of the surrender of personality, which is sin. Submission to poverty is the unpardonable sin against the body. Submission to unhappiness is the unpardonable sin against the spirit.
> ("Strindberg—The English Gentleman" 269)

Here, her initial concern with the damage that unhappy marriages cause to children quickly shifted into an egoistic argument that surrendering happiness to marital duty amounted to a sacrifice of the individual personality to the institution of marriage. She pursued this proposition further in the short story, "Indissoluble Matrimony," which was first published in *Blast* in 1914.[28]

---

[28] West later recalled that the "story was written in my teens to amuse some friends, as a pastiche of the stories Austin Harrison was then publishing in the *English Review*. It was published in *Blast*—a publication of which I knew nothing [...] for no other reason than that Wyndham Lewis found the manuscript in the chest of drawers in the spare room of Violet Hunt & Ford Madox Hueffer's home at Selsey, a week or so after I had left" (West, *Selected Letters of Rebecca West* 119–20).

In "Indissoluble Matrimony," West's depiction of the powerful and self-satisfied Evadne Silverton demonstrates the egoism inherent in the fully formed individuality of the New Woman. The story is told from the perspective of Evadne's husband, a sullen solicitor's clerk named George, who is, in turn, repulsed and captivated by his wife's sensualism and vitality. His disgust is compounded by "the fact that Evadne had, two years after their marriage, passed through his own orthodox Radicalism to a passionate Socialism, and that after reading enormously of economics she had begun to write for the Socialist press and to speak successfully at meetings" (West, "Indissoluble Matrimony" 102). Convincing himself that Evadne is engaged in an affair with the local socialist candidate, George pursues and apparently drowns his wife. Upon returning home, he discovers that she has clearly survived the exchange and is, in fact, sleeping soundly in their marital bed. Only now does George realize that "[h]e had imagined the wonder and peril of the battle as he had imagined his victory" and, in a final demonstration of his triviality, "[s]till sleeping, Evadne caressed him with warm arms" (117). Evadne's ego has thoroughly overwhelmed George. It is not so much that she has won, but that he was never worthy of even being considered an adversary. George lays down beside her, "as he had done every night for ten years, and as he would do every night until he died" (117). He was—and will now indefinitely remain—Evadne's property.

Regardless of whether it was Weston or West who first recommended *The Ego and His Own* to Marsden, the book fundamentally changed her view of the individual's relationship to society. Stirner's thought reverberated through her leading article for *The Freewoman* on August 8. Furthermore, Marsden developed her own form of egoism which continued to guide the general attitude of the journal for the length of her editorship and through two subsequent changes of name. She was immediately astonished by Stirner's book:

> It reads almost like an old man muttering. From point to point Stirner moves on, deposing all things and all powers in order that he may enthrone the Ego. The entire conceptual world, the complete thought-realm he attacks and overcomes and lays at the feet of the Ego.
>
> ("The Growing Ego" 222)

Her main doubt about the book was that Stirner had not yet proceeded far enough in his conclusions. She suggested that "if the Ego needs the realisation in itself of morality, or religion, or God, then, by virtue of its own supremacy, the realisation will be forthcoming" (222). God, religion, and morality were not enemies of the self, but products of the self's desire for expansive control. Unlike the philosophical anarchists, Marsden understood the implications that Stirner's thought had for anarchism. Stirner's thesis demolished the foundation of anarchist principles of liberty, justice, and equality as readily as it demolished the foundations of religion. The natural development of *Der Einzige und sein Eigentum* was not anarchism, but "archism"—total rulership.

Although she recognized that anarchist notions of liberty could not survive Stirner's criticisms, Marsden does not seem to have recognized the full implications of his egoism either. Her suggestion that the individual might create and own morals—even gods—was already addressed at length by Stirner in *Der Einzige und sein Eigentum*. It was Walker and Tucker who conceived of egoism as a struggle between the unique individual and society. Stirner went much further than this, conceiving of the material and conceptual world as a creation of the ego. By Stirner's logic there was no external otherness to struggle against. The state, society, humanity, even other individuals, were not external beings—at least not in any conceivable sense—but creations of the unique ego. Their capacity to dominate stemmed from the ego's failure to recognize itself as creator of all values. Stirner proposed that "I am not nothing in the sense of emptiness, but I am the creative nothing, the nothing out of which I myself as creator create everything" (*The Ego and Its Own* 7). Stirner certainly seemed to allow for the existence of matter, but matter only became meaningful when it was possessed by the individual. There was no question that the unique could create moralities or gods, but there was no point to creating gods beholden to the will of their creator. In the 1920s, Marsden's continued belief that the ego might realize itself in a more Nietzschean sense through the creation and delineation of God eventually led her away from egoism and into the realm of mysticism.

The Freewoman ran out of funding just as it was beginning its transformation into England's foremost organ of philosophical egoism. Its final number was published on October 10, 1912. The editorial, co-written by Marsden and Jardine, suggested that "[e]fforts have been made to bring out this issue in order to make clear to our friends something of the developments in the present financial situation—a situation which has confronted us with a suddenness equal to that which it must have for them" ("Our Last Issue" 401). It appealed for funding from its readership so that the journal might be revived at a later date. Money was eventually secured from Harriet Shaw Weaver, and the journal was relaunched in June 1913 as *The New Freewoman: An Individualist Review*. Ashford suggests that *The New Freewoman* represented "the concerted attempt on Marsden's part to apply her highly individual interpretation of Stirnerian egoism to every aspect of contemporary culture" (59). In the interim Benjamin Tucker had evidently become aware of Marsden's conversion to egoism. From the first number of *The New Freewoman* Tucker was a regular contributor to the journal. Within a matter of months, however, he and Marsden were at odds about the compatibility of egoism and anarchism.

From September 1913 to its subsequent rebranding as *The Egoist* in January 1914, *The New Freewoman* became host to a broader contest between Marsden, Tucker, and another regular contributor, Ezra Pound, for control of the future direction of the journal. David Moody observes that "Miss Marsden had been put on her guard by Rebecca West against Pound's looking to take over her review, and was quite justifiably suspicious of his intentions" (218). There are many accounts of this conflict, and in *Autarchies* David Ashford has already examined its implications for the spread of Stirnerian egoism. While a great deal has been made of Pound's attempt to seize control of the journal and turn it into a vehicle for Imagist poetry, at the time Marsden's attention was more firmly focused on her sallies with Tucker and Byington. Ashford observes that "in a series of arguments conducted across the correspondence and editorial sections of *The New Freewoman* and *The Egoist*, Marsden would take Tucker and Byington to task for failing to understand the full implications of Stirnerian egoism" (Ashford 60). Unlike Tucker and the philosophical anarchists, Marsden recognized that egoism was fundamentally incompatible with anarchism. In November 1913 she proposed in her "Views and Comments" editorial column that "[w]e frankly do not understand why Mr. Tucker, an egoist, and Stirner's English publisher, does not see the necessity of clearing current language of padding as a preliminary of egoistic investigation" (204). She went on to compare Proudhon's writings to "the workings of a private telephone, lucid and clear for respectable intervals, then a buzz which churns into one's head for quite long spells until one is tempted to put up the receiver—or close the book" (204). It was a deliberate provocation directed at Proudhon's English translator, intended to force him to choose between Stirner and Proudhon.

The name of the journal changed a final time to *The Egoist* in January 1914. In her editorial comments Marsden observed that a letter had been received by *The New Freewoman* from Allen Upward, Ezra Pound, Huntly Carter, Reginald W. Kauffmann, and Richard Aldington, asking her to "consider the advisability of adopting another title which will mark the character of your paper as an organ of individualists of both sexes, and of the individualist principle in every department of life" ("Views and Comments" 244). There is no reason to suggest that the choice of name was the result of this interference, but the letter may have been just the push that Marsden needed to shift the direction of the journal more openly toward egoism. Indeed, later in the editorial she used the change to further attack Tucker. Marsden suggested that "[t]he moment when we propose attaching to ourselves a new label seems the right one to answer an objection raised by a contributor, Mr. Benj. R. Tucker, in the present issue against a former statement that we 'stand for nothing'" (244). It was now clear that Marsden stood for egoism, but only on her own terms. She continued that "[t]he irony of 'standing for' a thing lies in the fact that the first return the thing stood for makes is to bring its advocates kneeling before it" (244). This was a typically Stirnerian position to take, and the fact that she leveraged her understanding of egoism against Tucker must have added insult to injury.

On March 16, 1914, Tucker finally cut his ties with Marsden's journal. He left with a whimper, suggesting that "[y]our comments on my letter to you (which was written by the way, not to attack you for being an Archist, but to excuse myself for ceasing to co-operate with you) show a most ludicrous misapprehension of the Anarchist position" (Tucker, "Why not put up the Shutters?" 118).[29] Ashford suggests that "Marsden had succeeded in persuading this early advocate of Stirner that he had been very wrong to think the philosophy compatible with more humanitarian forms of anarchist revolt" (Ashford 61–2). In an issue containing poetry, fiction, and articles by Joyce, Pound, and Williams Carlos Williams, Marsden's response to Tucker was one of the most fully realized statements of modernist rebellion to date:

We are sorry that *The Egoist*'s mottled label should so worry and—we fear—irritate Mr. Tucker. Irresistibly one thinks of the old song:
"By what name shall I greet her?
How shall I know her voice?"

---

[29] On March 2, 1914, Marsden observed that "one who is perhaps the best-known living exponent of Anarchism and hitherto an unwearying friend of *The Egoist* has informed us that we are not Anarchist" ("Views and Comments" 84). She added that "[i]f to be an Archist is to be what we are, then we prefer Archism to Anarchism which presumably would necessitate our being something different" (84). Tucker's suggestion was that Marsden did not stand for liberty but the political power of the individual. Tucker's criticism of Marsden's egoism effectively marked his own break with Stirner's ideas.

Perhaps if we made a few statements we might help matters somewhat.

1. We refuse to answer to "Rebel."
2. We *prefer* not to be called "Pragmatist."
3. We may not—according to Mr. Tucker—be called "Anarchist"—wherein we are quite willing to acquiesce.
4. We respond readily to "Egoist," and beg it be observed that throughout this battle about nomenclature, the "voice" remains the same: and that a well-meaning person could distinguish it anywhere.

("Why not put up the Shutters?" 118)

This series of numbered declarations belongs alongside the polemics in *Blast* as an example of the capacity of the manifesto to advance the cause of egoism. Marsden's use of the editorial "we" is almost indistinguishable from that of the egoistic manifesto writer. In this series of powerful statements, she demonstrated her control over the direction of the journal. Pound had not so much taken control of *The Egoist* as Marsden had imbued English modernism with the characteristic of Stirnerian revolt. Marsden's editorials and responses to her critics in the final number of *The New Freewoman* and first number of *The Egoist* were some of the earliest examples of openly egoistic polemical writing in English modernism.

Here the history of Stirner's reception once again intersects with the development of the modern literary manifesto. Marsden's editorial repudiation of Tucker's anarchism in favor of an idiosyncratic interpretation of Stirnerian egoism demonstrated the hallmarks of the modern manifesto, even if it stopped short of calling itself one. In attempting to formulate her own egoistic position Marsden had almost unconsciously fallen into the rhythms of the manifesto. In less than six months, Wyndham Lewis would produce the first volume of *Blast*, unleashing a torrent of manifestos directly informed by the thought of Stirner. In the work of Wyndham Lewis, the various threads of Stirner's reception terminated at a single point. Self-educated in the bohemian circles of Paris, a brief proponent of Marinetti's Futurism, and part of the modernist circle gathered around *The Egoist*, Lewis was uniquely placed to create the most self-consciously egoistic manifestos to be written before the First World War.

5

England: From Imagism to Vorticism

Wyndham Lewis was certainly not England's first manifesto writer, but English polemics that included the word manifesto in their title before 1914 tended to be narrowly political or stylistically dull. Nevertheless, by the time that the first manifestos of *Blast* were published in July 1914 English authors had already made innovative contributions to the field of literary polemic through works that eschewed—or rejected outright—the label of manifesto. In her anthology *Manifesto* (2001), for example, Mary Ann Caws includes James Abbott McNeil Whistler's famous "Ten O'Clock lecture" (1885) and two of Oscar Wilde's essays, "The Poets and the People: By One of the Latter" (1887) and the preface to *The Picture of Dorian Gray* (1891).[1] Whistler and Wilde were both associated with the Symbolist milieu in Paris, and through it had connections to intellectual aristocratism, anarchism and—if only indirectly in 1885—the newly arriving egoism of Stirner. As Caws points out, "[i]t was Mallarmé, Whistler's close friend, who, with the poets Francis Viélé-Griffin and George Moore, translated" Whistler's lecture "into French and helped to spread its renown" (2). There were other English pioneers in literary polemic, too, but early instances of the modern use of manifesto were far less innovative.[2] One such example was a tract written by George Bernard Shaw in 1884, which purported to be "A Manifesto" for

---

[1] While it is hard to know what Wilde knew of Stirner, it is worth pointing out that on at least two occasions he "explicitly referred to himself as an anarchist" (Goodway 75), and that he would have been aware of recent developments in the pederasty movement. There is certainly a Stirnerian aspect to Wilde's characterization of individuality being subsumed by possessions in "The Soul of Man under Socialism" (1891): "Private property has crushed true Individualism, and set up an Individualism that is false. It has debarred one part of the community from being individual by starving them. It has debarred the other part of the community from being individual by putting them on the wrong road, and encumbering them. Indeed, so completely has man's personality been absorbed by his possessions that the English law has always treated offences against a man's property with far more severity than offences against his person, and property is still the test of complete citizenship" (13).
[2] The mission statement found at the end of several volumes of the Pre-Raphaelite journal, *The Germ* (1850) is another example of the kind of works that should be considered as part of a broader English tradition of literary treatise.

the Fabian movement. Another "Fabian Manifesto" was written by Edward R. Pease, and it appeared in *The New Age* in November 1907, only months after the journal's first positive review of Stirner's book. Pease's manifesto was little more than an essay declaring the Fabian Society's position on privatizing the railways. By comparison Shaw's manifesto was strongly influenced by the work of Marx and Engels, but exhibited only the occasional glimmer of his usual wit:

> That the most striking result of our present system of farming out the national Land and Capital to private individuals has been the division of Society into hostile classes, with large appetites and no dinners at one extreme, and large dinners and no appetites at the other.
>
> (Shaw, "A Manifesto" np)

None of these works included numbered demands, gave the impression of collaborative authorship, or declared the founding of a radical new movement. These elements of manifesto writing only appeared in England after the translation of *Der Einzige und sein Eigentum*. There were, however, more direct precedents to the manifestos in *Blast*, and these had numerous connections to the reception of Stirner's book.

Several Imagist programs, including those by Pound, had circumstantial links to the spread of Stirnerian egoism. Pound was the ostensible leader of the Imagists in 1913, and even before he worked with Marsden he was espousing radical individualism and intellectual aristocratism. Once he became involved with Marsden's journal the connections between Imagism and egoism became more concrete. From the second half of 1913 references to Pound's school of poetry began to regularly appear in *The New Freewoman* and *The Egoist*. The first of these was an article by Rebecca West titled "Imagisme" that was published in *The New Freewoman* that August. West's piece quoted extensively from Frank Stuart Flint's essay of the same name, as well as from Pound's "A Few Don'ts by an Imagiste," both of which were originally published in the American journal *Poetry* in March 1913. A comparison of Pound's approach to manifesto writing before and after his contact with Stirnerian egoism hints at the importance of Stirner's ideas to the development of the manifesto in English modernist circles.

Pound first introduced American readers to Imagism in January 1913, when he discussed the new movement in an editorial for Harriet Monroe's Chicago-based journal, *Poetry* (1912–). Writing from London and maintaining an illusion of distance from what was fundamentally his movement, Pound observed that "[t]he youngest school here that has the nerve to call itself a school is that of the Imagistes" ("Status Rerum" 126). Imagism borrowed heavily from French Symbolism, but replaced the symbol—along with its associated notion of suggestion through correspondence—with the supposedly more precise concept of the image. Even the Gallicization of *Imagisme* reflected the extent of the French movement's influence on the new school. Pound differentiated Imagism by its focus on technical competence:

> Space forbids me to set forth the program of the Imagistes at length, but one of their watchwords is Precision, and they are in opposition to the numerous and unassembled writers who busy themselves with dull and interminable effusions, and who seem to think that a man can write a good long poem before he learns to write a good short one, or even before he learns to produce a good single line.
>
> (126)

At the very least, Imagists seemed to reject a dogmatic approach to aesthetics, and Pound suggested that "[t]o belong to a school does not in the least mean that one writes poetry to a theory" (126). Readers of *Poetry* would have to wait until March for a meaningful explanation of what was meant by the word image in this context.

Ironically, Flint observed in "Imagisme"—a work which set out the tenets of the movement—that Imagism had no manifesto. While he set forth three numbered rules for would-be Imagists, he denied any comparison to revolutionary art movements such as Futurism.³ He suggested:

> The Imagistes admitted that they were contemporaries of the Post Impressionists and the Futurists; but they had nothing in common with these schools. They had not published a manifesto. They were not a revolutionary school; their only endeavor was to write in accordance with the best tradition, as they found it in the best writers of all time,—in Sappho, Catullus, Villon.
>
> (Flint 199)

This program actively rejected the label of manifesto. Flint further differentiated "Imagisme" from the Futurist manifestos by refusing to acknowledge his connection to the movement. In contrast to the repeated use of "I" and "we" in Marinetti's manifestos, Flint and Pound maintained a façade of distance, and referred to the Imagists as though they were not members of the group. Even

---

³ Flint's three rules were:
  1. Direct treatment of the "thing," whether subjective or objective.
  2. To use absolutely no word that did not contribute to the presentation.
  3. As regarding rhythm: to compose in sequence of the musical phrase, not in sequence of a metronome (Flint 199).

in writing down the rules of the movement for publication, Flint maintained that the Imagists "had a few rules, drawn up for their own satisfaction only, and they had not published them" (199). The effect was a confected disinterest that correlated with Imagism's position that poetry was a science. It was no less a posture than Marinetti's bluster and swagger.

In some respects, "Imagisme" was a real example of what Martin Puchner calls "rear-guardism" in *Poetry of the Revolution* (2006). There, he suggests that "[r]ear-guardism, which culminates in Lewis but includes a wider range of figures, is a defensive formation that places itself within the field of advancement but is sceptical of its most extreme practitioners; it seeks to correct and contain the avant-garde's excess without falling behind and losing touch with it entirely" (108). Lewis's Vorticism was, much like Marinetti's Futurism, not so much a rear-guard action as an effort to reconcile egoistic will and collective might. Without recourse to Stirner's notion that the collective was in fact the property of the individual, Flint and Pound seem to have rejected the manifesto as a product of revolutionary dogmatism. After being forced to account for Marsden's egoism, however, Pound evidently shifted his opinion enough to become a signatory to the Vorticist manifesto—and contributed a manifesto of his own to *Blast*.

"The Serious Artist"

Nevertheless, there were aspects of Pound's Imagism which helped account for his subsequent transition to Vorticism, with its clear debt to egoism. On a personal level, Moody suggests that Pound's instincts "were all for an exclusive élite of superior individuals like himself" (215). Like Marsden and Stirner, "[h]e too would have the young learn to say 'I,' and to go in fear of conventions and abstractions and clichés" (Moody 220). These attitudes about the relationship between the individual artist and society found their way into the content of "A Few Don'ts by an Imagiste." Like Stirner, Pound warned against abstract concepts, and proposed that prospective poets should "[g]o in fear of abstractions" ("A Few Don'ts by an Imagiste" 201). He even cautioned against dogmatism in the context of Imagism itself:

> To begin with, consider the three rules recorded by Mr. Flint, not as dogma—never consider anything as dogma—but as the result of long contemplation, which, even if it is some one else's contemplation, may be worth consideration.
>
> (201)

For the first time Pound also attempted to clarify what Imagists meant by the term image, and he suggested that "[a]n 'Image' is that which presents an intellectual and emotional complex in an instant of time" (200). As a presentation of the subjective psychological experience, the image begins to resemble the "unspeakable self" which Lanson had seen as Mallarmé's debt to Stirner.

David Ashford suggests just how similar Imagist poetry must have initially appeared to Marsden's own egoistic aspirations for art. He observes that "the poems that Pound submitted to her journal must in themselves have seemed the most perfect vindication of her own hopes for the medium; a new mode of poetry that would represent that psychological process whereby the mind converts an object into Idea" (Ashford 77). If Pound did not see himself as an egoist, Marsden may nonetheless have seen nascent egoism in Pound. She invited him to justify his vision of poetry in the form of a leading article titled "The Serious Artist," the first instalment of which was published in October 1913. This article forced Pound to theorize about poetry in a way he generally avoided on principle, and at this hurdle he faltered:

> I take no great pleasure in writing prose about aesthetic. I think one work of art is worth forty prefaces and as many apologiæ. Nevertheless I have been questioned earnestly and by a person certainly of good will. It is as if one said to me: what is the use of open spaces in this city, what is the use of rose-trees and why do you wish to plant trees and lay out parks and gardens?
>
> ("The Serious Artist" 161)

Pound spent the rest of the article grappling with an argument that poetry was as much of a science as chemistry, and that the serious artist provided data necessary for understanding human nature. Marsden described the exercise as "agnosticism and the vague waving of hands" ("The Art of the Future" 182).

While Marsden was clearly unmoved by "The Serious Artist," the article revealed a significant effort on Pound's part to fuse intellectual aristocratism, psychological realism, and technical precision into a coherent approach to art. Partly due to Marsden's prompting, Pound seems to have developed a theory—though he would have suggested a *science*—of art which nonetheless accommodated elements of egoism. The subject of art was still Imagism's direct treatment of the "thing," but the thing in question was now a fluctuation of the individual artist's ego, and "[t]he serious artist is scientific in that he presents the image of his desire, of his hate, of his indifference as precisely that, as precisely the image of his own desire, hate or indifference" ("The Serious Artist" 163).

The serious artist, Pound suggested, did not commit the error of presenting false universalities where there were none. Art provided the measure of humanity, but the measure was the individual:

> The permanent property, the property given to the race at large is precisely these data of the serious scientist and of the serious artist; of the scientist as touching the relations of abstract numbers, of molecular energy, of the composition of matter, etc.; of the serious artist, as touching the nature of man, of individuals.
>
> (163)[4]

Pound suggested that the antithesis of the serious artist was the theorist, a person who erroneously attempts to draw conclusions about humanity from the work of the artist. The fact that Marsden seems to fit Pound's idea of a theorist surely contributed to her nonplussed response to his essay. He proposed that "[t]he theorist, and we see this constantly illustrated by the English writers on sex, the theorist constantly proceeds as if his own case, his own limits and predilections were the typical case, or even as if it were the universal" (163). Such a theorist was certainly an egoist, but in Feuerbach's sense of mistaking personal limitations for universal ones.

Marsden's eagerness to respond may have caused her to dismiss Pound's equivocations too easily. Pound was suggesting that the finest achievement of the serious artist was the accurate presentation of a sliver of the self. In contrast, Marsden proposed:

> all the senses are senses of touch, i.e., contact—the impinging of organised life upon the things foreign to itself; the shiver of difference, and the shrinking where the "I" is touched by the "not I"—suggestions merely, indicative of the things which await the insight of the artists of the future. To delineate these things is the work of art. In music, painting and sculpture to project them afresh in analogues of sound, colour and contortion; in drama in their hurtling against each other; in these arts, presented; in poetry, the highest manifestation of self-consciousness, *re*-presented in terms of self-recognised emotion.
>
> ("The Art of the Future" 183)

For his part, Stirner would not have abided the notion that the ego might in any way be "touched" by the non-ego. It was a view much closer to the dialectical egoism of Fichte and Proudhon than Stirner's radical conception of the self

---

[4] Pound's use of "property" in what appears to be a twofold sense of characteristic and possession—as well as a lingering preoccupation with "abstract" relations and the individual nature of collective "man"—also invites further comparison to Stirner's thought. Recall that a more accurate translation of *Der Einzige und sein Eigentum* is: "The Unique Individual and Its Property."

as the source of meaningful reality.⁵ Marsden's desire to demonstrate Pound's philosophical shortcomings led her to make a greater blunder, and slip from Stirnerian egoism into an idealization of the ego. Compare Stirner's defense of artistic creation in *Der Einzige und sein Eigentum*:

> But not only not for your sake, not even for truth's sake either do I speak out what I think. No:
>
> I sing as the bird sings
> That on the bough alights;
> The song that from me springs
> Is pay that well requites.
>
> I sing because—I am a singer. But I *use* you for it because I—need ears.
>
> (263)

Stirner's concept of the egoist only survived his own critique by absorbing all of reality into itself. He only allowed for the meaningful existence of the non-I in so far as it was a product of the ego. After all, the ego was the "creative nothing" which created everything—including the "non-I"—out of an instinctual desire to live itself out. Pound was closer to Stirner's own position regarding the subject of art, and the more convincing, if unconscious, egoist as a result.

The conflict between Marsden and Pound in *The New Freewoman* therefore (perhaps paradoxically) marked yet another juncture in the reception of Stirner's thought in England. Marsden went on to devote decades to the task of reintegrating abstract concepts into the very hierarchies that were shattered by *Der Einzige und sein Eigentum*. Stirner had proposed that God was a creation of the individual ego and governed only as a fixed idea—a spook. In 1913 Marsden was already hinting at a desire to restore God to her throne. Ashford observes that "Marsden can be seen to break with Stirner—and on precisely the issue she had anticipated in 1912 [...] that is to say, her superhuman ego *is* whatever absolute it can define and realize, and not nothing" (70). This was not an advance on Stirner's thought, but a regression born from the idealization of the self. Marsden went on to dedicate the first volume of her philosophical masterwork, *The Definition of the Godhead* (1928), to "Her, Heaven, The Mighty Mother of

---

⁵ Recall Proudhon's conception of the self, which has already been noted for its influence on Maurice Barrès's *culte du moi*: "Moi, c'était tout ce que je pouvais toucher de la main, atteindre du regard, et qui m'était bon à quelque chose; non-moi était tout ce qui pouvait nuire ou résister à moi" ("I was all I could touch with my hand, reach with my gaze, and that was good for something; not-I was all that could harm or resist me"; my trans.; *De la justice dans la révolution et dans l'Église* 209–10).

All." In the book she suggested that "all that 'abstraction' implies is a narrowing of the attention upon a part of a sensorily-apprehended complex in preference to the entire complex whole" (38). Marsden's egoism had collapsed into a dense mixture of philosophy, theology, and metaphysics. In 1935 she was admitted to Crichton Royal Hospital after a psychological breakdown. Pound was similarly admitted to St Elizabeth's Hospital in Washington D.C. for treatment ten years after her. Unlike him, Marsden would spend the rest of her life in care.

The failure of "The Serious Artist" to satisfy Marsden's demands in 1913 clearly did not cause Pound to refute egoism entirely. On the contrary, it seems to have pushed him to further develop his conception of the individual artist. In this regard, Ashford makes a stronger case than Moody for connecting the ideas of Pound, Marsden, and Stirner. He suggests that "Pound's failure to theorize his Modernist practice did not mean an immediate end to the Imagist presence at *The Egoist* (far from it): and there is even evidence to suggest that the two components within the journal, Marsden's egoism and Pound's Imagism, began to impact upon each other from this point on" (Ashford 79). In 1844 Stirner had forced Marx to account for the role of individual will in his theory of materialism, and now Marsden had forced Pound to engage with the role of egoism in modernist aesthetics. In both cases the result was a shift toward manifesto writing. From 1913 Pound's aristocratic individualism diverged further from Marsden's increasingly metaphysical approach to egoism but seems to have retained something of Stirner's more absolute egoism. In addition, Pound was now working with Wyndham Lewis, who was also engaging with Stirner's ideas at that time.

The Vortex as Ego

There is evidence to suggest that Lewis may have been aware of Stirner's thought well before Pound, and perhaps even before the publication of *The Ego and His Own* in 1907. While his approach to egoism is usually understood in the context of the contemporary vogue for Stirner in England in 1914, it is more likely that Lewis's first encounters with Stirner's ideas occurred on the Continent between 1904 and 1908. By most accounts the teenaged Lewis was an idle and mildly rebellious student with a remarkable talent for art but little else. After disappointing the schoolmasters at Rugby with his indolence, and being expelled outright from the Slade School in 1901, he spent much of his twenties traveling Europe in pursuit of intellectual and recreational interests.

Paul Edwards describes this period as "seven years of self-indulgent study and travel in Europe as an aspiring painter, supported by his mother and occasional subventions from his father's family" (9). By 1908 Lewis had become a typical example of the English expatriate bohemian in Europe:

> [H]e had the education that European travel provided, and his dormant intellect had been awakened to the current of anti-positivist thinking that flowed through the Paris of his student days. He read Nietzsche and Dostoyevsky in French translations, attended lectures by Henri Bergson and studied his writings. He also knew of George Sorel, syndicalism and the Action Française movement.
> (Edwards 9–10)[6]

Such an education was likely to have included some acquaintance with *l'unique et sa propriété*, given Stirner's perceived connection to many of the movements and individuals Edwards mentions. Although he proposes that "Stirner probably had little lasting influence on Lewis," Edwards acknowledges that Stirner's "influence in Paris during Lewis's student days had been even more important" than his English reception in the following decade (157). When Lewis refers to Stirner's book in *Blast* there is little reason to conclude that he had only just become acquainted with his ideas. The fact that Lewis described "Der Einige und Sein Eigenkeit" by "Stirnir" lying open in his protagonist's student lodgings in Germany may even obliquely suggest the conditions in which he first encountered Stirner's book ("The Enemy of the Stars" 76).[7]

Between returning home from his studies in Europe and the formation of Vorticism, Lewis became a brief but influential champion of Marinetti's Futurism. In 1910 he was back in England, and Marinetti had begun his efforts to win English artists over to his movement. Paul O'Keeffe observes that "[i]t is not known whether Lewis attended" Marinetti's first lecture at the Lyceum Club in 1910, "but it was to be another year or so before he had direct dealings with Marinetti beyond their

---

[6] In the absence of a definitive account of Lewis's reading habits, speculation about his studies seems to have produced an impressive list of European intellectuals. Geoffrey Wagner singled out Benda and Paul Bourget—Barrès's mentor—as influences on Lewis, and most biographers suggest that T. E. Hulme introduced Lewis to the art theorist Wilhelm Worringer.

[7] Lewis regularly incorporated his experiences abroad in his early writing, most notably in *Tarr* (1916–17). He certainly traveled to Munich as a student in 1906, though the reference to Stirner in "The Enemy of the Stars" takes place in Berlin. It is impossible to be sure if the book's mangled and ungrammatical title was an intentional act of parody, the product of sloppiness, or something more ambiguous. It is hard to know what to make of Lewis's use of *Einige* (few) instead of *Der Einzige* (the unique). Perhaps he is indicating the plurality of the author's self which is discussed later in this chapter. The use of *Eigenkeit* (characteristics) instead of *Eigentum* (property) suggests more may be at play here than mere typographical error.

coincidental proximity in *The Tramp*" (97).[8] At the same time that Marinetti was laying siege to the English art scene, Lewis was establishing himself as one of its key innovators. By 1912 "Lewis had undergone a remarkable development, from a poet and writer of occasional prose pieces to an artist whose work wrenched critical attention away from acres of other men's canvas in the Albert Hall or wherever it was shown" (O'Keeffe 121). That March an exhibition of thirty-five Futurist paintings was shown at the Sackville Gallery, but in 1913 Marinetti mounted a far more successful propaganda campaign in England that directly involved Lewis.

In 1913 Harold Monro dedicated a significant portion of the September number of his journal, *Poetry and Drama*, to Futurist writing. Poetry by the Imagist, Flint, appeared alongside Futurist poems by Paolo Buzzi, Aldo Palazzeschi, and Marinetti. More importantly the journal published a translation of one of Marinetti's manifestos, "Wireless Imagination and Words at Liberty: The New Futurist Manifesto." Monro suggested in the editorial:

> It may surprise, it may even shock, some of our readers that we devote the principal space of a whole number of *Poetry and Drama* to the publication of matter in a certain degree representative of a term at present closely, in fact almost exclusively, associated with that group of young Italian rebels led by the famous Marinetti.
>
> (262)

Monro went so far as to propose that "we claim ourselves, also, to be futurists" (262). Crucially, in "The New Futurist Manifesto" Marinetti explicitly connected Futurism to the Stirnerian illegalism of Jules Bonnot. The fourth declaration called for "[d]estruction of the feeling of *the beyond*, and increased value of the individual who, according to Bonnot's expression, must *vivre sa vie*" (Marinetti, "The New Futurist Manifesto" 320). The quote from Bonnot was in turn drawn from Stirner's suggestion that the egoist "lives himself out, careless of how well or ill humanity may fare thereby" (*The Ego and Its Own* 323). In seeking English converts to the cause, Marinetti and the other Futurists apparently made no effort to conceal their connections to illegalism and, as a result, the thought of Stirner.

Within months of the Futurist filibuster in *Poetry and Drama*, Marinetti returned to London to harangue English audiences once again. On November 18, a Futurist dinner was held in his honor. O'Keeffe points out that "Christopher

---

[8] Marinetti and Lewis both had their work published in the same volume of Douglas Goldring's journal, *The Tramp*, in 1910. O'Keeffe observes that Lewis's short story, "'A Breton Innkeeper,' shared the pages of the August issue with a translation of Filippo Tommaso Marinetti's first Futurist Manifesto" (97).

Nevinson organised the dinner, aided and abetted by Lewis" (139). At this stage Lewis clearly identified with the Futurist movement, and "there may even have been some rivalry between the two Englishmen when it came to greeting their celebrated guest" (O'Keeffe 139). Marinetti's visit culminated in an extravagant ball held at the Albert Hall, where the Private Secretary to Winston Churchill, Edward Marsh, paraded in a Futurist costume designed by Lewis himself.

Lewis's recent split with Roger Fry's Omega Workshop may have contributed to his willingness to be associated with Marinetti's Futurists at the end of 1913. Indeed, the grouping of artists that evolved into the Vorticist movement seems to have begun as a retributive attempt by Lewis to organize against Fry, after falling out with him over a commission offered by the *Daily Mail* in October 1913.[9] At the outset, philosophical concerns seem to have been secondary to the formation of a group of talented artists affiliated with the newly formed Rebel Art Centre at 38 Great Ormond Street. The studio space was paid for by Kate Lechmere, and by this time Lewis had begun collaborating with Pound. Together, the two men conceived a more revolutionary union of artists. Pound was in the midst of his debate with Marsden about the future of art and was becoming increasingly disenchanted with the possibilities afforded by Imagism. O'Keeffe suggests that "Lewis and Pound had first encountered one another at the Vienna Café near the British Museum, probably in late 1908 and in the company of their respective mentors: Sturge Moore and Laurence Binyon" (143). It was Pound who supplied the defining concept of the vortex, and with it an opportunity to take control of the direction of English art through a simultaneous insurrection against the Omega Workshop, Imagism, Futurism, and even the British Academy.

Lewis's now necessary break with Futurism precipitated when Nevinson and Marinetti attached the names of Atkinson, Bomberg, Epstein, Etchells, Hamilton, Wadsworth, and Lewis as signatories to the Futurist manifesto, "Vital English Art." O'Keeffe suggests that there was already "a growing realisation that if the English movement, based at 38 Great Ormond Street and led by Lewis, was to gain any credibility at all, it would not be under Marinetti's welcoming banner" (153). Nevinson's apparently unilateral attempt to characterize the Rebel Art Centre as

---

[9] In July an agent of the *Daily Mail* specifically invited Spencer Gore, Lewis, and Fry to provide decorations for an upcoming Ideal Home Exhibition. The invitation did not reach Lewis before Fry had reduced Lewis's role to the carving of a mantelpiece. He responded by storming out and penning a scathing letter, signed by Etchells, Hamilton, and Wadsworth, in which he wrote of Omega: "As to its tendencies in Art, they alone would be sufficient to make it very difficult for any vigorous art-instinct to long remain under that roof. The Idol is still prettiness, with its mid-Victorian languish of the neck, and its skin is 'greenery-yallery,' despite the Post-What-Not fashionableness of its draperies" (*Letters of Wyndham Lewis* 49).

the English branch of Marinetti's movement was a typical example of the egotistical power plays and shifting allegiances that dominated this union of egoists. Stirner's thought provided a means to rally against Marinetti's attempt to claim them as Futurists, but petty conflicts frequently boiled over into threats of violence. Lewis recalled some of these conflicts in *Blasting and Bombardiering* (1937):

> Gaudier [Brzeska] was spoiling for a fight. He threatened at Ford's to sock Bomberg on the jaw, and when I asked him why, he explained that he had an imperfect control over his temper, and he must not be found with Bomberg, for the manner adopted by that gentleman was of a sort that put him beside himself [...] On the other hand I seized Hulme by the throat; but he transfixed me upon the railings of Soho Square.
>
> (35–6)

In another incident David Bomberg and his brother—a professional boxer—threatened Lewis after finding that a "coveted position he had claimed for his picture the day before was now occupied by Lewis's *Christopher Columbus*" (O'Keeffe 149). The break with Marinetti did not come to blows, but when Marinetti and Nevinson delivered a lecture together at the Doré Gallery it descended into spectacle. O'Keeffe suggests that "[w]hile Gaudier stayed resolutely on his feet in the middle of the audience, hissing 'Vorti-ccc-iste' at the speaker, Lewis and the rest of his party 'maintained a confused uproar'" (154). It was in a similar climate of egoistic struggle that the first volume of *Blast*, edited by Lewis and published by John Lane appeared in July 1914.

Egoism in "The Enemy of the Stars"

Lewis's only surviving reference to Stirner's name and book appeared in the experimental play "The Enemy of the Stars," which is the longest single work in—and centerpiece of—the first volume of *Blast*.[10] O'Keeffe describes the piece as "a strange hybrid of play and novella, replete with dark metaphor" (156). Despite its

---

[10] Indirect references to Stirner's thought in "The Enemy of the Stars" are too numerous to count. Arghol is described as a "gladiator who has come to fight a ghost, Humanity" (Lewis, "The Enemy of the Stars" 61). He tells Hanp that the self is "the one piece of property all communities have agreed it is illegal to possess" (66). Arghol's "criminal instinct" is put to use by "unknown Humanity, our King, to express its violent aversion to Protagonist, statue mirage of Liberty in the great desert" (59). More obliquely, Ashford has written at length about the similarities between Stirner's and Lewis's use of the concept of shamanism. Even the fact that Arghol has abandoned Berlin to work in a wheelwright's yard recalls the English translation of Stirner's idiomatic insult: "Man, your head is haunted; you have wheels in your head!" (43).

impenetrable style, Edwards suggests that the story "is simple to reconstruct" (146). Arghol is a former student from Berlin who has abandoned his studies because "he felt that his social relationships and his studies were obscuring his true, original self with a layer of falsity" (Edwards 146). At the beginning of the play he is laboring in a wheelwright's yard two hundred miles south of the Arctic Circle, where his uncle subjects him to daily beatings. After a philosophical discussion about the nature of the self ends with him assaulting his co-worker Hanp, Arghol collapses and dreams of his earlier life as a student in Berlin. At the end of the play Hanp returns to murder Arghol in his sleep before throwing himself off a bridge. It is a strange but simple plot, which is obscured by an almost total rejection of exposition in favor of abstract, visual descriptions of the scenes and events as they take place.

In "The Enemy of the Stars" Stirner is treated with such a degree of ambivalence that it is impossible to assess Lewis's genuine opinion of his thought. Arghol expresses hatred for Stirner's book, but he struggles to free himself from it. When Stirner appears he is described in admiring terms, but Arghol immediately evicts the visitor. These direct references to Stirner appear in Arghol's dream, which Lewis identifies as a kind of psychological primer for the earlier conflict with Hanp. As Arghol collapses into sleep Lewis suggests that "[n]ow a dream began valuing, with it's [sic] tentative symbols, preceding events" ("The Enemy of the Stars" 76). Recalling his days as a student in Berlin, Arghol finds himself in "[h]is room in the city, nine feet by six, grave big enough for the six corpses that is each living man" (76). The room is strewn with books, bric-a-brac and assorted refuse. The bed is perpetually unmade. In disgust, Arghol sets about putting the room straight. Amidst the detritus of this "[a]ppalling tabernacle of Self and Unbelief" (76), only one book is named:

> The third book, stalely open, which he took up to shut, was the "Einige und Sein Eigenkeit."
> Stirnir.
> One of seven arrows in his martyr mind.[11]
> Poof! he flung it out of the window.
>
> (76–7)

Within minutes, however, the book comes back. A young man has found it out in the street, and knocks on Arghol's door to return it.

---

[11] "The Enemy of the Stars" is laden with inscrutable symbols that are never fully explained, but the seven arrows could be a reference to the Eastern Orthodox icon of the Mother of God being pierced by seven arrows. Whether Lewis is trying to suggest that Stirner's book represents one of the seven virtues or seven deadly sins—most obviously pride—is a matter of conjecture.

Arghol's attempt to rid himself of Stirner's influence begins a comedy of misunderstandings, in which repeated acts of repudiation seem to further confirm Arghol's allegiance with Stirner's insurrectionary egoism. Ashford suggests that "in attempting to effect a catharsis, to purify ego of a philosophy which has been recognised as parasitic, Lewis's puppet is reiterating the very conditions that render such a renunciation necessary—and this is reflected in the way that Stirner's book *comes back*—to be rejected over and over again" (90–1). By rejecting Stirner's book as an imposition on his self Arghol is effectively taking the course of action dictated by Stirner, beginning a never-ending cycle of repudiation. In the dream, the young man bearing Stirner's book undergoes a series of transformations: he first becomes Hanp; then "obliquely" becomes Stirner; and finally becomes "[a] middle aged man, red cropped head and dark eyes, self = possessed, loose, free, student—sailor, fingering the book: coming to a decision. Stirnir as he had imagined him" (Lewis, "The Enemy of the Stars" 77).[12] There is something of the romantic hero in this depiction of an imagined Stirner, and it is certainly a generous portrayal by Lewis's standards. With each transformation Arghol renews injunctions for his visitor to leave, culminating in an attempt to bribe him to go. Confusing the money to be for the purchase of the book, the guest hurls Stirner's book at Arghol's head in disgust. The ensuing fight is also a repetition of Arghol's earlier scuffle with Hanp, and once again Arghol is seemingly victorious and the visitor is evicted. Once alone, Arghol tears up his books and walks out into the street. Nevertheless, the repetition of these fights and Arghol's increasing psychological disturbance suggests it has been a contingent victory at best.

Much of the existing commentary about Stirner's role in "The Enemy of the Stars" proceeds from Paul Edward's reading of the play, but his interpretation depends on a particular understanding of Stirner's thought. Edwards suggests that it "can be seen as implying a critique of the Stirnerian ego, which can only exist untrammelled as a 'creative nothing'; so when it is most itself its activity will be saturated with this 'nothing'" (157). He sees the creative nothing as a "nihilism at the base of his philosophy," which Stirner imagines "can be constantly deferred simply by having the ego act" (Edwards 157). There are,

---

[12] There is an interesting level of detail in Lewis's physical description of Stirner. It seems to indicate that he had read Mackay's biography, which suggested that Stirner's "blond, reddish, lightly curled and short-cut, soft hair left completely free his massive, domed, quite strikingly high and conspicuous forehead" (86).

however, fundamental problems with this approach to Stirner's ideas. First, it has already been seen that logic forced Stirner to deny the independent existence of external influences. Values that appear to originate outside the self are, by necessity, alienated properties of the individual which have been mistaken for external influences.[13] To accept ideals as anything other than creations of the individual mind causes Stirnerian egoism to collapse, as the individual is no longer the creator of all values—the "creative nothing" which Stirner described. There is no possibility of cutting away external influence, only of recognizing— and thus realizing—the personal ownership of ideals. Second, Stirner actively rejected the idea of transcendental self-realization or, as Edwards phrases it, "the Romantic urge to realise the authentic self" (146). Self-realization was, for Stirner, merely a conscious recognition that all external values were actually the creations and properties of the unique individual.[14] Last, Stirner's creative nothing is less an expression of anarchistic nihilism—though it continues to be interpreted as such—than a suggestion that language is incapable of delimiting the individual who creates and owns language through use.[15]

Like Arghol, Lewis struggled against but maintained an ambiguous and ambivalent relationship with Stirnerian egoism. Through his dealings with others, Arghol is constantly creating the world he occupies, but he vainly attempts to cordon himself off from his creation in order to realize a transcendental selfhood. He parrots Stirner's aphoristic language, but refuses to accept his philosophical conclusions. Arghol tells Hanp that he is "an unclean little beast, crept gloomily out of my ego" and that "[y]ou are the world, brother, with its family objections to me" (Lewis, "The Enemy of the Stars" 73), but he cannot reconcile these two contradictory truths. For Arghol, the world he has created remains a parasitic reality that both erodes his pure self and serves as a barrier between himself and others. Meeting a friend in his dream, Arghol expresses his frustration by thinking that "[t]his man would never see anyone but Arghol he

---

[13] The idea that Stirner advocated rebellion against external influences is one of the most persistent misapprehensions about his thought. It is an interpretation that Stirner repeatedly contradicted: "[a]s I find myself behind things, and that as mind, so I must later find *myself* also behind *thoughts*, namely, as their creator and owner" (*The Ego and Its Own* 17). Lewis may have held this misapprehension, but there is certainly evidence to suggest he did not.

[14] Stirner distinguished between unconscious and conscious egoism, and suggested that "what I do unconsciously I half-do, and therefore after every victory over a faith I become again the *prisoner* (possessed) of a faith which then takes my whole self anew into its *service*" (*The Ego and Its Own* 316).

[15] The unique individual is only nothing insofar as it is not an idea, and Stirner suggested that "they say of God, 'Names name thee not.' That holds good of me: no *concept* expresses me, nothing that is designated as my essence exhausts me; they are only names" (*The Ego and Its Own* 324).

knew.—Yet he on his side saw a man, directly beneath his friend, imprisoned, with intolerable need of recognition" (78). The irony, of course, is that Arghol is not a unique self but Lewis's creation, and Lewis goes to significant lengths to emphasize the artificiality of Arghol's reality.[16] Arghol despises the unreality of a world that emerges out of and parasitizes his own sense of self, but Lewis as artist seems to take pleasure in the performances of his creations. In contrast to Arghol, who attempts to cut himself off from the inferior selves he produces in the world around him, Lewis has assembled a gallery of them—puppets and masks—and he sets them to work for his own artistic satisfaction.[17]

Another way to understand Stirner's role in Lewis's Vorticist philosophy is to consider that in "The Enemy of the Stars" Lewis, as the artist existing outside of the work, has created a reality occupied by his creations and properties. His will directs these creations to perform in ways that satisfy his own ego. The ever-present but indiscernible author is the sole egoist and creator of a reality which his characters occupy. As Ashford suggests, "[t]he universe Arghol inhabits is truly the creation of a demiurge—a minor and malicious god—that is to say, Lewis himself" (100). Although Lewis's characters are his property, they nevertheless share properties with their owner. Lewis has created Arghol, but because of this Arghol also resembles Lewis. Arghol is a "[g]reat mask" for Lewis to wear, while his "CHARACTERS AND PROPERTIES BOTH EMERGE FROM GANGWAY INTO GROUND AT ONE SIDE" (Lewis, "The Enemy of the Stars" 59).[18] Stirner's philosophy becomes the basis for a fracturing of the self into innumerable selves, which all suggest the existence of, but never restrict the qualities of, a shared and illimitable wellspring of personality.

---

[16] The structuring of "The Enemy of the Stars" as an un-performable play, replete with staging and dress instructions, reinforces the notion that these characters possess no will of their own and that the world they occupy is of Lewis's creation, not theirs.

[17] Stirner took similar pleasure in constantly creating and dissolving constructed selves, and suggested that "I on my part start from a presupposition in presupposing *myself*; but my presupposition does not struggle for its perfection like 'man struggling for his perfection,' but only serves me to enjoy it and consume it" (135). Arghol certainly struggles for perfection, but Lewis both creates Arghol and destroys him for his own artistic satisfaction.

[18] On a related note, Geoffrey Wagner suggests that "'The Code of a Herdsman,' originally published in *The Little Review* for July 1917, is mainly a set of instructions to the Herdsman, or inspired artist, not to come down from his mountain to the herd without some mask or disguise" (21). Wagner then outlines a number of such masks adopted by Lewis, including Cantleman, William Bland Burn (a pseudonym used to engage in correspondence with Pound's own alter ego, Walter Villerant) and The Enemy. "The Code of a Herdsman" itself satirizes *Thus Spoke Zarathustra*, particularly when read in the context of Lewis's later observations about Nietzsche in *The Art of Being Ruled*.

The *Blast* Manifestos

Once it has been acknowledged that Lewis's personal philosophy during his Vorticist period was influenced by Stirner's ideas, it is easy to recognize the traces of egoism that run throughout *Blast*'s many manifestos, vortices, and notes. Stirnerian virtues of individuality, instinct, and contradiction were all praised in the manifestos, and Lewis suggested in the journal's introduction that *Blast* "will not appeal to any particular class, but to the fundamental and popular instincts in every class and description of people, TO THE INDIVIDUAL" (Lewis "Long Live the Vortex" 7). The first formal manifesto in the volume is the famous series of "blasts" and "blesses" in which frequently contradictory positions were taken in relation to England, France, humor, the Victorian era, and even hairdressers.[19] "Manifesto I" also included lists of individuals who were either blasted or blessed for unspecified reasons. O'Keeffe suggests that "[t]he Blast and Bless lists, compiled by Lewis and Pound, [...] was a catalogue of despised establishment figures and personal *bêtes noires* on the one hand, and friends, rebels, suffragettes, music hall performers, and prizefighters, on the other" (156). Henri Bergson was singled out for blasting—presumably for his philosophy's preoccupation with the concept of time—but Stirner and Nietzsche are curiously absent from either list. Given the extent of Vorticism's reliance on a distinctly Stirnerian interpretation of the ego, silence on the subject of Stirner may indicate an effort to free the movement from a debt to preceding forms of egoism.

The Stirnerian aspect of "Manifesto I" is more conceptual than in the other polemics found in *Blast* and is suggested by Lewis's commitment to mutually exclusive positions. Like Stirner and Marsden before him, Lewis refused to be bound by ideological consistency. His defense against dogmatism involved satirically assuming simultaneous but contradictory positions such as in *The Diabolical Principle* (1931), where he suggested that his politics was "partly communist and partly fascist, with a distinct streak of monarchism in my Marxism, but at bottom anarchist with a healthy passion for order" (126).[20] Addressing similar contradictions in *Blast*, Lewis recalled in *Blasting and*

---

[19] O'Keeffe suggests that hairdressers are blessed for bringing "order to overgrown chaotic nature" (156).
[20] That is to say Lewis had no consistent political position beyond whichever one he decided to take at any given time. It probably would have been more accurate—though far less infuriating for his readers—for Lewis to suggest that his politics was founded on contrarianism and self-interest, rather than a consistent ideological perspective.

Bombardiering (1937) that "[a]gainst the tyranny of the 'sense of humour,' I, in true anglo-saxon fashion, humorously rebelled" (38). To add a further layer of contradiction, he added that "since there are two sides to every argument, you find me *blessing* what I had a moment before *blasted*" (Lewis, *Blasting and Bombardiering* 38). To prevent Vorticist positions from calcifying into fixed ideas, Lewis persistently subjected the tenets of his manifestos to parody and critique.[21] Stirner advised a similar approach to values:

> I want only to be careful to secure my property to myself; and, in order to secure it, I continually take it back into myself, annihilate in it every movement toward independence, and swallow it before it can fix itself and become a "fixed idea" or a "mania."
>
> (*The Ego and Its Own* 128)[22]

English humor is blessed for being "the great barbarous weapon of the genius among races" (26), but also blasted for being a "[q]uack ENGLISH drug for stupidity and sleepiness" (Lewis, "Manifesto I" 17). The layers of contradiction serve to destabilize humor as an objective ideal and counter the risk of the Vorticist approach to humor becoming dogmatic.

Stirner's thought had a more direct influence on "Manifesto II," where egoism can be seen to inform several tenets of the Vorticist program. This second, more serious, attempt at the formulation of a Vorticist manifesto makes numerous allusions to the thought of Stirner and Nietzsche. The manifesto consists of sixty-three numbered declarations and begins with the distinctly Nietzschean proposition that "[b]eyond Action and Reaction we would establish ourselves" (Lewis, "Manifesto II" 30). This opening statement also suggests that the Vorticists sought to establish their individual selves outside a cycle of action and reaction to external circumstances. Vorticism was certainly aligned with notions of contradiction and self-will, and Lewis proposed in another statement that "[w]e fight first on one side, then on the other, but always for the SAME cause, which is neither side or both sides and ours" (30). Stirner had already suggested that "I have no need to take up each thing that wants to throw its cause on us and show that it is occupied only with itself, not with us, only with its good, not with

---

[21] Parisian Dada took a similar approach to entertaining contradiction, and there too it marked a connection with Stirner's ideas.

[22] It is worth noting that the dissolution of ideals was not a prerequisite for maintaining the uniqueness of the self, but a means of remaining conscious of the dependence of ideals on the self. Stirner suggested that "if criticism says: You are man only when you are restlessly criticizing and dissolving! Then we say: Man I am without that, and I am I likewise" (127).

ours" (*The Ego and Its Own* 6), and now Lewis concurred: "Our Cause Is NO-MAN'S" ("Manifesto II" 31). With its apparent allusion to Stirner's opprobrium of "mankind's cause" (*The Ego and Its Own* 6), it is tempting to see a relationship between Stirner's use of *Unmensch* and Lewis's use of NO-MAN. At any rate, Lewis was not suggesting that Vorticism had no cause, but that its cause was either that of no man or the NO-MAN. Either interpretation owes a debt to Stirner's insurrectionary egoism.

Later statements in "Manifesto II" suggest that Vorticism's approach to humor also borrowed from Stirner's analysis of comedy. In the fifth sequence of declarations, Lewis variously described humor as "Chaos invading Concept and bursting it like nitrogen," and as "the Individual masquerading as Humanity like a child in clothes too big for him" ("Manifesto II" 38). He went on to propose that "[a]ny great Northern Art will partake of this insidious and volcanic chaos" (38). In satire the individual assumed the role of society more broadly, and destabilized concepts with savage mockery. Humor blew apart accepted ideals by putting them under unnatural and intolerable stress. Humor was the artist's weapon against convention. It has already been seen that Stirner, too, suggested that humor played the role of demolishing ideals. In "Kunst und Religion" he had proposed that comedy "displays the emptiness, or better, the deflation of the Object," and by doing so "frees men from the old belief" ("Art and Religion" 333). In *Der Einzige und sein Eigentum* laughter is used to express Stirner's ridicule of ideals, such as when Stirner looks forward to a time when "mankind is buried, and I am my own, I am the laughing heir!" (*The Ego and Its Own* 193).[23] Lewis was intimately familiar with Stirner's book, so it is only reasonable to suggest that his similarly insurrectionary approach to humor owed a debt to Stirner's praise of derisive laughter.

In a series of "Vortices and Notes" attacking Impressionism, Futurism, and other forms of art that he considered to be inferior, Lewis once more demonstrated his reliance on aspects of Stirner's thought. In the first of these manifestos and short polemical essays, "Life is the Important Thing!," Lewis used Stirner's criticism of ideals as the basis for an assault on Impressionism's obsession with nature:

> In the revolt against Formula, revolutionaries in art sell themselves to Nature. Without Nature's aid the "coup" could not be accomplished. They, of course,

---

[23] Earlier in the book, Stirner pauses during his account of the spirits haunting individual minds to tell his reader that we will "go along a bit of road together, till perhaps you too turn your back on me because I laugh in your face" (31).

become quite satisfied slaves of Nature, as their fathers were of Formula. It never occurs to them that Nature is just as sterile a Tyrant.

(129)

Lewis substituted Stirner's preoccupation with God and man for the artistic ideals of formula and nature, but his argument otherwise remained unchanged. Stirner suggested that "[t]he Christian may reform and revolt an infinite deal, may demolish the ruling concepts of centuries," but that "he will always aspire to a new 'principle' or new master again, always set up a higher or 'deeper' truth again, always call forth a cult again, always proclaim a spirit called to dominion, lay down a *law* for all" (*The Ego and Its Own* 307). Lewis did not merely borrow Stirner's logic; however, he also borrowed his language. No one familiar with *Der Einzige und sein Eigentum* could miss the implicit reference to Stirner when Lewis suggested that the Impressionist obsession with nature was "[a]n idea which haunts the head" ("Life is the Important Thing!" 129). Nature was, however, not the only fixed idea that Lewis singled out for contempt.

In "Futurism, Magic and Life" Lewis connected Impressionism with the thought of Bergson and Futurism with the thought of Nietzsche, and he proposed that in both cases the result was a romantic devotion to life at the expense of art. Lewis argued that "for the last half century, the intellectual world has developed savagely in one direction—that of Life," and that "[e]verywhere LIFE is said instead of ART" ("Futurism, Magic and Life" 132). In the case of Marinetti, an obsession with life was the product of Nietzsche's influence, and his "war = talk, sententious elevation and much besides, Marinetti picked up from Nietzsche" (132). On the other hand, Lewis observed that "Bergson, the philosopher of Impressionism, stands for this new prescience in France" (132). Vorticism was distinct from these European movements because it was not obsessed with either art or life, but turned these impulses to the service of the individual artist. Lewis proposed that art "is all a matter of the most delicate adjustment between voracity of Art and digestive quality of Life" but that in order to achieve this balance "a course of egotistic hardening, if anything, is required" (134). The reality that the artist sought to depict was the self, but the artist's engagement with nature could operate as a mirror for the ego. Recalling Pound's description of the image as psychological complex, Lewis suggested that "Reality is in the artist, the image only in life, and he should only approach so near as is necessary for a good view" (135). Bergson may have been the theorist of Impressionism and Nietzsche of Futurism, but both men, as well as Stirner, contributed to the theoretical positions of Vorticism.

There are further hints at Stirner's influence throughout the rest of Lewis's manifestos in the first volume of *Blast*, but "Our Vortex" suggests the complexity of pinning down Lewis's engagement with egoism.[24] It is also an important example of Vorticist manifesto writing that brings together many of the movement's—and Lewis's—chief concerns. In it, Lewis asserts that "[o]ur vortex regards the Future as as sentimental as the Past" because "[t]he Future is distant, like the Past, and therefore sentimental" ("Our Vortex" 147). The argument that sentimentality indicated a kind of false consciousness was a mainstay of British and American interpretations of egoism. In the first volume of *The New Freewoman* Marsden similarly suggested that "[a]n intellectual concept is not, strictly speaking, a concept at all" but rather "a verbal trick, put through from many different and mainly sub-conscious motives, and its immediate outcome is sentimentality—an intellectual 'fake' touched up with associated emotion" (Marsden, "The Lean Kind" 4). Lewis seems to agree with this reading of sentimentality when he suggests that "[t]he Past and Future are the prostitutes Nature has provided," while "Art is periodic escapes from this Brothel" ("Our Vortex" 148). Past and future are mere concepts masquerading as nature's truths, while art provides a temporary escape from the false reality of sentimentalism because it originates in the unique self of the individual artist rather than nature.

More tellingly, however, Lewis suggested in "Our Vortex" that Vorticism—like egoism—recognized no truth beyond the individual. He declared that "[w]e have no Verbotens" and that "[t]here is one Truth, ourselves, and everything is permitted" (148). The notion that "everything is permitted" was borrowed from either *Thus Spoke Zarathustra*, *The Genealogy of Morals*, or *The Brothers Karamazov*, but Lewis rejected an important aspect of Nietzsche's version of this maxim. In *Thus Spoke Zarathustra*, Zarathustra's shadow suggests that "[n]othing is true, everything is permitted" (Nietzsche 285). In *The Genealogy of Morals* (1887) Nietzsche attributed the maxim "Nothing is true, everything is allowed" to the Nizari Isma'ili assassins (109). Dostoevsky attributed variations

---

[24] For instance, Lewis suggested in "The New Egos" that "the modern town = dweller of our civilization" lives in a society that is "sufficiently organised for his ego to walk abroad" (141). In these conditions, "the old form of egotism is no longer fit for such conditions as now prevail, so the isolated human figure of most Ancient art is an anachronism" (Lewis, "The New Egos" 141). Modern egos "burrow into each other," and this new form of selfhood necessitated a new form of art (141). It is also worth remembering that many of Vorticism's strongest allies—including Pound and Lewis themselves—were associated with, or submitting to, *The Egoist*, the most important mouthpiece of egoism to be published in England at that time.

of a similar conclusion to Ivan Karamazov.[25] In one instance Ivan's belief that, in the absence of God, "crime must not only be permitted but recognised as the inevitable and the most rational outcome" was also associated with the word egoism in the English translation (Dostoevsky 33).[26] Rather than concurring with Nietzsche that "nothing is true," however, Lewis proposed that the selfhood of the artist was the only truth. He rejected the implied nihilism in Nietzsche's maxim in favor of egoistic affirmation. Nevertheless, he added that "[i]n a Vorticist Universe, we don't get excited at what we have invented" (Lewis, "Our Vortex" 148). Like Ivan Karamazov, Lewis was suggesting that egoism was a rational and even inevitable outcome, but in this case of a genuinely radical approach to art.

In their manifestos for *Blast*, Pound and Gaudier-Brzeska more obliquely suggested the importance of egoism to Vorticism. In his "Vortex," Pound's attitude to egoism remained ambiguous. He suggested that "man" could be considered as either "the TOY of circumstance, as the plastic substance RECEIVING impressions," or "as DIRECTING a certain fluid force against circumstance, as CONCEIVING instead of merely observing and reflecting" (Pound, "Vortex. Pound" 153). If Pound's Vorticism was associated with this second interpretation of the individual—as suggested by the use of "merely"—it was at least compatible with Lewis's more overtly egoistic approach to the movement. By comparison Gaudier-Brzeska was less equivocal about the importance of the artist's ego in Vorticism. In "Vortex. Gaudier Brzeska" he described a historical Hamite Vortex in the artwork of the ancient Egyptians. According to him, the Egyptian's "gods were self made," and "he built them in his image" (155). The individual Egyptian artist is the subject here, and Gaudier-Brzeska is suggesting that he made gods out of his self and in his own image. If there was any doubt that this same egoistic impulse was crucial to English Vorticism, Gaudier-Brzeska clarified his position in the final lines of the work:

> We have been influenced by what we liked most, each according to his own individuality, we have crystallized the sphere into the cube, we have

---

[25] The similarity of these passages in *The Brothers Karamazov* is such that it led Sartre to suggest in *Existentialism Is a Humanism* (1946) that "Dostoevsky once wrote 'If God did not exist, everything would be permitted'; and that, for existentialism, is the starting point" (294).

[26] Ivan suggests that for those who do not believe in God or the immortality of the soul "the moral law of nature must immediately be changed into the exact contrary of the former religious law, and that egoism, even to crime, must become not only lawful but even recognised as the inevitable, the most rational, even honourable outcome of his position" (Dostoevsky 33).

made a combination of all the possible shaped masses—concentrating them to express our abstract thoughts of conscious superiority.

Will and consciousness are our
VORTEX.

(158)

Simply put, Vorticism was the will and consciousness of the individual artist. It was artistic egoism. Gaudier-Brzeska's manifesto was the final piece to appear in the first volume of *Blast*, and it was immediately followed by advertisements for *Poetry* and the foremost organ of English egoism, *The Egoist*.

Vorticism certainly owed a theoretical debt to Stirner's egoism, but Lewis and Pound also took an egoistic approach to manifesto writing, as well as the management of the movement more broadly. A desire for personal ownership and control of artistic ideals dominated their involvement with Vorticism and its programs. In *Blasting and Bombardiering* Lewis claimed to have been the sole author of the six manifestos he reproduced in the memoir, suggesting that they were "written (by myself) immediately before the war" (37). He also described himself as the leader and voice of the movement, suggesting:

> I concluded that as a matter of course some romantic figure must always emerge, to captain the "group." Like myself! How otherwise could a "group" get about and above all *talk*. For it had to have a mouthpiece didn't it? I was so little of a communist that it never occurred to me that left to itself a group might express itself *in chorus*. The "leadership" principle, you will observe, was in my bones.
> (Lewis, *Blasting and Bombardiering* 32)

The same principle had underpinned Marx's approach to *The Communist Manifesto*, and other Vorticists were not ignorant of the "leadership" principle exhibited by Pound and Lewis. Marx had the benefit of using the manifesto to advance the cause of collective solidarity under the auspices of communism, but Lewis had proposed something altogether different. Vorticism was to be a movement of self-possessed individual artists, and such individuals were far less willing to be bound by his manifestos.

In *Cometism and Vorticism: A Tate Gallery Catalogue Revised* (1956), William Roberts rejected Lewis's egoistic claim that Vorticism simply referred to his own approach to art. Roberts recognized the political egoism inherent in Lewis's manifestos when he observed that "'accepted' ideas of the 'Leader' crystalise into a 'teaching' which the master afterwards 'repudiates' just as later the 'Colleagues' are repudiated in the famous phrase ... 'Vorticism, in fact, was what I, personally, did and said at a certain period'" (Roberts np). More importantly, Roberts called into question any notion of collective solidarity in the *Blast* manifestos:

> If anyone were to imagine we signed this Manifesto, pen in hand, in solemn assembly, they would be making a big mistake. I, in fact, personally signed nothing. The first knowledge I had of a Vorticist Manifesto's existence was when Lewis, one fine Sunday morning in the summer of 1914, knocked at my door and placed in my hands this chubby, rosy, problem-child Blast, the fruits of his own, Ezra Pound's and Nevinson's combined labours.
>
> (np)

Despite his best efforts, Lewis did not succeed in taking ownership of a broader Vorticist movement, but he did take personal ownership of the abstract concept of Vorticism—in his own mind at least—by writing its manifestos. The Vorticist manifestos claimed to encapsulate the shared ideals of a movement but represented attempts to take control of that movement and the abstract ideals associated with it. As in the case of *The Communist Manifesto*, "Le Symbolisme," and "Fondation et manifeste du Futurisme," the *Blast* manifestos were largely produced by a single individual working to commandeer the power of a movement. The collective "we" of Lewis's *Blast* was little different from the editorial we of Marsden's *The Egoist*. In each case the manifesto enshrined the egoism of its writer and subjected a movement's ideals to the will of a self-appointed leader.

War was declared in the same month that the first issue of *Blast* was published, and it marked a turning point for Stirner's reputation. In an article for the *English Review* in September 1914, Austin Harrison proposed that "[b]ased on a misreading of Nietzsche, Max Stirner, and egocentric theories of life, the general attitude of the Germans has been moulded on the copybook of the drill sergeant" ("Psychology and Motives" 242).[27] The idea of Stirner as the most extreme theorist of anarchism was replaced by the notion that he was a philosopher of autocratic militarism. This was perhaps the cruelest perversion of Stirner's thought to date—twisting his strident criticism of all

---

[27] A month later—in another article that referenced Stirner—Harrison argued that "[a]ll this 'new' psychology, new drama, new art impertinence is German. Whether the thing be called Secessionist, Futuristic, or Vorticist, its German brand is unmistakable; it comes straight from Bavaria, kibbled from the vats of Munich" ("The Kaiser's World War: World-Power or Downfall" 315). The connections between Vorticism, Futurism, Stirner, and German militarism seemed obvious to him, but it is worth noting that he considered this to result from a misreading of Stirner rather than an inherent aspect of his thought.

forms of authority to serve the cause of the state. By the mid-twentieth century those casually familiar with Stirner's thought were more likely to associate it with fascism or German National Socialism than anarchism. In either case he had become a bête noire of mainstream philosophy. Stirner's reputation was permanently tarnished, but his influence on the manifesto persisted. Manifestos continued to be used as a means of codifying and owning the abstract ideals that underpinned radical movements in artistic, literary, and political spheres. In some instances, such as in the case of Paris Dada and Russian Futurism, his influence was obvious. Where writers remained unaware of Stirner's historical importance to the development of the manifesto the weight of his influence was nonetheless felt in appeals to individual liberty and rejections of traditional notions of moral and artistic value. He had provided the justification for Marx to take ownership of communism in *The Communist Manifesto*, and Stirner's demand for personal ownership of abstract ideals reverberated through every instance of the manifesto that followed.

Conclusion: A History of Possession

When Max Stirner first wrote *Der Einzige und sein Eigentum* in 1844 he could not have foreseen the extent to which his sustained critique of ideals and essences would be adapted, developed, reinterpreted, taken out of context, and enlisted into the service of abstract ideals. Egoism did not so much disappear after the First World War as continue to evolve into ever less recognizable forms. Similarly, egoism's influence on manifesto-writing became more nebulous and, in some cases, existed as an unacknowledged current of individualistic rebellion within otherwise collective movements. By the time that the second volume of *Blast* was published in 1915, many contemporary interpretations of egoism would have been entirely unrecognizable to Stirner himself. Philosophical anarchists claimed to be egoists but held liberty and contractual rights to be objective virtues. Illegalists espoused insurrection but treated the concept of crime as though it was an abstract ideal. Barrès, D'Annunzio, and Mussolini proclaimed the importance of individual rebellion but were possessed by the fixed idea of national identity. Italian Futurists worshipped newly imagined gods of speed and technology. Still others equated egoism with Nietzsche's deification of a transcendent *Übermensch*.[1] In each case, Stirner's most insightful conclusion—the tyrannizing power of abstract ideals—was the first aspect of his thought to be cast aside. Movements, while dismissing their opponents' ideals as hauntings of the mind, clung to their own abstractions all the more fiercely. Very few readers of Stirner engaged with his book on its own terms, and fewer still read it in the narrow context of mid-nineteenth-century German idealism.

---

[1] While it is tempting to see Stirner's egoism as espousing an ideal of self-realization, Stirner went to significant lengths to clarify that his concept of the ego was not an ideal: "Enough, there is a mighty difference whether I make myself the starting-point or the goal. As the latter I do not have myself, am consequently still alien to myself, am my *essence*, my 'true essence,' and this 'true essence,' alien to me, will mock me as a spook of a thousand different names" (*The Ego and Its Own* 290). For Stirner the egoist was not something for an individual to become, but a conscious recognition of what the individual already was.

Nevertheless, elements of egoism survived in many aesthetic movements well after the First World War. The manifesto, too, retained qualities of egoistic revolt, even as Stirner's popularity continued to wane.

One of the few clear-eyed English critics of *Der Einzige und sein Eigentum* after the First World War was the historian, philosopher, poet, and anarchist, Herbert Read.[2] In *The Tenth Muse* (1941), he recalled his first contact with Stirner's book: "I bought my copy in 1915, and it is a book I have never lost sight of—it is a book which once read is persistently recalled to memory" (76). Read frequently discussed the implications of Stirner's thought in his writing, and *The Forms of Things Unknown* (1935), *The Contrary Experience* (1962), and several essays on anarchism and existentialism contain assessments of Stirner's legacy in the twentieth century. An entire essay in *The Tenth Muse* is devoted to Stirner. In these works Read connected egoism not only to his own personal intellectual development, but also to the development of existentialism, Surrealism, and psychology. His assessment of Stirner's importance before, and indeed after, the Second World War suggests the changing nature of egoism after recognition of Stirner's contributions had faded.

Although his conception of anarchism was markedly different from the insurrectionary egoism of Stirner, Read acknowledged the unavoidable logic of Stirner's assault on abstract ideals. In *The Forms of Things Unknown*, Read observed:

> To say that [*Der Einzige und sein Eigentum*] had a great influence on me would not be correct, for influences are absorbed and become part of one's mind. This book refused to be digested—to use our vivid English metaphor: it stuck in the gizzard, and has been in that uncomfortable position ever since.
>
> (173)

According to Read, Stirner's "outrageous book, which subsequent philosophers have somewhat guiltily ignored" (*The Forms of Things Unknown* 173), did not provide the basis for his philosophy, but served as a persistent warning against the dangers of abstraction. Read observed that "[w]arned by Stirner, I for one do not seek an abstracted essence, an illusion to which I give an irrational adherence" (175). Instead, Stirner's thought led Read to pursue a desire for beauty and order on a more personal basis. Although he expressed a distaste for

---

[2] Read made many contributions to British culture in a variety of fields. He was an important proponent of Surrealism and existentialism, and also championed the work of British artists such as Paul Nash. He published criticism on English Romanticism and Imagism and was a close friend of T. S. Eliot.

unrestrained egoism, Read's focus on the abstract nature of ideals rather than a need for constant insurrection against established institutions suggests he was one of the few readers genuinely to consider the implications of Stirner's assault on idealism.

In his intellectual autobiography, *The Contrary Experience*, Read reflected on the role egoism had played in his personal philosophy. Like Stirner—and Nietzsche—he acknowledged that atheism necessitated a new foundation for moral values. God had provided a justification for Christian morality that had no equivalent in an atheist conception of the world. Read proposed that Stirner's egoism represented one of only two rational foundations for ethics afforded to atheists:

> Having rejected any code of morality dependant on a supernatural sanction, the only alternatives seemed to be, either an egoism as extreme as Max Stirner's, or a social code determined by the needs and guaranteed by the laws of the community of which one was a member. This latter solution was too relative and too pragmatic for my taste; and fundamentally I had no belief in social sanctions of any kind—they are only an excuse for tyranny.
> (*The Contrary Experience* 347)

Read's choice was between a personal or social basis for morality, and the choice was a reiteration of the fundamental disagreement between Stirner and Marx about the individual's role in society. Like Stirner, Read gravitated toward a personal foundation for morality and he observed that "I therefore fell back upon some form of egoism, but though I recognised the logicality of the extremest position, and its freedom, [...] I was not prepared for its consequences" (347). The logic of egoism seemed to Read "to involve hedonism (a life of unrestricted sensuousness, which always ends in despair) rather than a desirable eudemonism" (348). Unwilling to accept what he saw as the Dionysian implications of Stirner's logic, Read arrived at a conception of egoism moderated by his artistic taste for beauty. In some respects, Read's aesthetic view of anarchism was similar to that of other writers, artists and thinkers confronted by the horrors of total war.[3] Sharing elements in common with the thought of Camus, Sartre, and Breton,

---

[3] Camus is the obvious example here, but George Orwell's sympathetic account of Spanish anarchists in *Homage to Catalonia* (1935) captures a similar sense of beauty in anarchist thought that is absent from the brutish efficiency of Marxist communism: "my desire to see Socialism established [was] much more actual than it had been before. Partly, perhaps, this was due to the good luck of being among Spaniards, who, with their innate decency and their ever-present Anarchist tinge, would make even the opening stages of Socialism tolerable if they had the chance" (Orwell 105).

Read's approach to rebellion was a profound development upon the absolute egoism of Stirner.

The influence of Stirner's thought on Read's anarchism is a good example of the way in which elements of egoism were incorporated into interwar theory even as Stirner was becoming an increasingly peripheral figure. While Barrès, Marinetti, and Lewis had developed egoistic approaches to art, Read instead proposed an aesthetic approach to egoism. Because egoism concluded that all values originated in the ego of the unique individual, Read observed that "the principles I was working out in the aesthetic sphere could, as Plato had already suggested, be carried over into the ethical sphere, and that a valid analogy exists between the order of the universe, the order of art and the order of conduct" (*The Contrary Experience* 348). The application of his artistic values to the formation of a personal morality led Read to conclude that "[v]ulgarity is the only sin, in life as in art" (348).[4] He went on to describe a theory of ethical egoism restrained by the guiding forces of beauty and taste. Furthermore, Read suggested that similar approaches to ethics were apparent in several European contemporaries associated with Surrealism and existentialism—particularly Breton, Sartre, and Camus. He acknowledged that "[i]t was on the basis of this philosophy of art that I gave my support to that movement in contemporary art known as Surrealism" (349). Read seems to have detected a note of qualified egoism in the Surrealist movement which it had almost certainly inherited from its origins in Paris Dada.

Stirner's Legacy

In the case of Dada, an interest in egoism was once again concurrent with the flourishing of a manifesto writing tradition. Theresa Papnikolas, David Weir, and David Ashford have all written at length about the connections between the aesthetics of Paris Dada and the ideas of Stirner. Many members of the broader Dada movement—including Tzara, Hugo Ball, Francis Picabia, and Marcel Duchamp—expressed sympathy with Stirner's ideas, and egoism was

---

[4] Nevertheless, Read accepted the existence of an egoistic desire for greatness, and he suggested that "[a]t certain moments the individual is carried beyond his rational self, on to another ethical plane, where his actions are judged by new standards" (*The Contrary Experience* 348). He called this impulse to irrationality "the sense of glory," and admitted that it was "a phrase which is sometimes misunderstood, but which I find too appropriate to abandon" (348).

of particular importance to Dadaism in Paris.[5] Papanikolas observes that "the newly assembled Paris Dadaists gave concrete expression to Tzara's vision of a supremely egoist, tradition-shattering 'new man' by offering poetry readings and performances that [...] shamelessly promoted Stirnerian absolute individualism" (84). Although she does not directly attribute Dadaist manifesto writing to the influence of Stirner's thought, Papanikolas does suggest that Ball and Tzara were both proponents of Stirnerian anarcho-individualism at the dawning of the Dada movement. Furthermore, she argues that "with increased exposure came a transformation in Dada performance, as the obliquely polemical simultaneous poem gave way to the overtly political manifesto, and Ball's optimistically spiritual anarcho-individualism was given, thanks to Tzara, a revolutionary twist" (96). In the light of a broader history of Stirner's influence on manifesto writers, this transformation of Dadaism's polemical style can be seen as yet another instance of contact with Stirner leading to the writing of manifestos.

The schism between Tzara and Breton led to the broader collapse of Dada in the 1920s and also obscured Surrealism's debt to Stirnerian egoism. Papanikolas suggests that "by 1919, Zurich Dada had become polarized along anarcho-communist and anarcho-individualist lines, motivating Tzara to bring his revolutionary Dadaism to Paris, where it found a willing sympathizer in André Breton" (105). Within two years, however, Paris Dada was also beginning to fracture along similar lines. Conflicts within Dada, and specifically between Tzara and Breton, "translated into debates that brought about the decline of Paris Dada and catalyzed the development of Surrealism, for they forced Breton to redefine his Dadaism, his individualism, and his anarchism" (Papanikolas 145). Breton formulated "a new theory of cerebral revolt in which 'revolution' and 'construction' merged in the poetic liberation of the individual subconscious" (145). Tzara's more conventionally egoistic approach to artistic revolt became increasingly incompatible with Breton's desire to effect revolutionary changes in the realms of art and society.

When the tensions within Dada finally ruptured into conflict in 1921, Stirnerian egoism was an important aspect of the argument. The disagreement within Paris Dada centered on Maurice Barrès, a man who had himself played

---

[5] Stirner's influence on Picabia and Duchamp has already been noted, while Hugo Ball wrote "his doctoral dissertation on Nietzsche" and "moved in the anarcho-expressionist circles associated with the magazines *Die Aktion* and *Der Sturm*, where writers and artists inspired by Nietzsche and Stirner were formulating an anarcho-individualist alternative to revolutionary anarchism" (Papanikolas 89).

an important role in the reception of egoism in France. On May 13, 1921, Dadaists held a mock trial of Barrès for what Breton described as an "attack on the security of the spirit" (Papanikolas 148). Breton suggested that Barrès's shifting allegiance from *le culte du moi* to *la terre et la morts* represented a betrayal of the author's duty to ideological consistency. Barrès's sense of self was, however, indistinguishable from his sense of the national character. His nationalism was certainly a betrayal of what Dadaists saw as anarchist values, but both Barrès's anarchism and nationalism represented egoistic expressions of the self.[6] Breton argued that Barrès's transformation "suggested the potential for a similar decline into despotism of unmanaged individualism in all of its forms" (Papanikolas 151). While Tzara seems to have found the nature of Barrès's politics repellent—describing him as a *"vieille oie"* (old goose) during the trial—he was understandably unwilling to condemn an individual on the grounds of self-contradiction. Tzara "reluctantly agreed to participate as a witness [...] only to have his interrogator (Breton) force him to defend his Stirnerian anarcho-individualism and what Breton wished to expose as an apparent lack of ideological focus" (Papanikolas 150). The outcome of the trial was yet another split within Dada, this time leading to the development of Surrealism.

The similarities that Read perceived between his own refiguring of egoistic anarchism and Surrealism were, at least in part, the result of an effort by Breton to escape the nihilistic implications of Dada. In a note to his *Manifesto of Surrealism* (1924), Breton suggested that once "Surrealist methods begin to enjoy widespread favour [...] a new morality must be substituted for the prevailing morality, the source of all our trials and tribulations" (44). Breton's desire to dismantle existing moral codes and replace them with a Surrealist one certainly suggested that Stirnerian and Nietzschean attitudes to morality were relevant to Surrealism, and the manifesto remained an important method of creating and imposing new moral structures on the collective. For Read, however, the anarchist—and egoist—aspects of Surrealism were more keenly felt in the movement's approach to irrationality. He suggested that "[t]he impulse which moves [individuals] to irrational action I have called the sense of glory" (*The Contrary Experience* 348). The desire for glory and honor was dangerous

---

[6] Ashford similarly recognizes that Barrès's egoism was not incompatible with his nationalism when he suggests that "[t]he philosophy that had provided the single most important theoretical foundation for Paris Dada is shown to be compatible with (perhaps the driving force behind) a long career in far right politics" (48).

and deeply romantic, but Read also connected it with the egoistic drive to consume one's own life in pursuit of glory and self-satisfaction:

> No considerations of utility or expediency can explain the actions of men who at the inspired moment will throw away life itself to achieve their glory or to safeguard their honour; but without these concepts, life is reduced to a routine and cautious existence only worthy of meaner animals.
>
> (348)[7]

It was for its combination of anarchic egoism, revolutionary aspiration, commitment to aesthetics, and periodic flights into Dionysian extravagance that Read expressed his support for "Surrealism as a first step towards a revindication and re-integration of the romantic tradition" (349). The joyful heights of Surrealist self-expression were, according to Read, demonstrations of egoistic temerity.

Read also saw indications of Stirner's legacy elsewhere in the landscape of twentieth-century literature, particularly in writing associated with absurdist and existentialist thought. In various essays collected in *Anarchy and Order* (1971) Read connected Stirner's ideas with those of Camus and Sartre. He suggested that Camus's concept of rebellion in *L'Homme revolté* and Stirner's notion of insurrection in *Der Einzige und sein Eigentum* were interchangeable terms for a counterpoint to the Marxist meaning of revolution.[8] Read concurred that a distinction must be drawn "between revolution and insurrection; or as Albert Camus does, between revolution and rebellion" (*Anarchy and Order* 17). In contrast to revolution, "[r]ebellion and insurrection [...] being guided by instinct rather than reason, being passionate and spontaneous rather than cool and calculated, do act like shock therapy on the body of society, and there is a chance that they may change the chemical composition of the societal crystal" (17). Revolution sought to overthrow the institutions in power, but rebellion challenged institutional power itself. Indeed, rebellion was the strongest limit on "the kind of machinery which, at the end of a successful revolution, would merely be taken over by the leaders of the revolution, who then assume the functions of a government" (51). Like Read, however, Camus parted ways with Stirner on

---

[7] Compare Stirner's suggestion that "[w]hen one is anxious only to *live*, he easily, in this solicitude, forgets the *enjoyment* of life. If his only concern is for life, and he thinks 'if I only have my dear life,' he does not apply his full strength to using, that is, enjoying, life. But how does one use life? In using it up, like the candle, which one uses in burning it up. One uses life, and consequently himself the living one, in *consuming* it and himself. Enjoyment of life is using life up" (*The Ego and Its Own* 283).

[8] A more substantial discussion of Camus's reading of Stirner in *L'Homme Revolté* and its subsequent excision from most English translations of the book can be found in the introduction of this book.

the grounds of his absolutism, suggesting that the "law of moderation equally well extends to all the contradictions of rebellious thought" (295). For Camus, Stirner's "bitter and imperious logic can no longer be held in check, except by an I which is determined to defeat every form of abstraction and which has itself become abstract and nameless through being isolated and cut off from its roots" (Camus, *The Rebel* 64). Camus may have had a dim view of Stirner's extremism, but he no doubt felt the weight of Stirner's logic.

Stirner's importance to Camus's conception of rebellion lies in egoism's crucial role in the history of metaphysical revolt. When Camus suggests that the slave's "insurrection against his condition becomes an unlimited campaign against the heavens for the purpose of bringing back a captive king who will first be dethroned and finally condemned to death" (25), the allusions to both Stirner's and Nietzsche's efforts to pronounce the death of God are obvious. Camus continues by proposing that "Human rebellion ends in metaphysical revolution," and that "[w]hen the throne of God is overturned, the rebel realizes that it is now his own responsibility to create the justice, order, and unity that he sought in vain within his own condition, and in this way to justify the fall of God" (25). Rather than forging a path toward a revolutionary change in the human condition, however, the rebel becomes mired in an intractable effort to secure his own power through crime and murder. In many cases, Camus argues, the rebel "forgets his original purpose, tires of the tremendous tension created by refusing to give a positive or negative answer, and finally abandons himself to complete negation or total submission" (25). In Stirner, Camus finds the full trajectory of the rebel's path from insurrection to total nihilism.

Read was forced to be more speculative about the influence of Stirner on existentialism because, unlike Camus, Sartre never mentioned *Der Einzige und sein Eigentum* in his writing.[9] Nevertheless, Read repeatedly observed the similarities between egoism and existentialism. In the essay, "Existentialism, Marxism and Anarchism" (1949), Read proposed that the greatest contribution of existentialism "is saying that man is the reality—not even man in the abstract, but the human person, you and I; and that everything else—freedom, love,

---

[9] As Read noted, however, Martin Buber did write about the importance of Stirner's thought. In *Between Man and Man* (1947), Buber suggested: "What Stirner with his destructive power successfully attacks is the substitute for a reality that is no longer believed: the fictitious responsibility in face of reason, of an idea, a nature, an institution, of all manner of illustrious ghosts, all that in its essence is not a person and hence cannot really, like father and mother, prince and master, husband and friend, like God, make you answerable" (52-3). Buber considered Stirner to be an important figure, who "leads towards his contemporary Kierkegaard" (52).

reason, God—is a contingency depending on the will of the individual" (147). From this point of view it was natural for Read to conclude that "existentialism has much in common with Max Stirner's egoism," although "[a]n existentialist like Sartre differs from Stirner in that he is willing to engage the ego in certain super-egoistic or idealistic aims" (147). Read returned to the subject in "Chains of Freedom" (1946–52), where he openly confessed his suspicion that Sartre was more familiar with Stirner than his silence implied:

> The existentialists speak often of Nietzsche's influence on Husserl, and Stirner is recognised as one of the precursors of Nietzsche. But I suspect a more direct liaison. Stirner is one of the most existentialist of all the philosophers, and whole pages of *The Ego and His Own* read like anticipations of Sartre.
> (*Anarchy and Order* 165)

It was a sentiment he had already expressed in *The Tenth Muse*, where he suggested that he saw "no resemblance at all [...] between Kierkegaard and Sartre," but that "the characters in Sartre's plays and novels are constructed round a philosophy which seems to me to be identical with Stirner's (plus a little American pragmatism)" (Read 81). Read was correct to suggest that there were fundamental correlations between the ideas of Stirner and Sartre, and his suspicions about Sartre's silence were not without merit.

Setting aside the fundamental incompatibility of any existentialist notion of becoming with Stirnerian egoism, there is clearly some common ground between Sartre and Stirner. Certainly, Sartre's definition of *being-for-itself* in *Being and Nothingness* (1943) "as being what it is not and not being what it is" (*Being and Nothingness* lxv), recalled Stirner's negative conception of the self as a creative nothing.[10] What Sartrean existentialism shares with egoism is the position that experience preceded—and indeed created—the world of ideals, morals, and essences. Nevertheless, the likely reason for this similarity was that, working forward from Kierkegaard, Nietzsche, and Heidegger, Sartre could reasonably come to several conclusions that Stirner had arrived at in response to Hegel and Feuerbach. Over time, any common ground between egoism and existentialism was subsumed by notions of self-realization that more rightly belonged to the thought of Nietzsche than Stirner. In *Existentialism Is a Humanism* (1946) Sartre reiterated the similarity between his own understanding of individual experience

---

[10] Stirner repudiated Fichte's conception of the self-positing ego by suggesting that only "the self-dissolving ego, the never-being ego, the—*finite* ego is really I" (*The Ego and Its Own* 163).

and Stirner's concept of the creative nothing. Sartre proposed that "[i]f man as the existentialist sees him is not definable, it is because to begin with he is nothing" (*Existentialism Is a Humanism* 290). This conclusion led to the "first principle of existentialism" that "[m]an is nothing else but that which he makes of himself" (291). Although much of *Existentialism Is a Humanism* was later rejected by Sartre, both existentialism and egoism relied on a negative conception of the ego as an inexpressible self that preceded language and abstract ideas.

In addition to Dada, Surrealism, and existentialism, Read indicated that developments in the field of psychology provided another haven where Stirner's ideas found continued relevance in the twentieth century.[11] Once again his ideas were absorbed, according to Read, without due acknowledgment. He suggested that "most modern psychologists—certainly Jung, Burrow, Rank, and Fromm—would subscribe to what is the essence of Stirner's claim that freedom, 'in the full amplitude of the word' is 'essentially self-liberation—i.e. that I can only have so much freedom as I procure for myself by my ownness'" (*The Tenth Muse* 80). If these psychologists had not actively engaged with Stirner's thought, egoism nonetheless anticipated contemporary developments in their theories. Read rejected the view that egoism was a philosophy of simple selfishness, and observed that "Stirner's doctrine is, in fact, a plea for the integration of the personality, and on that basis the charge of 'selfishness' becomes somewhat naïve" (80). This was perhaps most apparent in Stirner's discussion of egoistic love, for which Read seemed to express unqualified support. He suggested that "[t]he whole of Stirner's treatment of the subject of love is of great subtlety and profundity, and Marxian criticism does not touch it at all" (81). Egoistic love was one of the few aspects of Stirner's work not to become subsumed into and subsequently associated with the theories Read described.

There were, however, psychologists who appear to have at least been familiar with the ideas of Stirner, including Otto Gross and Wilhelm Reich. A former student of Freud, Gross is infamous for his radical approaches to sexuality and psychology; his involvement in the Ascona anarchist commune; and for his affairs with Frieda and Else von Richthofen.[12] Arthur Mitzman suggests

---

[11] Later still, Stirner's ideas demonstrably influenced deconstruction and the thought of Jacques Derrida. In *Specters of Marx* (1993) Derrida suggested that "let us not try to hide the fact here, although this is not exactly the right moment, that we take seriously the originality, audacity, and, precisely, the philosophico-political seriousness of Stirner who also should be read without Marx or against him" (151).

[12] This is yet another interesting connection between D. H. Lawrence and various purveyors of Stirnerian egoism. D'Annunzio and the Futurists drew his attention, and his familiarity with Gross's psychological theories may help explain his use of egoism when discussing D'Annunzio's writing.

that a "shift in ground from Stirnerian individualism to a communitarian ideology, or rather the attempt to make the two compatible [...] characterizes a fundamental turning point in Gross' ideas during the war" (90). Carl Levy also observes a connection between "the Stirner revival through Mackay's blending of Nietzsche with Stirner, the romantic libertarian Jewish intelligentsia [...] and the erotic movement of Gross" (87). There is less ambiguity about Wilhelm Reich's attitude to Stirnerian egoism. In his autobiography he described Stirner in adulatory terms:

> Communist gibberish and egotistical reality! Look at Russia! Max Stirner, the god who saw in 1844 what we do not see today in 1921! Somehow I am growing increasingly secure in my conviction that a system of economic communism which lacks a candid acknowledgment of egotism is an impossibility.
>
> (158)

Ultimately, however, the connections between Stirner and the fringes of psychology are yet to be fully charted. As in the cases above, historians of psychology have largely ignored any intellectual debt that the field might owe to Stirner's theories of the ego.

Exorcizing Modernity

The reality is that various aspects of Stirner's thought thrived both between and after the two World Wars, but they increasingly became associated with thinkers who rarely acknowledged Stirner's importance. Throughout the twentieth century, Marxism became a hegemonic force in radical politics. Anarchism was relegated to the status of a fringe movement, while forms of individualist anarchism became inconsequential subsets of that fringe. Significant opponents of Marx in his lifetime, such as Bakunin and Stirner, became footnotes in the history of communism, while connections between Stirner's ideas and the development of fascism poisoned his reputation. Stirner's contributions to theories of art were portioned out to others; rebellion became the purview of Camus; the abstract foundations of language were associated with existentialism; the contingent nature of morality became the contribution of Nietzsche; and the inexpressible ego belonged to the psychologists. The only aspects of Stirner's thought that remained his own were his failings: an unworkable theory in which the individual strove for total ownership and a desire to carve out a unique existence that seemed to many mere selfishness.

This book has not sought to provide an exhaustive account of the various connections between Stirnerian egoism and instances of avant-garde manifesto writing. It could not hope to. Many more movements, including Expressionism, Fauvism, and Russian Futurism, at least superficially, suggest the influence of Stirner's thought. By 1920, Stirner had found a wide international audience through his contributions to anarchism, Futurism, and Dada. Stirner's first Japanese translator, Jun Tsuji, also described himself as Japan's first Dadaist. In Australia, the influential literary critic A. G. Stephens reviewed Huneker's *Egoists* in 1909 and suggested that "Stendhal, Baudelaire, Flaubert, Anatole France, Huysmans, Maurice Barres, Nietzsche, Ibsen, Max Stirner—these names make an attractive bill of fare" (20). Stephens went on to propose that "altruism is plainly hyperegoism" and suggested that the real "opposition pressed by Huneker is rather that of rebels and martyrs which makes the deepest psychical division of humanity" (20). Even now, Stirner continues to find new readers from the disenchanted fringes of anarchism and nationalism. *Der Einzige und sein Eigentum*, as Read prophesized, still refuses to be digested.

What this book does establish, I hope, is that the character of the avant-garde manifesto—even the modern manifesto more broadly—owes a debt to Stirner's ideas. From Marx's *The Communist Manifesto* through to the manifestos of Marinetti and Lewis, Stirner has remained an ambiguous but influential figure. His suggestion that ideals are the creations and properties of the individual provided an important justification for the codification of ideals into manifestos. Egoism suggested that values—aesthetic or otherwise—are always contingent on the will of the individual, but if they are not treated as such they can come to dominate their creators. Despite Marx's distaste for Stirner's egoism, he recognized the importance of creating and controlling the moral code of communism. He was not prepared to let another dictate the terms of his ideology. *The Communist Manifesto* was not founded on collective solidarity, but on a philosopher's will to change the course of history. The manifesto was, and remained in the hands of early avant-gardists, a manifestation of will, rather than intellect; praxis rather than strategy. The early development of the avant-garde manifesto was underpinned by a conscious effort on the part of individuals to rise above abstract ideals of their own creation while imposing these same ideals on movements they regarded as their property. Even if no longer consciously, egoism remains implicit in the manifesto writer's desire to codify the moral values of a group. The manifesto continues to carry, within its polemic, a manifestation of egoism.

Stirner comprehensively destroyed the essences of Hegelian idealism, but the tragedy of his reception is that he was persistently read as though he had come after Marx, Bakunin, and Nietzsche. At his best, Stirner provided a fateful warning about the capacity of unquestioned ideas to imprison the mind. He described no universal template for how life should be lived because he argued that the conditions of life were as unique and multitudinous as the individuals who experienced them. In this one regard his thought transcended that of Marx and Nietzsche. The individual was not the product of history; history was the property of the individual. Nor was human experience a bridge to the universal *Übermensch*; it was the expansion of a singular reality produced at every moment by the consumption of one's own life. Abstract ideas were not external threats, but alienated properties that had been permitted to take possession of their owner. Stirner's critique of untrammeled abstraction was no less relevant to his readers in the twentieth century—enthralled as they were by abstract notions of communism, nationalism, liberalism, and fascism—than it had been in his own lifetime, but it was largely ignored in favor of anarchist and reactionary interpretations of his thought.

Connections to the development of anarchism and fascism poisoned Stirner's reputation, but they also ensured that aspects of his thought survived in the individualistic and insurrectionary currents of modern thought. It was largely because of polemicists, terrorists, and radical bohemians that Stirner's ideas endured the silence and disdain of his contemporaries. Marx believed he had defeated Stirner, but his opponent's ideas lived on in the modern manifesto, a genre that Marx himself had helped to popularize. Nevertheless, the time to consider Stirner beyond the context of Marx and Nietzsche is long-overdue. To confine him to the role of Marx's enemy or Nietzsche's precursor does a disservice to the originality of his thought. More importantly, it ignores his own conclusions about the uniqueness of individual experience. Indeed, abstractions continue to run unchecked in the twenty-first century, and Stirner's critique is as pertinent as ever. It is certainly possible to see shades of egoism in the cynicism and self-interest of the modern political operator—whether revolutionary or reactionary—but Stirner was not a proponent of authoritarianism. In fact, he denied the existence of state authority entirely. If he helped provide tyrants with the tools of oppression, it was only because he accurately described how individuals could be imprisoned by their own fixed ideas. It must be remembered that Stirner did not attempt to break the shackles of moral training for the benefit of others, but out of an egoistic desire for self-satisfaction. It is unsurprising that those who borrowed his ideas rarely gave him the due credit. Perhaps a history of repeated appropriation and alteration was a fitting fate for the ideas of a man who once declared that "[y]our thoughts are *my* thoughts, which I dispose of as I will, and which I strike down unmercifully; they are my property, which I annihilate as I wish" (Stirner, *The Ego and Its Own* 302). History suggests that manifesto writers who read Stirner's book took this advice to heart.

Works Cited

Albright, Daniel. *Putting Modernism Together: Literature, Music, and Painting, 1872-1927*. Johns Hopkins UP, 2015.
Antliff, Allan. *Anarchy and Art: From the Paris Commune to the Fall of the Berlin Wall*. Arsenal Pulp P, 2007.
Ashford, David. *Autarchies: The Invention of Selfishness*. Bloomsbury, 2017.
Ashton, Rosemary. *The German Idea: Four English Writers and the Reception of German Thought, 1800-1860*. Cambridge UP, 1980.
Baginski, Max. "Stirner: 'The Ego and His Own.'" *Mother Earth*, vol. 2, no. 3, May 1907, pp. 142-51.
Bakunin, Michael. *Bakunin on Anarchy: Selected Works by the Activist Founder of World Anarchism*. Edited and translated by Sam Dolgoff, Alfred A. Knopf, 1972.
Bakunin, Michael. *Statism and Anarchy*. Translated and edited by Marshall Shatz, Cambridge UP, 1990.
Barrès, Maurice. "From Hegel to the Workmen's Canteens of the North." *The French Right: From de Maistre to Maurras*, edited by J. S. McClelland, Harper, 1970, pp. 145-58.
Barrès, Maurice. *L'Ennemi des lois*. Paris, Perrin et Cie, 1893.
Barrès, Maurice. *Sous l'œil des barbares*. Emile-Paul, 1911.
Basch, Victor. *L'Individualisme anarchiste*. Félix Alcan, 1904.
Baudelaire, Charles. "Correspondences." *The Flowers of Evil*, translated by James McGowan, Oxford UP, 2008, p. 19.
Baudelaire, Charles. "The Life and Work of Eugène Delacroix." *The Painter of Modern Life and Other Essays*, translated and edited by Jonathan Mayne, Phaidon, 1964, pp. 41-68.
Baudelaire, Charles. "The Painter of Modern Life." *The Painter of Modern Life and Other Essays*, translated and edited by Jonathan Mayne, Phaidon, 1964, pp. 1-40.
Bauer, J. Edgar. "On the Nameless Love and Infinite Sexualities: John Henry Mackay, Magnus Hirschfeld and the Origins of the Sexual Emancipation Movement." *Journal of Homosexuality*, vol. 50, no. 1, 2005, pp. 1-26.
Beales, Derek and Eugenio Biagni. *The Risorgimento and the Unification of Italy*. Routledge, 2013.
Berghaus, Günter. *Futurism and Politics: Between Anarchist Rebellion and Fascist Reaction, 1909-1944*. Berghahn, 1996.
Birmingham, Kevin. *The Most Dangerous Book: The Battle for James Joyce's Ulysses*. Head of Zeus, 2014.

Blissett, William. "D. H. Lawrence, D'Annunzio, Wagner." *Wisconsin Studies in Contemporary Literature*, vol. 7, no. 1, 1966, pp. 21–46.

Borelli, Elena. *Giovanni Pascoli, Gabriele D'Annunzio, and the Ethics of Desire: Between Action and Contemplation.* Fairleigh Dickinson UP, 2017.

Bourdeau, Jean. "Nouvelles modes en philosophie: Max Stirner et Frédéric Nietzsche." *Journal des débats politiques et littéraires*, Thursday night, 16 March 1893, pp. 1–2.

Breton, André. "Manifesto of Surrealism." *Manifestoes of Surrealism*, translated by Richard Seaver and Helen R. Lane, U of Michigan P, 1972, pp. 1–47.

Brobjer, Thomas H. "A Possible Solution to the Stirner-Nietzsche Question." *Journal of Nietzsche Studies*, no. 25, 2003, pp. 109–14.

Buber, Martin. *Between Man and Man.* Translated by Ronald Gregor-Smith, Routledge, 2002.

Calasso, Roberto. *La Folie Baudelaire.* Translated by Alistair McEwen, Penguin, 2013.

Calasso, Roberto. *The Forty-Nine Steps.* Translated by John Shepley, Pimlico, 2002.

Camus, Albert. *L'Homme revolté. Albert Camus: Essais.* Edited by R. Quilliot and L. Faucon, Gallimard, 1965, pp. 407–709.

Camus, Albert. *The Rebel.* Translated by Anthony Bower, Penguin, 1973.

Camus, Albert. *The Rebel.* Translated by Anthony Bower, Vintage, 1991.

Carr, E. H. *Michael Bakunin.* Alfred A. Knopf, 1961.

Carroll, John. *Break-Out from the Crystal Palace: The Anarcho-Psychological Critique: Stirner, Nietzsche, Dostoevsky.* Routledge, 1974.

Carroll, John. Introduction. *The Ego and His Own.* Edited by Carroll, translated by Steven Byington, Jonathan Cape, 1971.

Carswell, John. *Lives and Letters: A. R. Orage, Beatrice Hastings, Katherine Mansfield, John Middleton Murry, S. S. Koteliansky.* New Directions, 1978.

Carus, Paul. "Max Stirner, the Predecessor of Nietzsche." *The Monist*, vol. 21, no. 3, 1911, pp. 376–97.

Caws, Mary Ann. *Manifesto: A Century of Isms.* U of Nebraska P, 2001.

Cunningham, Valentine. "Imagining *The Essence of Christianity*: Religion, Heart, and Mind in George Eliot." *The George Eliot Review*, no. 49, 2018, p. 15.

Curtis, Michael. *Three against the Third Republic: Sorel, Barrès and Maurras.* Princeton UP, 1959.

D'Annunzio, Gabriele. *La gloria: Tragedia.* Milan, Fratelli Treves, 1899.

D'Annunzio, Gabriele. *La Reggenza Italiana del Carnaro: Disegno di un nuovo ordinamento dello stato libero di Fiume.* Fionda, 1920.

D'Annunzio, Gabriele. *The Triumph of Death.* Translated by Georgina Harding, Dedalus, 1990.

Derrida, Jacques. *Specters of Marx: The State of the Debt, the Work of Mourning and the New International.* Translated by Peggy Kamuf, Routledge, 2006.

Dostoyevsky, Fyodor Mikhailovich. *The Brothers Karamazov.* Translated by Constance Garnett, William Benton, 1952.

Edwards, Paul. *Wyndham Lewis: Painter and Writer*. Yale UP, 2000.
Eliot, George. "GE to Sara Sophia Hennell, London, [29 April 1854]." *The George Eliot Letters*, edited by Gordon S. Haight, vol. 2, Oxford UP, 1954, p. 153.
Eliot, George. *Middlemarch*. Penguin, 2003.
Eliot, T. S. "Egoists." *Harvard Advocate*, vol. 88, no. 1, 5 October 1909, p. 16.
Ellman, Richard. *James Joyce*. Oxford UP, 1959.
Engels, Frederick. "Engels to Marx." 19 November 1844. *Karl Marx Frederick Engels: Collected Works*, edited by Jack Cohen et al, translated by Peter and Betty Ross, vol. 38, Lawrence & Wishart, 1982, pp. 9–14.
Engels, Frederick. "Engels to Marx." 20 January 1845. *Karl Marx Frederick Engels: Collected Works*, edited by Jack Cohen et al, translated by Peter and Betty Ross, vol. 38, Lawrence & Wishart, 1982, pp. 15–20.
Engels, Frederick. "Engels to Max Hildebrand." 22 October 1889. *Karl Marx Frederick Engels: Collected Works*, edited by Eric Hobsbawm et al, translated by Peter and Betty Ross et al, vol. 48, Lawrence & Wishart, 2001, pp. 393–5.
Feuerbach, Ludwig. *Das Wesen des Christentums*. Leipzig, Otto Wigand, 1841.
Feuerbach, Ludwig. *The Essence of Christianity*. Translated by Marian Evans, London, John Chapman, 1854.
Feuerbach, Ludwig. "*The Essence of Christianity* in Relation to *The Ego and Its Own*." *The Philosophical Forum*, translated by Frederick M. Gordon, vol. viii, nos. 2-3-4, 1978, pp. 81–91.
Feuerbach, Ludwig. "Über das *Wesen des Christentums* in Beziehung auf den *Einzigen und sein Eigentum*." *Wigands Vierteljahrsschrift*, no. 2, September 1845, pp. 193–205.
Fichte, Johann Gottlieb. *Foundations of Natural Right: According to the Principles of the Wissenschaftslehre*. Edited by Frederick Neuhouser, Cambridge UP, 2000.
Fichte, Johann Gottlieb. *Grundlage des Naturrechts nach Principien der Wissenschaftslehre*. Jena, Christian Ernst Gabler, 1796.
Flint, F. S. "Imagisme." *Poetry*, vol. 1, no. 6, March 1913, pp. 198–200.
Forth, Christopher E. "Nietzsche, Decadence, and Regeneration in France, 1891–95." *Journal of the History of Ideas*, vol. 54, no. 1, 1993, pp. 97–117.
France, Anatole. "La vie à Paris." *Le Temps*, 26 September 1886, pp. 2–3.
Funck-Brentano, Théophile. *Les Sophistes allemands et les nihilistes russes*. Paris, Plon, 1887.
Gaudier-Brzeska, Henri. "Vortex. Gaudier Brzeska." *Blast*, vol. 1, no. 1, 1914, pp. 155–8.
Glassford, John. "Did Friedrich Nietzsche Plagiarise from Max Stirner." *Journal of Nietzsche Studies*, no. 18, 1999, pp. 73–9.
Goldman, Emma. *Anarchism and Other Essays*. Mother Earth, 1917.
Goldman, Emma. *Living My Life*. Penguin, 2006.
Goodway, David. *Anarchist Seeds beneath the Snow: Left-Libertarian Thought and British Writers from William Morris to Colin Ward*. Liverpool UP, 2006.

Hamilton, Paul. *Coleridge and German Philosophy: The Poet in the Land of Logic.* Bloomsbury, 2007.

Härmänmaa, Marja. "Beyond Anarchism: Marinetti's Futurist (Anti-)Utopia of Individualism and 'Artocracy.'" *The European Legacy*, vol. 14, no. 7, 2009, pp. 857–71.

Harrison, Austin. "The Kaiser's World War: World-Power or Downfall." *The English Review*, vol. 18, 1914, pp. 312–26.

Harrison, Austin. "Psychology and Motives." *The English Review*, vol. 18, 1914, pp. 233–47.

Von Hartmann, Eduard. *Philosophy of the Unconscious.* Translated by William Chatterton Coupland, vol. 3, London, Kegan Paul, 1893.

Heller, Erich. *The Importance of Nietzsche.* University of Chicago P, 1988.

Hemingway, Ernest. *Across the River and into the Trees.* Jonathan Cape, 1950.

Hess, Moses. "The Recent Philosophers." *The Young Hegelians: An Anthology*, edited by Lawrence S. Stepelevich, Cambridge UP, 1983, pp. 359–75.

Hughes-Hallett, Lucy. *The Pike: Gabriele D'Annunzio, Poet, Seducer and Preacher of War.* Fourth Estate, 2013.

Huneker, James. *Egoists, a Book of Supermen: Stendhal, Baudelaire, Flaubert, Anatole France, Huysmans, Barrès, Nietzsche, Blake, Ibsen, Stirner, and Ernest Hello.* Charles Scribner's Sons, 1909.

Ialongo, Ernest. *Filippo Tommaso Marinetti: The Artist and His Politics.* Fairleigh Dickinson UP, 2015.

Jackson, Holbrook. "Book Notes." *The New Age*, vol. 1, no. 1, 2 May 1907, p. 13.

Jackson, Holbrook. "Marginalia." *The New Age*, vol. 1, no. 12, 18 July 1907, p. 188.

Jensen, Richard Bach. "The International Anti-Anarchist Conference of 1898 and the Origins of Interpol." *Journal of Contemporary History*, vol. 16, no. 2, April 1981, pp. 323–47.

Joannou, Maroula. "The Angel of Freedom: Dora Marsden and the Transformation of *The Freewoman* into *The Egoist*." *Women's History Review*, vol. 11, no. 4, 2002, pp. 595–611.

Jones, Gareth Stedman. *Karl Marx: Greatness and Illusion.* Penguin, 2016.

Kahn, Gustave. "Stirner et l'individualisme." *La Nouvelle Revue*, no. 30, 1 September 1904, pp. 131–6.

Kant, Immanuel. *Anthropology from a Pragmatic Point of View.* Translated by Victor Lyle Dowdell and edited by Hans H. Rudnick, Southern Illinois UP, 1978.

Kelly, Gertrude B. "A Letter of Protest." *Liberty*, vol. 5, no. 1, 13 August 1887, p. 7.

Kelly, John F. "A Final Statement." *Liberty*, vol. 4, no. 26, 30 July 1887, p. 7.

Kenny, Anthony. *The Rise of Modern Philosophy: A New History of Modern Philosophy, Volume 3.* Clarendon, 2006.

Laing, Kathryn. "*The Sentinel* by Rebecca West: A Newly Discovered Novel." *Notes and Queries*, vol. 45, no. 2, 1998, pp. 234–7.

Lange, Friedrich-Albert. *The History of Materialism and Criticism of Its Present Importance*. Translated by Ernest Chester Thomas, vol. 2, Boston, Houghton Osgood, 1880.
Lansdown, Richard. "Byron and the Carbonari." *History Today*, vol. 41, May 1991, pp. 18–25.
Lanson, Gustave. "La Poésie contemporaine: M. Stéphane Mallarmé." *Revue Universitaire*, vol. 2, no. 7, 15 July 1893, pp. 121–31.
Lasvignes, Henri. Introduction. *L'Unique et sa propriété*, translated by Lasvignes, Editions de la Revue Blanche, 1900.
Lawrence, D. H. *Kangaroo*. William Heinemann, 1923.
Lawrence, D. H. *The Letters of D. H. Lawrence: Volume II 1913–16*. Edited by George J. Zytaruk and James T. Boulton, Cambridge UP, 2002.
Lawrence, D. H. *Twilight in Italy*. Duckworth, 1916.
Lazare, Bernard. "Anarchistes." *Entretiens*, vol. 5, no. 29, August 1892, pp. 96–7.
Lee, Vernon. *Gospels of Anarchy and Other Contemporary Studies*. T. Fisher Unwin, 1908.
Leopold, David. Introduction. *The Ego and Its Own*, edited by Leopold, translated by Steven Byington, Cambridge UP, 1995.
Lévy, Albert. *Stirner et Nietzsche*. Société nouvelle de librairie et d'édition, 1904.
Levy, Carl. "Max Weber, Anarchism and Libertarian Culture: Personality and Power Politics." *Max Weber and the Culture of Anarchy*, edited by Sam Whimster, Macmillan, 1999, pp. 83–109.
Levy, Oscar. "Jack Ashore." *Supplement to the New Age*, vol. 9, no. 23, 5 October 1911, pp. 1–7.
Lewes, George Henry. *A Biographical History of Philosophy*. Series 2, vol. 4, London: G. Cox, 1853.
Lewis, Wyndham. *The Art of Being Ruled*. Edited by Reed Way Dasenbrock, Black Sparrow press, 1989.
Lewis, Wyndham. *Blasting and Bombardiering: An Autobiography (1914–1926)*. Calder and Boyars, 1967.
Lewis, Wyndham. "Enemy of the Stars." *Blast*, no. 1, 1914, pp. 51–86.
Lewis, Wyndham. "Futurism, Magic and Life." *Blast*, no. 1, 1914, pp. 132–5.
Lewis, Wyndham. *Letters of Wyndham Lewis*. Edited by W. K. Rose, New Directions, 1963.
Lewis, Wyndham. "Life Is the Important Thing!" *Blast*, no. 1, 1914, pp. 129–31.
Lewis, Wyndham. "Manifesto I." *Blast*, no. 1, 1914, pp. 10–28.
Lewis, Wyndham. "Manifesto II." *Blast*, no. 1, 1914, pp. 30–43.
Lewis, Wyndham. "The New Egos." *Blast*, no. 1, 1914, p. 141.
Lewis, Wyndham. "Our Vortex." *Blast*, no. 1, 1914, pp. 147–9.
Lewis, Wyndham. *Tarr: The 1918 Version*. Black Sparrow Press, 1990.

Low, B. "The Freewoman Discussion Circle." *The Freewoman*, vol. 2, no. 32, 27 June 1912, p. 115.

Löwith, Karl. *From Hegel to Nietzsche*. Constable, 1964.

Lyon, Janet. *Manifestos: Provocations of the Modern*. Cornell UP, 1999.

Mackay, John Henry. *The Anarchists: A Picture of Civilization at the Close of the Nineteenth Century*. Translated by George Schumm, Boston, Benjamin R. Tucker, 1891.

Mackay, John Henry. *Max Stirner: His Life and Work*. Translated by Hubert Kennedy, Peremptory, 2005.

Mackay, John Henry. Untitled letter. *The Eagle and the Serpent*, vol. 1, no. 3, 15 June 1898, p. 47.

Mallarmé, Stéphane. "Crisis in Verse." *Divagations*, translated by Barbara Johnson, Harvard UP, 2007, pp. 201–11.

Mallarmé, Stéphane. "Hamlet." *Divagations*, translated by Barbara Johnson, Harvard UP, 2007, pp. 124–8.

Mallarmé, Stéphane. "Henri Cazalis." *Selected Letters of Stéphane Mallarmé*, edited and translated by Rosemary Lloyd, U of Chicago P, 1988, pp. 59–61.

Mallarmé, Stéphane. "An Interrupted Performance." *Divagations*, translated by Barbara Johnson, Harvard UP, 2007, pp. 23–5.

Mallarmé, Stéphane. "Jean Moréas." *Selected Letters of Stéphane Mallarmé*, edited and translated by Rosemary Lloyd, U of Chicago P, 1988, pp. 173–4.

Mallarmé, Stéphane. "Maurice Barrès." *Selected Letters of Stéphane Mallarmé*, edited and translated by Rosemary Lloyd, U of Chicago P, 1988, pp. 141–2.

Mallarmé, Stéphane. "Restricted Action." *Divagations*, translated by Barbara Johnson, Harvard UP, 2007, pp. 215–19.

Mallarmé, Stéphane. "A Throw of Dice Not Ever Will Abolish Chance." *Manifesto: A Century of Isms*, edited by Mary Ann Caws, U of Nebraska P, 2001, pp. 28–49.

Marcus, Jane. Introduction. *The Young Rebecca: Writings of Rebecca West, 1911–1917*. Selected by Marcus, Macmillan, 1982, pp. 3–11.

Marinetti, Filippo Tommaso. "Against Academic Teachers." *F.T. Marinetti: Critical Writings*, edited by Günter Berghaus, translated by Doug Thompson, Farrar Straus and Giroux, 2006, pp. 81–4.

Marinetti, Filippo Tommaso. "The Foundation and Manifesto of Futurism." *F. T. Marinetti: Critical Writings*, edited by Günter Berghaus, translated by Doug Thompson, Farrar Straus and Giroux, 2006, pp. 11–17.

Marinetti, Filippo Tommaso. "Futurism: An Interview with Mr. Marinetti in *Comœdia*." *F. T. Marinetti: Critical Writings*, edited by Günter Berghaus, translated by Doug Thompson, Farrar Straus and Giroux, 2006, pp. 18–21.

Marinetti, Filippo Tommaso. "Futurism's First Battles." *F. T. Marinetti: Critical Writings*, edited by Günter Berghaus, translated by Doug Thompson, Farrar Straus and Giroux, 2006, pp. 151–7.

Marinetti, Filippo Tommaso. *La conquête des étoiles; poème épique*. E. Sansot, 1909.

Marinetti, Filippo Tommaso. "Lecture to the English on Futurism." *F. T. Marinetti: Critical Writings*, edited by Günter Berghaus, translated by Doug Thompson, Farrar Straus and Giroux, 2006, pp. 89–93.

Marinetti, Filippo Tommaso. "Le Futurisme." *Le Figaro*, 20 February 1891, p. 1.

Marinetti, Filippo Tommaso. *Mafarka the Futurist: An African Novel*. Translated by Carol Diethe and Steve Cox, Middlesex UP, 1998.

Marinetti, Filippo Tommaso. "The Necessity and Beauty of Violence." *F. T. Marinetti: Critical Writings*, edited by Günter Berghaus, translated by Doug Thompson, Farrar Straus and Giroux, 2006, pp. 60–72.

Marinetti, Filippo Tommaso. "Self Portrait." *F. T. Marinetti: Critical Writings*, edited by Günter Berghaus, translated by Doug Thompson, Farrar Straus and Giroux, 2006, pp. 5–8.

Marinetti, Filippo Tommaso. *The Untameables*. Translated by Jeremy Parzen, Green Integer, 2016.

Marinetti, Filippo Tommaso. "War the Sole Cleanser of the World." *F. T. Marinetti: Critical Writings*, edited by Günter Berghaus, translated by Doug Thompson, Farrar Straus and Giroux, 2006, pp. 53–4.

Marinetti, Filippo Tommaso. "We Renounce Our Symbolist Masters, the Last of All Lovers of the Moonlight." *F. T. Marinetti: Critical Writings*, edited by Günter Berghaus, translated by Doug Thompson, Farrar Straus and Giroux, 2006, pp. 43–6.

Marinetti, Filippo Tommaso. "Wireless Imagination and Words at Liberty: The New Futurist Manifesto." *Poetry and Drama*, vol. 1, no. 3, September 1913, pp. 319–26.

Marsden, Dora. "The Art of the Future." *The New Freewoman*, vol. 1, no. 10, 1 November 1913, pp. 181–3.

Marsden, Dora. "Bondwomen." *The Freewoman*, vol. 1, no. 1, 23 November 1911, pp. 1–2.

Marsden, Dora. *The Definition of the Godhead*. Egoist P, 1928.

Marsden, Dora. "The Growing Ego." *The Freewoman*, vol. 2, no. 38, 8 August 1912, pp. 221–2.

Marsden, Dora. "Interpretations of Sex." *The Freewoman*, vol. 1, no. 26, 16 May 1912, pp. 501–2.

Marsden, Dora. "The Lean Kind." *The New Freewoman*, vol. 1, no. 1, 15 June 1913, pp. 1–2.

Marsden, Dora. "Views and Comments." *The Egoist*, vol. 1, no. 1, January 1, 1914, pp. 3–5.

Marsden, Dora. "Views and Comments." *The Egoist*, vol. 1, no. 5, 2 March 1914, pp. 83–5.

Marsden, Dora. "Views and Comments." *The New Freewoman*, vol. 1, no. 6, 1 September 1913, pp. 104–6.

Marsden, Dora. "Views and Comments." *The New Freewoman*, vol. 1, no. 11, 15 November 1913, pp. 203–5.

Marsden, Dora. "Views and Comments." *The New Freewoman*, vol. 1, no. 13, 15 December 1913, pp. 244-5.
Marsden, Dora and Grace Jardine. "Our Last Issue." *The Freewoman*, vol. 2, no. 47, 10 October 1912, pp. 401-2.
Marshall, Peter. *Demanding the Impossible: A History of Anarchism*. Harper Perennial, 2008.
Marx, Karl. "Marx to Engels." 20 July 1852. *Karl Marx Frederick Engels: Collected Works*, edited by E. J. Hobsbawm et al, translated by Peter and Betty Ross, Lawrence & Wishart, 1983, vol. 39, pp. 134-5.
Marx, Karl. "Marx to Engels." 26 September 1856. *Karl Marx Frederick Engels: Collected Works*, edited by E. J. Hobsbawm et al, translated by Peter and Betty Ross, vol. 40, Lawrence & Wishart, 1983, pp. 70-2.
Marx, Karl. "Marx to Heinrich Börnstein." 1844-1845. *Karl Marx Frederick Engels: Collected Works*, edited by Jack Cohen et al, translated by Peter and Betty Ross, vol. 38, Lawrence & Wishart, 1982, p. 14.
Marx, Karl. "Marx to Pavel Vasilyevich Annenkov." 9 December 1847. *Karl Marx Frederick Engels: Collected Works*, edited by Jack Cohen et al, translated by Peter and Betty Ross, vol. 38, Lawrence & Wishart, 1982, pp. 150-1.
Marx, Karl. "Theses on Feuerbach." *Karl Marx Frederick Engels: Collected Works*, edited by Jack Cohen et al, vol. 5, Lawrence & Wishart, 1976, pp. 3-9.
Marx, Karl and Frederick Engels. *The Communist Manifesto*. Translated by Samuel Moore, edited by Joseph Katz, Pocket Books, 1964.
Marx, Karl and Frederick Engels. *The German Ideology. Karl Marx Frederick Engels: Collected Works*, edited by Jack Cohen et al, translated by Clemens Dutt et al, vol. 5, Lawrence & Wishart, 1976, pp. 19-539.
Mazgaj, Paul. *Imagining Fascism: The Cultural Politics of the French Young Right, 1930-1945*. U of Delaware P, 2007.
McCall, John Erwin. "A Course of Reading for Young Egoists." *The Eagle and the Serpent*, vol. 1, no. 2, 15 April 1898, p. 28.
McGuiness, Patrick. *Poetry and Radical Politics in fin de siècle France: From Anarchism to Action Française*. Oxford UP, 2015.
McLellan, David. *The Young Hegelians and Karl Marx*. Billing and Sons, 1969.
McLelland, J. S. *The French Right: From de Maistre to Maurras*. Harper, 1970.
Meredith, George. *The Egoist: A Comedy in Narrative*. Constable, 1914.
Michaud, Guy. *Mallarmé*. Translated by Marie Collins and Bertha Humez, New York UP, 1965.
Mitzman, Arthur. "Anarchism, Expressionism and Psychoanalysis." *New German Critique*, no. 10, 1977, pp. 77-104
Monro, Harold. "Varia." *Poetry and Drama*, vol. 1, no. 3, September 1913, pp. 262-72.
Moody, A. David. *Ezra Pound: Poet*. Vol. 1, Oxford UP, 2007.

Moréas, Jean. "Le Symbolisme." *Le Figaro: Supplément littéraire du dimanche*, 18 September 1886, pp. 150–1.

Moréas, Jean. "Symbolist Manifesto." *Manifesto: A Century of Isms*, edited by Mary Ann Caws, U of Nebraska P, 2001, pp. 50–1.

Moréas, Jean. "Une nouvelle école." *Le Figaro*, 13 September 1891, p. 1.

Morgan, Peter. "Pederasty and Anarchist Individualism in the Work of John Henry Mackay." *Kulturrebellen – Studien zur anarchistischen Moderne*, edited by Christine Magerski and David Roberts, Springer, 2019, pp. 119–37.

Mussolini, Benito. "In tema di neutralità: Al nostro posto!" *Opera Omnia di Benito Mussolini*, edited by Edoardo and Duilio Susmel, vol. 6, Fenice, 1954, pp. 331–2.

Mussolini, Benito. "La filosofia della forza." *Opera Omnia di Benito Mussolini*, edited by Edoardo and Duilio Susmel, vol. 1, Fenice, 1954, pp. 174–84.

Mussolini, Benito. "Mussolini to Berti." 3 November 1911. *Opera Omnia di Benito Mussolini*, edited by Edoardo and Duilio Susmel, vol. 4, Fenice, 1954, pp. 257–8.

Mussolini, Benito. *My Autobiography*. Translated by Richard Washburn Child, Mayflower P, 1936.

Mussolini, Benito. "Vecchie Usanze." *Opera Omnia di Benito Mussolini*, edited by Edoardo and Duilio Susmel, vol. 14. Fenice, 1954, pp. 192–4.

Newman, Saul. *From Bakunin to Lacan: Anti-Authoritarianism and the Dislocation of Power*. Lexington, 2001.

Nietzsche, Friedrich. *On the Future of Our Educational Institutions*. Edited by Oscar Levy, translated by J. M. Kennedy, T. N. Foulis, 1909.

Nietzsche, Friedrich. *The Gay Science*. Edited by Bernard Williams, translated by Josefine Nauckhoff and Adrian Del Caro, Cambridge UP, 2001.

Nietzsche, Friedrich. *The Genealogy of Morals*. Translated by Horace B. Samuel, Dover, 2003.

Nietzsche, Friedrich. *Thus Spoke Zarathustra*. Translated by R. J. Hollingdale, Penguin, 2003.

O'Keeffe, Paul. *Some Sort of Genius: A Life of Wyndham Lewis*. Pimlico, 2001.

Orwell, George. *Homage to Catalonia*. Harcourt Brace, 1980.

Papanikolas, Theresa. *Anarchism and the Advent of Paris Dada: Art and Criticism, 1914–1924*. Routledge, 2016.

Parry, Richard. *The Bonnot Gang: The Story of the French Illegalists*. PM, 2016.

Paterson, Ronald and William Keith. *The Nihilistic Egoist Max Stirner*. Oxford UP, 1971.

Pound, Ezra. "A Few Don'ts by an Imagiste." *Poetry*, vol. 1, no. 6, March 1913, pp. 200–6.

Pound, Ezra. *Guide to Kulchur*. New Directions, 1968.

Pound, Ezra. "The Serious Artist." *The New Freewoman*, vol. 1, no. 9, 15 October 1913, pp. 161–3.

Pound, Ezra. "Status Rerum: London, December 10, 1912." *Poetry*, vol. 1, no. 4, January 1913, pp. 123–7.

Pound, Ezra. "Vortex. Pound." *Blast*, no. 1, 1914, pp. 153–4.

Proudhon, Pierre-Joseph. *De la justice dans la révolution et dans l'Église*. Paris, C. Marpon et E. Flammarion, 1870.

Proudhon, Pierre-Joseph. *System of Economical Contradictions: Or, The Philosophy of Misery*. Translated by Benjamin R. Tucker, Boston, Benjamin R. Tucker, 1888.

Puchner, Martin. *Poetry of the Revolution: Marx, Manifestos, and the Avant-Gardes*. Princeton UP, 2006.

Quincey-Jones, Steven. "Herbert Read's Egoist Roots." *Modernism/modernity*, vol. 25, no. 2, 2018, pp. 389–405.

Rabaté, Jean-Michel. *James Joyce and the Politics of Egoism*. Cambridge UP, 2001.

Randal, Théodore. "Le Livre Libérateur." *Entretiens*, vol. 5, no. 30, September 1892, pp. 117–28.

Randall, A. E. "Reviews: *Anarchism* by Dr Paul Eltzbacher." *The New Age*, vol. 3, no. 6, 6 June 1908, pp. 114–15.

Randall, A. E. "Reviews: *Gospels of Anarchy* by Vernon Lee." *The New Age*, vol. 3, no. 17, 22 August 1908, pp. 335–6.

Randall, A. E. "Views and Reviews." *The New Age*, vol. 10, no. 25, 18 April 1912, pp. 592–3.

Read, Herbert. *Anarchy and Order: Essays in Politics*. Souvenir P, 1974.

Read, Herbert. *The Contrary Experience: Autobiographies*. Horizon P, 1973.

Read, Herbert. *The Forms of Things Unknown: Essays towards an Aesthetic Philosophy*. Faber and Faber, 1935.

Read, Herbert. Forward. *The Rebel*. Translated by Anthony Bower, Penguin, 1973.

Read, Herbert. *The Tenth Muse: Essays in Criticism*. Routledge and Kegan Paul, 1957.

Reich, Wilhelm. *Passion of Youth: An Autobiography, 1897–1922*. Edited by Mary Boyd Higgins and Chester M. Raphael, translated by Philip Schmitz and Jerri Tompkins, Farrar, 1988.

Rhodes, Anthony. *The Poet as Superman: A Life of Gabriele D'Annunzio*. Weidenfeld and Nicolson, 1959.

Roberts, William. *Cometism and Vorticism: A Tate Gallery Catalogue Revised*. 1956, accessed 29 September 2020. http://www.englishcubist.co.uk/cometism.html.

Roger, Thierry. "Art and Anarchy in the Time of Symbolism: Mallarmé and His Literary Group." *Journal of the Circle for Lacanian Ideology Critique*, vol. 9, 2016, pp. 58–81.

Sartre, Jean-Paul. *Being and Nothingness: An Essay on Phenomenological Ontology*. Translated by Hazel E. Barnes, Philosophical Library, 1956.

Sartre, Jean-Paul. "Existentialism Is a Humanism." *Existentialism: From Dostoevsky to Sartre*, edited and translated by Walter Kaufmann, Meridian Books, 1958.

Scruton, Roger. *A Short History of Modern Philosophy: From Descartes to Wittgenstein*. Routledge, 1981.

Shaw, George Bernard. "A Manifesto." *Fabian Tracts Number 2*, London: Standring, 1884.
Shaw, George Bernard. "The Impossibilities of Anarchism." *Essays in Fabian Socialism*, Constable, 1961, pp. 63–99.
Shaw, George Bernard. *The Sanity of Art*. Benjamin R. Tucker, 1908.
Shone, Steve. *American Anarchism*. Haymarket Books, 2014.
Somigli, Luca. *Legitimizing the Artist: Manifesto Writing and European Modernism, 1885–1915*. U of Toronto P, 2003.
Soucy, Robert. *Fascism in France: The Case of Maurice Barrès*. U of California P, 1972.
Spencer, Herbert. *The Data of Ethics*. New York: D. Appleton and Company, 1881.
Spencer, Herbert. *The Principles of Psychology Volume II. A System of Synthetic Philosophy Volume 5*. London, Williams and Norgate, 1881.
Stedman Jones, Gareth. *Karl Marx: Greatness and Illusion*. Penguin, 2017.
Stepelevich, Lawrence S. "The Revival of Max Stirner." *Journal of the History of Ideas*, vol. 35, no. 2, 1974, pp. 323–8.
Stephens, Alfred George. "The Bookfellow." *The Sunday Times, Perth, West Australia*, 22 August 1909, p. 20.
Stirner, Max. "Art and Religion." *The Young Hegelians: An Anthology*, edited by Lawrence S. Stepelevich, Cambridge UP, 1983, pp. 327–34.
Stirner, Max. *Der Einzige und sein Eigentum*. Edited by Bernd Kast, Verlag Karl Alber, 2016.
Stirner, Max. *The Ego and His Own*. Translated by Steven Byington, Benjamin R. Tucker, 1907.
Stirner, Max. *The Ego and His Own*. Translated by Steven Byington, A. C. Fifield, 1912.
Stirner, Max. *The Ego and His Own*. Edited by John Carroll, translated by Steven Byington, Jonathan Cape, 1971.
Stirner, Max. *The Ego and Its Own*. Edited by David Leopold, translated by Steven Byington, Cambridge UP, 1995.
Stirner, Max. *The False Principle of Our Education: Humanism and Realism*. Translated by Robert H. Beebe, edited by James J. Martin, Ralph Myles, 1967.
Stirner, Max. *L'Unico*. Edited and translated by Ettore Zoccoli, Fratelli Bocca, 1902.
Stirner, Max. *L'Unique et sa propriété*. Translated by Henri Lasvignes, Editions de la Revue Blanche, 1900.
Szeliga. "Über *Der Einzige und sein Eigenthum*." *Norddeutsche Blätter für Kritik, Literatur, und Unterhaltung*, vol. 2, no. 9, March 1845, pp. 1–34.
Taillandier, Saint-René. "De la crise actuelle de la philosophie hégélienne: les partis estrêmes en Allemagne." *Revue des deux Mondes*, vol. 19, 1847, pp. 238–68.
Taillandier, Saint-René. "La démagogie et l'athéisme." *Études sur la Révolution en Allemagne*, vol. 1, Paris, A. Franck, 1853, pp. 333–400.
Thorel, Jean. "Les pères de l'anarchisme: Bakounine, Stirner, Nietzsche." *Revue Bleue*, vol. 51, no. 15, April 1893, pp. 449–55.

Tucker, Benjamin R. "*Lego et Penso*: A Rebel against War." *The New Freewoman*, vol. 1, no. 13, 1913, pp. 254–5.

Tucker, Benjamin R. "Why Not Put Up the Shutters?" *The Egoist*, vol. 1, no. 6, 16 March 1914, p. 118.

"The Unique Individual." *The New Age*, vol. 1, no. 16, 15 August 1907, pp. 250–1.

Wagner, Geoffrey. *Wyndham Lewis: A Portrait of the Artist as the Enemy*. Routledge and Kegan Paul, 1957.

Walker, James L. *The Philosophy of Egoism*. Denver, K. Walker, 1905.

Walker, James L. Introduction. *The Ego and His Own*, translated by Steven Byington, Benjamin R. Tucker, 1907, pp. xii–xviii.

Walker, James L. (Tak Kak). "The Rational Utilitarian Philosophy." *Liberty*, vol. 4, no. 13, 22 January 1887, p. 8.

Walker, James L. (Tak Kak). "What Is Justice?" *Liberty*, vol. 3, no. 25, 6 March 1886, p. 8.

West, Rebecca. "Letter to Dora Marsden in June 1912." *Selected Letters of Rebecca West*, edited by Bonnie Kime Scott, Yale UP, 2000, p. 13.

West, Rebecca. "Minor Poets." *The Freewoman*, vol. 2, no. 29, 6 June 1912, pp. 48–9.

Weston, Selwyn. "A Gospel of Goodwill." *The Freewoman*, vol. 1, no. 5, 21 December 1911, pp. 81–2.

Weston, Selwyn. "Millennium." *The Freewoman*, vol. 1, no. 8, 11 January 1912, pp. 148–9.

Wilde, Oscar. *Soul of Man under Socialism*. The Floating Press, 2009.

Valesio, Paolo. *Gabriele D'Annunzio: The Dark Flame*. Translated by Marilyn Migiel, Yale UP, 1992.

Varèsc, Edgard et al. "Dada Excites Everything." *Manifesto: A Century of Isms*, edited by Mary Ann Caws, U of Nebraska P, 2001, pp. 290–1.

Woodhouse, John. *Gabriele D'Annunzio: Defiant Arcangel*. Oxford UP, 1998.

Youmans, Charles. *Richard Strauss's Orchestral Music and the German Intellectual Tradition*. Indiana UP, 2005.

Zoccoli, Ettore. Introduction. *L'Unico*. Edited and translated by Zoccoli, Torino, Fratelli Bocca, 1902.

Index

Albert, Henri 80
altruism 79, 123–4, 126–7, 143, 145–6, 190
American interlude 128–34
Anarchism and the Advent of Paris Dada (Papanikolas) 79 n.53
anarchist theory 1, 44, 61, 87–92, 96, 122
Angiolillo, Michele 90
Anthropologie in pragmatischer Hinsicht (Kant) 6–7
Antliff, Allan 2
Arghol 164 n.10, 165–8, 168 n.17
Ashford, David 2, 37, 54 n.2, 134, 149–51, 157, 159–60, 164 n.10, 166, 168, 182, 184 n.6
atheist 26 n.14, 28, 181
Auban, Carrard 57, 78–9, 128
Aufstand 11
Autarchies (Ashford) 2, 79 n.53, 150

Baginski, Max 136 n.19
Bakunin, Michael 25, 40 n.28, 42–4, 43 n.29, 51, 55–6, 59, 61, 66, 68, 77, 87–90, 88 n.5
Ball, Hugo 183 n.5
Barnhill, John Basil 137 n.20
Barrès, Maurice 54, 62, 62 n.24, 65, 80, 83, 83 n.60, 84, 86, 88, 104–5, 109–10, 112–14, 117, 120, 129, 136, 136 n.17, 141 n.24, 159 n.5, 182–4, 184 n.6
  De Hegel aux cantines du Nord 77
  Le culte du moi 54, 72–80
  L'Ennemi des lois 78–80
  Sous l'oeil des barbares 73–6, 114
Basch, Victor 94, 94 n.11
Baudelaire, Charles 5, 54–5, 61, 63, 68, 70–2, 83
Bauer, Bruno 21, 30, 36, 36 n.24, 37
Bauer, J. Edgar 135
Berghaus, Günter 93, 95–7, 97 n.17, 100 n.19, 107 n.21

Bergson, Henri 96, 161, 169, 172
Bernhardt, Sarah 93
Between Man and Man (Buber) 186 n.9
A Biographical History of Philosophy (Lewes) 122, 125 n.3
Bonnot, Jules 54 n.2, 81, 87, 162
Börnstein, Heinrich 35
Bourdeau, Jean 58–60, 78
  Nouvelles modes en philosophie: Max Stirner et Frédéric Nietzsche 58, 78
Bourget, Paul 74
Breton, André 79, 79 n.53, 136 n.17, 183–4
Brobjer, Thomas H. 48–50
Bronte, Cesare 113–14
The Brothers Karamazov (Dostoyevsky) 174 n.25
Buber, Martin 8, 186 n.9
Byington, Steven 1 n.1, 27 n.17

Cafiero, Carlo 89
Calasso, Roberto 61–2, 71, 80, 85–6
Camus, Albert 1, 3–4, 6, 8, 181, 181 n.3, 182, 185, 185 n.8, 186, 189
Carnot, Marie François 90
Carr, E. H. 43
Carroll, John 2, 6, 17 n.4, 33–4, 51, 119–20
Carus, Paul 49
Caws, Mary Ann 82, 82 n.57, 153
Cazalis, Henri 65
Chambre des députés 61, 74
Cometism and Vorticism: A Tate Gallery Catalogue Revised (Roberts) 175–6
Costa, Andrea 89

Dähnhardt, Marie 17, 23
Daily Mail 163, 163 n.9
D'Annunzio, Gabriele 73–4, 79, 86–7, 87 n.3, 88, 91–2, 109–18, 110 n.25, 111 n.26, 111 n.28, 117 n.38, 119 n.41, 120, 129, 136, 188 n.12

Darwin, Charles 126
De Ambris, Alceste 87 n.3, 111 n.27, 118
Der Einzige und sein Eigentum (Stirner)
  1, 4–5, 9–10, 15–17, 19–20, 22–39,
  42, 44, 46–9, 51–2, 58–9, 66, 73, 76,
  78–80, 95, 107, 126, 131, 138, 145,
  149, 154, 171–2, 179–80, 185
  artistic creation in 159
  Calasso on 61–2
  Kahn on 93–5
  liberalism in 28–9
  Marx on 38–9
  Reclaire and Lasvignes on 53
  Zoccoli on 89–91
Derrida, Jacques 38 n.26, 99 n.18,
  188 n.11
Desmond, Arthur 136, 136 n.18
Die letzten Philosophen (Hess) 37
Die Neuen 26, 26 n.14
Dostoevsky, Fyodor 2, 6, 51, 161, 173–4
Duchamp, Marcel 135, 183 n.5
Duhamel, Georges 96

The Eagle and the Serpent (McCall) 137–8
Edwards, Paul 108, 161, 165–7
egoism *(Egoismus)* 6–8, 7 n.8, 8, 10–13, 43,
  43 n.30, 73 n.40, 79, 79 n.51, 123–4,
  124 n.2, 126 n.4
  in anarchist theory 87–92
  and the avant-garde 63
  Barrès on 73–4
  Bordeau on 79
  in D'Annunzian politics 113
  divergent 134–7
  Feuerbach and 122–8
  insurrectionary 16–17, 25, 42, 51, 108,
    112, 166, 171, 180
  and manifesto 80–4
  Meredith 144
  Symbolism and 68
  in "The Enemy of the Stars" 164–8
egoistic anarchism 128, 184
egoistic manifesto 9–13, 70, 152
egoistic tradition 5–9, 69
Egoists: A Book of Supermen (Huneker) 5,
  5 n.6, 49, 70, 72
Eliot, George 121–8, 124 nn.1–2, 125 n.3,
  130

Eliot, T. S. 5, 121
Empörung 10–11, 32, 32 n.22
Engels, Frederick 13, 17, 17 n.4, 20–1, 25,
  34–7, 39–40, 42, 44, 59, 96, 154
Existentialism is a Humanism (Sartre)
  174 n.25, 187–8

Fabian Manifesto (Pease) 154
Fauro, Giordano 113–14
Feuerbach, Ludwig 7, 7 n.7, 9–10, 17, 19,
  24, 24 n.12–24 n.13, 25–6, 28, 35–9,
  41–2, 52, 59, 83, 86, 91, 124 n.2, 126
  n.4, 144, 158, 187
  Das Wesen des Christentums 7, 24, 26,
    124 n.1
  and egoism 122–8
Fichte, Johann Gottlieb 7 n.8, 32, 59, 76,
  158
First World War 2, 4–5, 110–11, 120, 152,
  179–80
Flamma, Ruggero 112–14
Flint, Frank Stuart 154–5, 155 n.3, 156
  Imagisme 155–6
  Poetry 154–5, 175
Forth, Christopher E. 68
France 53–6, 60–1, 77–9, 86–8, 93, 96,
  135, 137
France, Anatole 10, 82–3
freedom 8, 20, 32–3, 43, 57, 115, 131–2,
  136 n.19, 188
Fry, Roger 163, 163 n.9
Funck-Brentano, Théophile 56
Futurism 13, 92, 95, 97–108, 134, 155–6,
  161–3, 171

Garibaldi, Giuseppe 88, 88 n.4
Gaudier-Brzeska, Henri 164, 174–5
The Germ 153 n.2
Glassford, John 50
Goethe 34, 80 n.54
Goldman, Emma 90 n.7, 136, 142
Gospels of Anarchy (Lee) 141, 141 n.24
Gross, Otto 188, 188 n.12, 189

Harding, Georgina 116 n.37
Härmänmaa, Marja 96, 104
Harrison, Austin 147 n.28, 176, 176 n.27
Harvard Advocate (Eliot) 5

Hegel, Georg Wilhelm Friedrich 18, 18 n.6
Heinsius, Theodor 21
Heinzen, Karl 42
Hess, Moses 21 n.8, 35–7, 40
The History of Materialism and Criticism of Its Present Importance (Lange) 15, 48
Hughes-Hallett, Lucy 73, 111
Hulme, T. E. 161 n.6, 164
humane liberalism 30
humanist 21, 24, 24 n.13, 31
Huneker, James 5–6, 5 n.6, 48–9, 70, 70 n.35, 72, 121, 190

Ialongo, Ernest 92, 96, 105
Il trionfo della morte (D'Annunzio) 112
Indissoluble Matrimony (West) 147–8
Individualisme anarchiste: Max Stirner (Basch) 94, 94 n.11, 96
Italy 85–91, 93, 110, 110 n.25, 115–17, 123, 137
Ivan Karamazov 174, 174 n.26

Jackson, Holbrook 138, 138 n.22, 139
James Joyce and the Politics of Egoism (Rabaté) 109 n.24, 127 n.5
Jefferson, Thomas 92
Joyce, James 109, 109 n.24, 116, 122
Junghegelianer (Young Hegelians) 18, 20, 24 n.12, 125 n.3

Kahn, Gustave 84, 84 n.61, 92–7, 93 n.10, 94 n.11
Kant, Immanuel 6–7, 121–3
Kapp, Christian 19
Karl Marx: Greatness and Illusion (Stedman Jones) 6
Kelly, Gertrude B. 132, 132 n.11, 133

Laing, Kathryn 146 n.27
Lange, Friedrich Albert 15, 44, 48–9, 128, 130
Lansdown, Richard 88 n.5
Lanson, Gustave 60–6, 68, 70, 72, 157
Lasvignes, Henri 53, 80, 115
Lauterbach, Paul 47

Lawrence, D. H. 109, 117, 117 n.38, 188 n.12
Lee, Vernon 141, 141 n.24
Legitimizing the Artist: Manifesto Writing and European Modernism (Somigli) 81 n.55
Leopold, David 1 n.1, 25, 27 n.17
Le Révolté 55, 55 n.3
Le Symbolisme (Moréas) 10, 73 n.38, 81–3, 176
Lévy, Albert 49
Levy, Carl 189
Levy, Oscar 141
Lewes, George Henry 122
Lewis, Wyndham 121, 161 n.7
  Blast 147, 147 n.28, 152–4, 156, 161, 164, 169–77, 179
  Blasting and Bombardiering 164, 169–70, 175
  The Diabolical Principle 169
  "Enemy of the Stars" 95 n.16, 99 n.18, 161 n.7, 164–8, 164 n.10, 165 n.11, 168 n.16
  Futurism, Magic and Life 172
  Manifesto II 170–1
  The New Egos 173 n.24
  NO-MAN 171
  Our Vortex 173
L'Homme révolté (Camus) 1, 3–6, 185, 185 n.8
Libertad, Albert 135
Liberty 122–3, 128–34, 138–9, 141
L'Unico (Zoccoli) 85, 91
L'Unique et sa propriété (Lasvignes) 58, 94, 94 n.12, 112, 115, 161
Lyon, Janet 9

Machiavelli, Niccolo 51, 57, 83, 113
Mackay, John Henry 15–25, 15 n.1, 20 n.7, 29, 48–9, 51, 53, 78, 87, 122, 130, 135–7, 139, 142, 189
  The Anarchists 128
  Die Anarchisten 16, 16 n.3, 48, 53, 56–7, 78–9
  Max Stirner: Sein Leben und sein Werk 15, 20, 25, 49
Malatesta, Errico 89, 105

Mallarmé, Stéphane 54, 60–1, 64, 64 n.29, 66 n.34, 68, 82–4, 83 n.60
   Hamlet 67, 71
   literary anarchist 62–72
   Mardis 63 n.25
   Restricted Action 68–9
Manifesto of Surrealism (Breton) 184
Marinetti, Filippo Tommaso 10, 12–13
   Fondation et manifeste du Futurisme 82, 98, 100–1, 176
   and Futurism 92–7
   La conquête des étoiles 95, 100
   Le Figaro 81, 86, 97–8
   Le Futurisme 86, 98, 100
   Mafarka le futuriste 99, 105–6
   The New Futurist Manifesto 162
   Poesia 98
   Poetry and Drama 162
   The Untameables 97
Marsden, Dora 10, 122, 127, 130, 133, 142–52, 151 n.29, 154, 156–60, 163, 169, 173, 176
   The Egoist 1, 10, 122, 127, 144, 150, 151 n.29, 152, 154, 160, 175–6
   The Freewoman 122, 127, 135, 143–50
   The New Freewoman 10, 122, 134, 149–50, 152, 154, 159, 173
Marshall, Peter 55, 88–9
Marx, Karl 1–2, 5–6, 17, 18 n.6, 20, 21 n.8, 25, 29 n.19, 34–45, 38 n.26–38 n.27, 40 n.28, 43 n.29, 52
   The Communist Manifesto 6, 9–10, 12–13, 39–42, 83, 99, 99 n.18, 118, 175–7, 190
   Die deutsche Ideologie 1, 37–8, 91
   The Theses on Feuerbach 10, 39, 41, 83
McCall, John Erwin 136 n.18, 137, 137 n.20
McClelland, J. S. 73
McElroy, Wendy 132 n.12
McGuiness, Patrick 66–7, 69
McLellan, David 6, 23–4, 26–7
Meredith, George 123–7, 127 n.5, 128, 144
Michaud, Guy 63, 63 n.25
Middlemarch (George Eliot) 125–6
Middleton, Clara 127, 144
Might is Right or The Survival of the Fittest (Desmond) 136 n.18

Mitzman, Arthur 188–9
modernity 101, 189–92
monomaniac prolixity 38
Monro, Harold 154, 162
Moody, A. David 150, 156, 160
Moréas, Jean 10, 73 n.38, 80–4, 97
Morgan, Peter 15 n.1, 135 n.16
Mussolini, Benito 74, 86, 91–2, 105, 109–10, 117–20, 136, 179

Nevinson, Christopher 162–4
The New Age (Carswell) 138–42, 138 n.22, 154
Nietzsche, Friedrich 2–4, 6, 16, 44–52
   Also sprach Zarathustra 46–7
   Die fröhliche Wissenschaft 46
   The Genealogy of Morals 173–4
   Letzter Mensch 47
   Übermensch 45, 47–8, 50–1, 71–2, 94–5, 106, 112–13, 117, 135, 145, 179, 191

O'Keeffe, Paul 161–4, 162 n.8, 169, 169 n.19
Orage, Alfred 138–9, 141
Overbeck, Franz 49
ownness 30 n.20, 32, 120, 131, 135, 188

Papanikolas, Theresa 2, 79 n.53, 135, 136 n.17, 183
Parry, Richard 55
Paterson, Ronald 18–19, 33, 35, 50
Patterne, Willoughby 127
Pease, Edward R. 154
Phänomenologie des sittlichen Bewusstseins (von Hartmann) 48, 76
philosophic anarchism 129
Philosophie des Unbewussten (von Hartmann) 48, 49 n.33, 76, 130, 130 n.7
The Philosophy of Egoism (Walker) 129 n.6
Picabia, Francis 135, 183 n.5
Poetry of the Revolution (Puchner) 156
political liberalism 29
Pound, Ezra 92, 109, 150–2, 154, 169, 172, 173 n.24, 174–6
   Imagism 154–7, 160, 163

property, use of 158 n.4
The Serious Artist 156–60
Proudhon, Pierre-Joseph 3, 25, 29 n.19, 42–4, 52, 55–6, 59, 61, 66–9, 73, 76–7, 88, 90–1, 97, 123, 128–9, 131, 131 n.9, 133, 150, 158, 159 n.5
Puchner, Martin 9–10, 39, 41, 81–3, 86, 156

Rabaté, Jean-Michel 109 n.24, 127 n.5
Randall, A. E. 141–2
Randal, Théodore 57–8, 60
Read, Herbert 3–4, 6, 9
  The Contrary Experience 181
  Existentialism, Marxism and Anarchism 186–7
  The Forms of Things Unknown 180–1
  The Tenth Muse 9, 180, 187
Reclaire, Robert L. 53–4, 80
Redbeard, Ragnar 136 n.18, 137
Reich, Wilhelm 188–9
Revue universitaire (Lanson) 60–1
Roberts, William 175
Roger, Thierry 66, 69, 163

The Sanity of Art (Shaw) 139, 141
Sartre, Jean-Paul 174 n.25, 187–8
Scott, Bonnie Kime 146 n.26
Shaw, George Bernard 137–9, 138 n.22, 139 n.23, 141 n.24, 153–4
Shone, Steve 20
Silverton, Evadne 148
social liberalism 29–30
Somigli, Luca 81 n.55
Sorel, George 58, 80, 97, 104, 161
Specters of Marx (Derrida) 38 n.26, 99 n.18, 188 n.11
Spencer, Herbert 121, 123–30, 143, 146–7
  The Data of Ethics 126
  The Principles of Psychology 126
  System of Synthetic Philosophy 126
Stedman Jones, Gareth 6
Stepelevich, Lawrence S. 1
Stephens, Alfred George 190
Stirling, J. H. 122
Stirner et Nietzsche (Lévy) 49
Stirner, Max (Johann Caspar Schmidt) 1–13, 1 n.1, 21 n.9. *See also Der Einzige und sein Eigentum* (Stirner)
  on anarchist and the avant-garde 2, 4–6, 9–10, 12, 15–17, 23, 27, 42–4, 63, 66–70, 85–92, 129, 190
  on Barrès 54
  on Christianity 24, 145
  on creative nothing 12, 34, 149, 159, 166–7, 187–8
  on Dada 2, 25–6, 92, 170 n.21, 182–4, 184 n.6, 190
  on dialectical egoism 8, 18 n.6, 25–8, 27 n.16, 37, 158–9
  Die Freien (the free ones) 16–17, 19–21, 20 n.7, 23, 27, 27 n.15, 28
  on Duchamp 135, 183 n.5
  The Ego and His Own 1 n.1, 119, 129, 130 n.7, 134–5, 136 n.19, 137–43, 145–6, 148, 160, 187
  Eigenheit 30, 30 n.20
  on French anarchism 5, 8, 29 n.19, 42, 54, 56, 64, 66, 84, 91, 149
  his influence 2–4, 5 n.6, 6, 10, 13, 15, 18, 42–4, 48, 54, 61, 66, 90, 92, 130, 134, 147, 166, 173, 182–3, 183 n.5, 186, 190
  on humanism 21–2, 28–30, 30 n.20, 31, 38, 41, 43, 124–5
  on idealism 8, 19, 25, 33, 38, 52–3, 84, 96, 181, 191
  on Imagism and Vorticism 154–7, 160–1, 163, 169–76, 174 n.24
  on Joyce 109, 122
  Kunst und Religion (Art and Religion) 22–3, 31, 67–8, 106, 171
  on law 42
  legacy 182–9
  on Lewis 121, 152, 160–76
  on Marsden 10, 122, 142–52, 156, 159–60, 169
  on materialism 9, 39, 43, 122, 130, 160
  on Nietzsche (*See* Nietzsche, Friedrich)
  on Picabia 135, 183 n.5
  on property 11–12, 42, 156, 170
  on Rand 2
  Rheinische Zeitung 20–1, 21 n.8, 22
  on society 6, 11, 28–31, 131–2, 136, 149
  on the State 121–2, 128–30, 132, 134, 138–9

translation 54–62
Vortices and Notes 171
Strauss, Richard 48
Szeliga 36, 36 n.24

Taillandier, Saint-René 53, 53 n.1, 56
  La demagogie et l'athéisme
    (Demagoguery and Atheism)
    53 n.1
  Revue des deux mondes 53
Thorel, Jean 59–60
Tucker, Benjamin 43, 43 n.30, 58, 91,
  91 n.9, 122, 131–4, 131 n.9, 139,
  139 n.23, 141–2, 149–52, 151 n.29
Tzara, Tristan 70, 183–4

Umberto I, King 85, 90 n.7

Valesio, Paolo 116
Vanitas! Vanitatum Vanitas! (Goethe) 34,
  80 n.54
Verbrecher 46, 46 n.31
Vildrac, Charles 96

von Bülow, Hans 17, 48, 87
von Hartmann, Eduard 44, 48–9, 49 n.33,
  72, 76, 78, 130, 130 n.7
Vorwärts! Pariser Deutsche Monatsschrift
  (Börnstein) 35–6

Wagner, Geoffrey 65, 161 n.6, 168 n.18
Walker, James L. 15 n.2, 53, 58, 128–34,
  129 n.6, 130 n.7, 132 n.10, 133 n.13,
  136 n.19, 141–2, 149
Weston, Selwyn 144–6, 148
West, Rebecca 122, 143–7, 147 n.28, 150,
  154
Whistler, James Abbott McNeil 153
Wiener, Georg Benedikt 19
Wigand, Otto 23
Wilde, Oscar 153, 153 n.1
Wissenschaftslehre (Science of Knowledge)
  (Fichte) 7 n.8, 32
Woodhouse, John 110, 110 n.25, 111,
  111 n.28, 112–13, 116, 116 n.37

Zoccoli, Ettore 56, 85–7, 89–91

www.ingramcontent.com/pod-product-compliance
Lightning Source LLC
Chambersburg PA
CBHW052041300426
44117CB00012B/1928